THE JEDBURGHS

THE
JEDBURGHS

The Secret History of the
Allied Special Forces, France 1944

LT. COL. WILL IRWIN,
U.S. ARMY (RET.)

PUBLICAFFAIRS
NEW YORK

Published in the United States by PublicAffairs™, a member of the Perseus Books Group.

Book Design by Janet Tingey

Library of Congress Cataloging-in-Publication Data
Irwin, Will, 1950-
The Jedburghs : The secret history of the Allied Special
    Forces, France 1944 / Will Irwin.—1ˢᵗ ed.
p.   cm.
Includes index.
ISBN–13 978–1–58648–307–4
ISBN–10 1–58648–307–2
1. World War, 1939–1945—Secret service—France. 2. World
    War, 1939–1945—Campaigns—France—Normandy. 3.
    World War, 1939–1945—Underground movements—
    France. 4. Special forces (Military science) 5. Special
    operations (Military science) 6. Normandy (France)—
    History, Military. I. Title.
D810.S7I79 2005
940.54′86′0944—dc22
                                            2005050917

First Edition

10 9 8 7 6 5 4 3 2 1

This book is dedicated to the Jeds
lost in the campaign for France.

"For always, no matter how powerful one's armies, to enter a conquered territory one needs the good-will of the inhabitants."

Niccolò Machiavelli, *The Prince*, 1513

"Any nation that uses [partisan warfare] intelligently will, as a rule, gain some superiority over those who disdain its use."

Karl von Clausewitz, *On War*, 1833

"The difficulties [for an invader] are particularly great when the people are supported by a considerable nucleus of disciplined troops. The invader has only an army: his adversaries have an army, and a people wholly or almost wholly in arms . . . even the noncombatants have an interest in his ruin and accelerate it by every means in their power."

General Baron de Jomini, *A Treatise on the Art of War*, 1838

CONTENTS

A NOTE ON MILITARY UNITS

The following table gives readers an idea of the organization and typical authorized strength of the various ground force units—both Allied (American, British, Canadian, and Free French) and German—referred to in the book. The "composition" column in the table shows only the major combat elements at each level of organization; in addition to these, organizations at the division level and above also had additional artillery, engineer, signal, medical, or other specialty units. As the weeks and months passed following D-Day, virtually all units operated below their authorized strength, even with replacements. Many German units, in particular, were at a fraction of their authorized strength by the late summer of 1944.

Throughout the book, specific unit designations are shown following conventional U.S.-European practice: Arabic numerals for divisions, regiments, battalions, and platoons (*e.g.*, 2nd SS Panzer Division, 16th Infantry Regiment); spelled-out numbers for field armies (*e.g.*, French First Army, Third U.S. Army); Roman numerals for corps (*e.g.*, VII Corps); and letters for companies (*e.g.*, Company B).

CHART 1

Organization	Typical Composition	Typical Strength
Army Group	Two or more field armies	200,000–300,000
(Field) Army	Two or more corps	100,000–150,000
Corps	Two or more divisions	25,000–50,000
Division	Three or more regiments, brigades, or combat commands	10,000–15,000
Regiment, Brigade, or Combat Command	Two or more battalions	1,000–3,500
Battalion or Squadron	Four to six companies	400–1,000
Company or Troop	Three to five platoons	100–250
Platoon	Two to four squads	16–50
Squad		8–12

PROLOGUE

A lone bomber climbed slowly into the darkness from the airfield in Northamptonshire, in central England. It was a little more than an hour before midnight on July 8, 1944, a warm Saturday night. To anyone outside at that hour in the nearby village of Harrington, the B-24 Liberator looked like hundreds of others based throughout Britain; but residents of Harrington knew that nothing at this particular airfield could be taken at face value. Something strange went on there, though no one could say exactly what. Planes took off at about this time—or even later—almost every night, and they always returned before dawn. Nearly always, the planes were silhouetted against a moonlit sky and bore no telltale running lights. Anyone who'd paid any attention at all during the past two years knew that the Americans stationed at every other base in England flew only daytime bombing missions.

The young airmen of the U.S. Eighth Air Force who worked at the base—they called themselves "Carpetbaggers"—were friendly enough. They often spent their free time drinking the weak wartime beer in local pubs, and many had accepted invitations from villagers to come by for a home-cooked meal. But if asked about what they did, the young men grew tight-lipped and evasive. Once it became clear that their work was a military secret, people stopped asking—as if they knew of some flaw in your family's past, but liked you and respected you enough not to bring it up.

Closer examination of the bomber lifting off at 2240 hours that night would have revealed that it was no ordinary Liberator. This B-24 was cloaked in a non-reflective black paint. Gun turrets had been removed from the nose, waist, and belly of the fuselage, leaving two gun mountings—one in the top of the fuselage and one in the tail. The crew had been reduced from the standard ten men to eight. Bomb racks had been stripped from the aircraft and replaced by specially designed racks for carrying supply containers; both the racks and the containers were of British manufacture. A plywood trapdoor had been fitted over the hole in the floor where the belly gunner's turret usually was—a hole meant to allow parachutists to exit the aircraft, one at a time. The air force called it the "Joe hole," referring to their universal name for jumpers.

Advanced avionics had been added to the plane, as well as a primitive "friend or foe" identification system. There also was advanced radio equipment and an early radar device designed to help prevent the plane from hitting the ground when flying at low altitudes. Oxygen bottles had been removed; this plane wouldn't be flying high enough to need them. The only light left to burn continuously once a mission was underway was a small one in the navigator's compartment that gave off an eerie green glow, providing just enough illumination for the navigator to read his charts.

Seated on the airplane's plywood floor were three young men—parachutists who would jump on the first pass over the drop zone. The leader of the team was a tall, handsome twenty-nine-year-old American army captain, an aircraft armaments officer before volunteering for duty with the Office of Strategic Services. Bernard Knox, a naturalized citizen of the United States, was a native Briton, a Cambridge graduate, and a veteran of the Spanish Civil War. His second-in-command, a French captain named Paul Lebel, had come from a Free French infantry regiment in North Africa, and the third member of the team, Sergeant Gordon Tack, was a British army radio operator assigned to that country's Special Operations Executive. All three men wore battledress uniform with a winged patch on the upper sleeve. In the center of the patch's spread white wings was a red circle with the letters SF, for Special Forces, in light blue.

Their equipment was an odd mixture—British radios, American M1 carbines and .45-caliber pistols, and British compasses. The men wore canvas money belts stuffed with hundreds of thousands in French francs and a smaller amount of American dollars. Over their uniforms they wore standard British jump smocks, their pockets crammed with code books and radio crystals. On their heads they wore British parachutist helmets, on their feet American jump boots.

Positioned above the bomb bay were twelve Type C containers—man-sized tubular-shaped canisters filled with weapons and other equipment for the resistance fighters. These would be dropped during the aircraft's second pass over the planned drop area, followed by twelve more from a second B-24. The containers were stamped from sheet metal, with reinforcing ribs on the surface. Each had an opening which ran the length of the container and was fastened closed with three latches. A small compartment at one end held a parachute. Protruding from a hole in the compartment was a static line that was fastened to a bar in the aircraft's interior; when the container left the aircraft the line would pull out the parachute. Carefully packed in the larger main compartment was a standard load of submachine guns, ammunition, grenades, explosives, radios, boots, and other gear—the impedimenta of guerrilla warfare.

The drop zone was a field two miles north of the town of Briec, near the westernmost tip of the Brittany peninsula—that dog-ear-like appendage of northwestern France that points into the North Atlantic. The field was ideal for receiving a parachute drop of men and equipment—a rolling, pastoral stretch of countryside with no high-tension wires or other obstacles on the field itself or along the plane's approach path.

The previous evening's French-language news broadcast by the BBC had been followed, as it was every evening, by coded "personal messages" intended for various French resistance groups. Nonsensical phrases that were pointless to anyone but those who knew their hidden meanings: "Jacques has a tall brother," or "The first snow fell in November," or some other such silliness.

One such message had meaning for members of the Finistère resistance, which picked up the BBC broadcast on a hidden radio in defiance of an edict by the German occupation authorities. One of the personal messages informed the members of the impending arrival of the three-man team and had directed that the reception committee—the men and women who would await the parachutists at the drop zone—should use a light to flash a pre-arranged letter in Morse code as the aircraft approached, indicating that the drop zone was secure—that no Germans were in the immediate vicinity.

Monsieur Arzel, deputy police chief of Quimper, a large market town to the southwest, organized the reception committee. Around midnight, members of the resistance from nearby villages converged on the drop zone and began preparation for the team's arrival. A small truck and a few horse-drawn wagons were pulled out of sight into the nearby woods, partly to remain hidden from anyone who might pass by and partly to keep the horses from being frightened by the low-flying aircraft. Armed men took up positions on approaching roads and trails to provide security against possible German patrols. Other men broke up into small groups for retrieving the metal containers packed with arms and ammunition and loading them onto the wagons—it usually took four to handle each container. Still others prepared three small bonfires; these were arranged to form the corners of a large triangle to mark the drop zone and were not to be lit until the aircraft could be heard approaching from the expected direction.

When all was ready, the reception teams hid along the edge of the woods. Shortly before one o'clock in the morning, the drone of the plane was heard and the bonfires were lit. Once the unmistakable shape of the Liberator loomed in the pale moonlit sky, a man standing on the drop zone aimed a flashlight skyward, with a tubular attachment to hide its beam from anyone but those in the bomber. He blinked the appropriate dashes and dots to indicate the pre-arranged letter.

Aboard the Liberator, an air corps sergeant—called the dispatcher—stood near the Joe hole. Only minutes earlier he had removed the plywood trap door in the floor of the bomber. The pilot, however, unable to spot any lights marking the drop zone, circled for twenty minutes searching for the triangle of small bonfires, the center of which would be his target. While the triangle lighting system of marking drop zones was common, it was only one of four methods used during the war.

Special operations piloting was something more than an acquired skill, and it demanded the very best pilots. It was low-level, seat-of-the-pants flying in a ponderous heavy bomber designed for formation flying at high altitudes. The B-24 could be cumbersome at these lower altitudes; the machine had to be manhandled. After circling for a time, the pilot informed the dispatcher that he had finally spotted the fires. Then the pilot leveled the plane off and began his run in—at an altitude of around six hundred feet above ground level—lowering the flaps halfway and slowing the bulky plane to about 125 miles per hour, barely above stall speed.

For everyone aboard the airplane, nervous tension rose in proportion to the slackening of the engines. With the bomber on final approach, the sergeant shouted, "Running in!" loudly enough to be heard over the groan of the four huge Pratt & Whitney engines. The dispatcher then busied himself re-checking the static lines leading from the men's parachutes, which he had moments before hooked to an anchorage in the floor just behind the Joe hole. Within seconds, a red light above the seated men came alive with a dim ruby glow. And, on its cue, the sergeant yelled, "Action stations!" Captain Knox scooted to the edge of the opening, dangling his feet in the slipstream below the plane, watching the grayish green patchwork that defined the ground some six hundred feet below. Only seconds later, a green light came to life as the red one died, and the dispatcher screamed, "Go!" In prearranged order, Captain Knox, then Sergeant Tack, and finally Captain Lebel dropped through the hole and were swallowed up by the darkness.

Thus began the mission of an Allied special forces team in German-occupied France, one of dozens carried out by these three-man units known as "Jedburghs." The secret Jedburgh project entailed dropping up to one hundred hybrid special forces teams into occupied France—hundreds of miles ahead of conventional ground forces. The men, commonly referred to as Jeds, were a mix of

British, American, and French operatives. Only about one team in ten, however, included a member of each of those nationalities; on most teams, two of the men were from the same country. But all teams included at least one Frenchman. The Jeds' mission was to organize, arm, and train groups of French resistance guerrillas.

But, more importantly, these teams were to orchestrate the sabotage and guerrilla warfare activities of these resistance groups to ensure that they complemented operations of the advancing Allied ground forces. The bands of underground partisan fighters with whom they worked were commonly called maquis (pronounced mah-kee)—named for a scrub brush that thrives in the hills of Corsica much as the partisans thrived in the more remote terrain of mainland France. Such maquis bands were initially formed by young men, many of them teenagers, who'd fled to the hills to avoid German labor drafts.

American Jeds belonged to the Office of Strategic Services (OSS); their British counterparts were from the Special Operations Executive (SOE). They were joined by men of General Charles de Gaulle's Free French organization. Espionage agents they were not. They all were military officers and noncommissioned officers who jumped and worked far behind German lines, most often in uniform. Joining them in this effort, and usually working hand in hand with them in the field, were other uniformed special forces, particularly the British and French Special Air Service (SAS) and the American Operational Groups.

The Jedburghs, along with a few other British and American special forces created at about the same time, were the first such units in history. Never before had nations institutionalized a uniformed military force organized, trained, and equipped to rally and direct the operations of irregular partisans deep in enemy territory. These units functioned in much the same way that their descendants— the U.S. Army Special Forces* (the Green Berets), Britain's SAS, and France's Premier Régiment Parachutiste d'Infanterie de Marine—do today.

But how and for what purpose were such units initially formed?

---

* Throughout this volume, references to special forces in general are lowercased. The capitalized term "Special Forces" specifically refers to the U.S. Army Special Forces, a standing organization added to the U.S force structure in 1952.

The original concept for such special forces in World War II Europe was to support British Prime Minister Winston Churchill's idea of engaging the people of occupied Europe in a guerrilla war against the Germans. In this way, Churchill hoped to tie down enemy forces by compelling them to engage in counter-guerrilla operations far from the front lines. Guerrillas could also sabotage railways and ambush enemy columns, delaying reinforcements from reaching the front and improving the prospect for Allied victory and a reduction in Allied casualties.

Unconventional warfare, as conducted during the Second World War, was unprecedented in its scope and methods. New technologies allowed for methods of clandestine and irregular warfare never before even imagined. The airplane provided a means for delivering not only intelligence agents and special forces teams, but also the ordnance and supplies to sustain the men in the field. Modern short-wave communications equipment made it possible for these elements to receive instructions from headquarters in friendly territory, hundreds of miles away. In turn, soldiers operating deep behind enemy lines could use such equipment to report enemy activity and to request supplies or reinforcement from the base station.

The Jedburgh concept was born in the minds of political and military leaders at the highest levels and developed by a small group of dedicated, imaginative Allied army officers (both regulars and soldier-civilians). It was supported with varying degrees of enthusiasm by Allied field commanders and executed by a few hundred highly motivated and adventurous soldiers. The British had devised a strategy of supporting partisan forces in occupied Europe as early as February 1941, and the Jedburgh plan had been first proposed the following year. Planning and preparation began almost in isolation. But over the next three years, with the backing of Churchill and General Dwight D. Eisenhower, it became more and more an integral part of the plan for Operation Overlord—the return of Allied forces to France.

The ideas and efforts of these men of imagination, however, would have counted for little without the remarkably capable young men who were selected and trained to carry out these missions. It took a special type of man to fight the unconventional war;

the work required extraordinary nerve. Once on the ground in German-occupied territory, there was no falling back when things got hot. Retreat or withdrawal was out of the question; there was no rear area to fall back to. And if a member of a Jedburgh team was killed or seriously wounded the loss represented a 33 percent reduction in the unit's strength and capability. Unlike in an infantry battalion, where units could eventually expect a replacement for such a loss, field replacements in the Jeds were almost unheard of and certainly were not expected.

In conventional combat units, men drew strength from the very nearness of large numbers of their comrades. In the Jedburghs, on the other hand, men had only their inner strength and that of a couple of teammates to pull them through some extraordinarily terrifying experiences.

These men were asked to parachute hundreds of miles behind enemy lines and establish contact with battle-hardened resistance fighters who had grown leery of strangers as a result of German infiltration ploys. The Jeds' task was to gain the confidence of these underground leaders and work with them to support the Allied ground campaign. It was work that left little margin for error, and it called for top-drawer men.

So who were these men and where did they come from? Some were army regulars, but many more came into the military from civilian life after the war began. And they were a tremendously mixed lot, coming from all walks of pre-war life: brewery worker, scholar, Hollywood stuntman, lawyer, silver polisher, business executive, whiskey taster, stockbroker, physical therapist, bank auditor, lumberjack, musician, restaurateur, foundry worker, French nobleman, grocery deliveryman, chemical lab assistant, photoengraver, politician, tennis pro, oil executive, and cattle rancher. There were engineers, radio repairmen, newspaper reporters, college undergraduates, medical and law school students, taxi drivers, university lecturers, high school teachers, and athletic coaches.

They hailed primarily, and in roughly equal numbers, from France, Britain, and the United States. Into this mélange were sprinkled, as if for flavoring, a Belgian, a Canadian, a handful of Dutch, and a South African. Just under three hundred men in all.

But, as diverse as their backgrounds were, they also had much in common. They all were men of adventurous spirit—not inclined to shrink from a challenge or to look for the easy way out. And they were men who liked to think for themselves.

The Americans among them could recall the anti-war movement in the United States in the pre–Pearl Harbor days—a movement whose sentiments some of them shared at the time—but since their country's entrance into the war these men were anxious to do their part. The British had seen the devastation and withdrawal of their army from France in 1940, and the costly German bombing of their cities and the evacuation of children and whole families to the countryside. The French had seen firsthand the theft of their country and the humiliation of its population. All the men were products of the Depression—a bleak and fearful time for most, regardless of nationality. And, as a result, most of them had become accustomed to risk, austerity, and hardship.

Then, as these men were finishing high school or college—generally during the late 1930s and early 1940s—their world started coming apart. Nations had once again failed to resolve their differences short of going to war. And, characteristically, these young men chose a most challenging and atypical way in which to help put the world right again.

These were the few men who remained in their seats at OSS and SOE recruitment briefings, even after hearing of the risks involved. Their motives for volunteering may have differed, but self-confidence was a common trait. They stayed because, regardless of what else they were, they were men of action—athletes, travelers, adventure seekers—tough guys, both physically and mentally.

The officers were graduates of some of the best colleges and universities in the world. Even the Jedburgh radio operators—noncommissioned officers (although the French made a practice of commissioning theirs just prior to deployment)—often had completed one or two years of college. And this was at a time when the average soldier had but two years of high school. Despite their tender ages, the noncoms were catapulted in rank, promoted at a pace unheard of in conventional units.

If you walked into a room full of Jeds, you could likely find someone with whom to discuss Greek tragedy or epidemiology or tort law or bel canto opera. Any number of them, as a result of their radio training, might get you in over your head on the subject of electromagnetic wave propagation—and many of them could do so in two or more languages. But, given cause, they could also knock you on your ass.

Although they were brassy, cocksure, boundlessly self-confident, these men were not without human emotion. In the field—hunted like wild animals by the Germans—some knew fear so strong that they clearly recalled it more than forty years later. But they never let that fear overcome them; they prevailed in spite of it. Some felt a need to prove something. But most were simply determined to serve with only the best—in other words, with men like themselves. In doing so, they formed a lifelong brotherhood.

General Eisenhower himself, supreme commander of Allied forces in Europe, recognized the special forces' contribution in the campaign for France when he said, "In no previous war, and in no other theater during this war, have resistance forces been so closely harnessed to the main military effort."[1]

Details of their activities were not widely known at the time because the operations were classified, and remained so until well after the war. As records emerge through declassification efforts begun in the 1980s, however, it is clear that these special forces, and the resistance movements they supported, did a great deal to help drive Hitler's army from France in the summer of 1944. Eisenhower praised their actions on numerous occasions, according to his naval aide, Captain Harry C. Butcher. As Butcher noted in his wartime diary, Ike considered the maquis to have been "far more effective than many doubting Thomases thought before D-Day."[2] And the Jedburghs contributed significantly to their success.

Fewer than three hundred men deployed on Jed teams—a third the strength of an American infantry battalion of the time;[3] indeed, only half again the size of a rifle company. Yet, this group of men earned an impressive number of decorations. Of the eighty-three American Jeds, for example, no less than fifty-three were decorated. The awards include twelve Distinguished Service Crosses, two Navy Crosses, eight Silver Stars, six Legion of Merit medals, and fourteen Bronze Star Medals;[4] and more than three dozen men earned the French Croix de Guerre.

If postwar careers of Jedburgh veterans are any indication, those who ran the exhaustive recruitment, assessment, and selection process did a remarkable job. Many of those chosen for the Jedburghs went on to become successful statesmen and diplomats, military and intelligence professionals, doctors and lawyers, scholars and educators, journalists and authors, businessmen and tradesmen. The French, British, and American contingents each included future generals (a dozen in all) and statesmen of cabinet, minister, and ambassadorial rank. Two would become members of Britain's parliament. There was a future director of the Central Intelligence Agency, a top columnist for *The Saturday Evening Post* and *Newsweek*, an acclaimed scholar and professor of Hellenic studies, and a world-renowned cardiac surgeon. The Jeds also produced an Episcopalian priest and a Benedictine monk, a cotton plantation manager and a wine grower, an artist and a novelist, and a public relations agent for Princess Grace of Monaco. One former Jed would become a television producer, another a psychiatrist, and still another an accomplished chef. Quite a showing for a group of roughly two hundred and eighty men. And all were true heroes—in a day when that label was not carelessly applied.

It is an unfortunate irony that most of these self-sacrificing heroes have lived unnamed and uncredited among us for decades. They taught us in school, they treated our illnesses, they sold us insurance, they saw to our legal affairs, but few ever spoke of their wartime experiences. Many of their immediate family members told me that they had no idea of the part their father or husband or brother had played in the war. The majority of them remained silent because they had been ordered to do so. Their role in the war was classified, and they were sworn to secrecy by their respective governments. In most cases, even family and friends only learned of their wartime deeds when the CIA began declassifying the relevant records in 1985. Wide exposure came even later in Britain, where the Official Secrets Act delayed declassification until more recently. And, until now, there never has been a complete account of how these men were selected and trained and how they operated in the field.

Ernie Pyle, the great war correspondent, wrote in 1944: "The story of the French underground, when the day comes for it to be written, will be one of the most fascinating stories in all history."[5] And the Jedburghs and other Allied special forces who did so much to help the resistance are an important part of that story.

Space restrictions compel me to limit this account to a representative half-dozen teams, allowing their stories to be told in greater detail. But the reader should keep in mind that for each Jedburgh team whose story is told here a dozen more were engaged in similar operations. I also should caution readers against comparing the Jedburghs to elite infantry strike forces such as the British Commandos or the U.S. Army's Rangers. The Jeds were not organized or equipped as those units were because the Jeds had a different and much broader mission. The Jedburghs were fighters, but they also were teachers and advisors, counselors and advocates, combat leaders, negotiators—the first diplomat-soldiers.

1

CALL TO ACTION

THE alert came on a clear and sunny Friday morning. The date was June 2, 1944, and Sergeant Bob Kehoe and his teammates were on a training exercise in central England. Unknown to the men, the long-awaited cross-channel invasion of occupied France, called Operation Overlord, was scheduled to begin on Monday morning, the fifth. In military planners' terminology, that gave June 5 the designation "D-Day."

The coming weeks were to bring adventure beyond anything that Kehoe, a young GI from New Jersey, ever had expected. More than six months of training ensured that he possessed the necessary skills and that his body was in peak condition. But no training could prepare young men like Kehoe for the human dimension of combat—especially behind enemy lines. He and his Jedburgh teammates soon would experience firsthand the deadly and unpredictable—yet exhilarating—war of the partisan. The men would come to know its inconceivable treachery, its unsung valor, its abrupt and unanticipated violence—its unimagined fear and excitement.

That spring, with D-Day drawing near, Allied rehearsals of all types had been stepped-up throughout Britain—everything from amphibious landings, with naval forces supporting infantry and armor as they splashed ashore on unchallenged Devon beaches, to

1

mass parachute landings by the airborne regiments. And to fine-tune the unconventional part of the grand scheme, the Jedburgh training staff had staged a series of field exercises. The Jeds were one of three special forces elements which General Eisenhower planned to drop throughout occupied France to sever German communications and to delay the movement of enemy reinforcements to the Normandy beachhead. They would do so by stiffening the French resistance and by relaying operational direction to the partisans from Eisenhower's headquarters.

Formal training for the multinational three-man Jedburgh teams, some six to eight months of it, was complete by the first week of June. The final and most extensive Jedburgh war game, Exercise Lash, put the teams in the hilly picture-postcard terrain of the Charnwood Forest, in Leicestershire.

For the past few days, Jeds had been lurking about the wooded upland, through its secluded valleys and up its rocky summits, organizing and controlling surrogate partisan groups. The field exercise required the men to put six months of guerrilla warfare lessons into practice—stealth, sabotage, clandestine communications, ambush. Fit young men worked at becoming shadows. Bodies had hardened, wits sharpened—they were ready. Lash was, in a sense, their final exam. It had kicked off on the last day of May under unsettled skies and occasional rain showers and was to continue until June 8.[1]

Kehoe had enlisted in the U.S. Army Signal Corps in September 1942. Less than two years later, he was the radio operator for—and the youngest member of—one of the few Jedburgh teams that was tri-national in makeup. All teams had at least one French officer; in some cases, the radio operator also was French and the third member was either an American or a British officer. On most other teams, the French officer was accompanied by an officer and radio operator who were both either American or British. Only about one team in ten featured an American-British-French combination. At twenty-one years of age, Kehoe looked much younger—too young, by appearance, to be served alcohol, and much too young to be in this deadly business. He was a good-looking kid, with a head of hair that the older Jeds must have envied, and sharp-nosed in a way that gave him a distinguished look, like the mature Joe DiMaggio, underwriting his youthful innocence with a no-nonsense image.

Friday had begun warm and clear, a perfect early summer day, and Sergeant Kehoe's team was in the middle of the Lash exercise. Then, without much in the way of a sensible explanation, Kehoe and the two officers he was teamed with were ordered to return to the country estate that served as the Jedburgh training center. By afternoon, they were back at the sprawling brownstone mansion known as Milton Hall—a seventeenth-century Elizabethan, set amidst sporadic hardwood groves in an otherwise pastoral flatland. The men saw that another team, led by a Frenchman, Captain Erard, and an American, Captain Cyr (pronounced "sear"), had also been called back. Kehoe had seen Captain Cyr before and knew who he was, but he had never really gotten to know him. Both teams were told to pack for a five-day exercise with the British Special Air Service (SAS). The men were forewarned that, just in case the exercise extended beyond five days, they should pack thoroughly. In fact, they should prepare as they would for combat. The teams were to be ready to depart on Sunday morning, June 4, 1944.

Leading Kehoe's team was Captain Adrian Wise of the British army. Wise had come to the Jedburghs from the Royal Warwickshire Regiment, was a graduate of the Royal Military Academy at Sandhurst, and was a veteran of two commando raids on the coast of Norway early in the war. Kehoe liked Wise and admired the captain's command of French, which he was told had been cultivated during the summers Wise had spent with his family in Normandy. The twenty-six-year-old Wise, with his beaming, handsome face and his dark, wavy hair, looked as if he'd been picked for the role of guerrilla leader by a Hollywood casting director. More to the point, though, his experience as an infantry officer in combat was invaluable.

Kehoe found himself agreeing with Wise's hunch that this "exercise" story was just that—a cover—and that what lay ahead was the real thing. Many soldiers currently engaged in field exercises throughout England, after all, had noticed the steady increase in convoys of troop-laden trucks and trains carrying military vehicles southward. Such activity only added to the nationwide speculation that the big invasion was near. Two other teams that had returned to Milton Hall over the last couple of days now were nowhere to be seen. Plus, being withdrawn from one exercise to be carted off to another just sounded too phony; they must have been pulled out for a real mission. They were sure of it. Still, anything was possible in the army.

The third member of the team, a French officer and Wise's second in command, was skeptical about the prospect that the team was embarking on anything other than another exercise. A moon-faced Parisian with deep-set eyes and a high forehead, the amiable Lieutenant Paul Aguirec was a bit older than Wise and Kehoe. He was an experienced army officer, having been activated from the reserves in the late 1930s, and, like many of the French Jeds, he had been recruited for the secret special forces project in North Africa. Wise and Kehoe enjoyed the company of the fun-loving Frenchman, despite his limited command of English. In keeping with a practice followed by all French men and women taking part in the shadow war, the lieutenant had adopted a nom de guerre to protect his relatives still in France in the event of his capture. His real name was, in fact, Paul Bloch-Auroch. But Aguirec was the only name Kehoe and Wise knew him by.[2]

Kehoe had first met the two officers when he was teamed with them on a recent exercise, and they had asked him to permanently join them a week later. He'd come to like both officers and was delighted to become their radio operator, and in the ensuing weeks he grew to appreciate their sense of teamwork. Although his job was communications, nothing on Captain Wise's team was the exclusive domain of the officers. During the exercises in the weeks since their team had been formed, Kehoe helped with the planning right alongside them.[3]

But, on the chance that this might be more than just another exercise, the two teams packed their gear carefully with an eye toward the prospect of months of combat rather than a week or two of training. The next day, all six men and their equipment were inspected and deemed ready. That afternoon, gloomy skies descended over southern England.

*   *   *

On the Channel coast that Saturday night, rain, driven by a howl-
ing wind, hammered General Eisenhower's tent camp. The great
Allied invasion, Operation Overlord, was about to be launched
from staging bases throughout southern England, and the supreme
commander and a few senior members of his staff had left their
London headquarters on May 29 and established an advanced command post at Southwick, seven miles north of Portsmouth.

Tucked away in a patch of woods atop a bluff, it was a GI tent
and trailer affair, spread along trails in the manner of a tourist
campground. Not far away, amid manicured lawns and gardens, sat
a mansion called Southwick House which served as the headquarters of Admiral Bertram Ramsay, Eisenhower's naval commander
in chief. The view from the house overlooking Portsmouth harbor
showed it to be crowded with naval vessels—battleships, destroyers, landing craft, and transports and tenders of all types.

Eisenhower held a special meeting in the library of the big house
for his senior commanders at two o'clock on Sunday morning, June
4. Because of the terrific storm raging outside, he announced a postponement of the invasion for at least twenty-four hours, pushing
D-Day from June 5 to June 6.[4]

Later that morning, the six Jeds threw their gear on the back of a
truck, climbed aboard, and began the two-hour drive to London. At
about eleven o'clock, the truck turned into Devonshire Close, an
attractive side street just south of Regent's Park, and stopped in
front of a handsome row house, just a few blocks east of Madame
Tussaud's wax museum in north London. The house, the men were
told, would be their home for the next few days. Oddly, there was
no sign of security in the area; it was a typical London residential
street. But such tedious benignity provided its own kind of security. The British Special Operations Executive (SOE) and the American Office of Strategic Services (OSS) had taken over many such
flats and houses in the Marylebone district of the city. The buildings were used as temporary quarters and briefing rooms for agents
and special forces teams awaiting transport to the Continent. This

one was less than half a mile from Special Operations Executive headquarters on Baker Street and Special Force Headquarters in nearby Montagu Mansions.[5]

A British officer from the London Jedburgh staff arrived at the Devonshire house and introduced himself as Major Horton. He would be the teams' escort and briefing officer. And yes, there was a real mission. No more exercises.

The Jeds soon learned that they would be jumping into Brittany, but also that they would not be going in alone. In the months leading up to the invasion, as it turned out, there had been heated debate at the highest levels about the role Britain's Special Air Service was to play. In the end, it was decided that SAS parties would parachute deep behind enemy lines and establish bases of operation from which to perform their mayhem. In North Africa, the SAS had made good use of heavily armed jeeps during raids on German air bases. Current plans called for these same jeeps to be dropped by parachute, or landed by glider, to allow similar mobile raiding parties in France. By the spring of 1944, the SAS had grown to brigade size with more than two thousand men organized in two British regiments, two French parachute infantry battalions, a Belgian parachute squadron, and supporting signal units.[6] In Brittany, the 4th French SAS was to be used. The 4th included many native Bretons, and their mission would be to arm and train the local maquis there, while adding their own firepower and leadership.

Unfortunately, there had been little coordination or planning between the SAS and the Jedburghs, and there were important differences in their approaches to unconventional warfare. Where the Jedburghs had been taught the importance of mobility in guerrilla warfare, constantly moving and never remaining long in one place, the SAS insisted on establishing and operating from fairly permanent and sizable bases deep behind enemy lines. While operating from such bases is a reasonable procedure in some parts of the world and against less capable enemies, plans which called for special forces and guerrillas to defend such bases in occupied France against attacks by the highly mechanized Wehrmacht at least should have raised some eyebrows.

The French SAS was to establish two bases in Brittany. One, code-named Samwest, would be in the Forêt de Duault, a forest west of the medieval cathedral town of St-Brieuc on Brittany's north coast. The other would go farther south, where the SAS would set up a somewhat larger base under the code name Dingson.

Captain Wise's Jed team, assigned the code name Frederick, was to accompany the Samwest party and, at least initially, operate under the command of the SAS leader, Captain André Leblond. Being subordinated to the SAS rankled Wise and Kehoe, but they bit their tongues, knowing that the mission would, at least, soon get them into France. On the eve of D-Day, the men learned, the SAS would drop two officers and sixteen soldiers as a lead element to find a site for a camp and prepare for the arrival of the remainder of the party. That remainder amounted to about one hundred men to be dropped over two consecutive nights. Jed team Frederick was to jump with the first contingent of forty-five SAS troopers on Friday night. They were to be dropped just southwest of the crossroads town of Guingamp, about a dozen miles in from the coast, west of St-Brieuc, in the department known as the Côtes-du-Nord (today called the Côtes d'Armor), one of five administrative departments that made up the region of Brittany. It was an area of farmlands and scattered hilly woodlands, with charming villages and towns that, like Guingamp, featured cobblestone streets and granite buildings with gray slate roofs.

The other team, with Captain Erard and Captain Cyr, was codenamed George. This team would be attached to the Dingson SAS party and would jump with them into an area near Redon in the department of Morbihan in southern Brittany.

Once on the ground, the Jeds were to contact local resistance elements, about which very little was known, and enlist their aid in defending the SAS camps. Any additional arms and supplies needed were to be delivered by airdrop arranged by the Jeds. The teams also were to provide London an assessment of the resistance potential in their respective areas. Additionally, if circumstances warranted it they were to request the deployment of additional Jedburgh teams and designate suitable drop zones for their delivery.

At one point, a communications expert arrived at the house and took Sergeant Kehoe to a separate room and went over communications procedures with him.[7] All radio messages, to and from the field, would be via wireless telegraphy and would be kept secure through the use of a cipher system known as the one-time pad. This pad of eight-inch-square sheets provided a key for enciphering and deciphering messages and was matched by an identical pad at the receiving station. Each sheet, different from all the rest, was used only once and then was destroyed, enabling the rendering of a brief message in a cipher that was unbreakable to anyone not possessing an identical pad.

For added security, Kehoe and the other radio operator memorized security checks. These were code words or letters or numbers which served as danger signals—to either be included in a message or omitted from it, according to the individual operator's instructions—to indicate to London that the operator had been captured and was transmitting under duress. Sergeant Kehoe was grilled until he and the briefer were certain that he had the codes down cold. For obvious reasons, they could not be written anywhere.

Security also could be enhanced by keeping messages as brief as possible. To assist in this, Kehoe was issued a twenty-inch-square piece of silk—which would outlast paper in the field—printed with four-letter brevity codes designed to replace often-used phrases in all messages. He also received a schedule of radio contacts to be made. The schedule designated times for both sending and receiving messages.

Next, the teams learned about German forces known to be in the area. Every scrap of available information was provided—unit designations and locations, and sites of headquarters and supply depots. Brittany had been vital to the German naval war, providing bases for the U-boat wolf packs that had decimated Allied shipping in the North Atlantic. Some fifty thousand German troops occupied Brittany, intent on defending those strategic bases. There were first-rate parachute divisions, other units comprised largely of Russians captured on the Eastern Front and thrown into German uniform, and everything in between. Intelligence estimated that the Germans could move three divisions from Brittany to reinforce front-line units in Normandy once the Allied landings began. They had to be delayed or stopped, and that responsibility fell largely to the resistance and Allied special forces.

The men were also reminded of German intelligence and security measures and units, including the Abwehr (military intelligence) and the Geheime Staatspolizei (secret state police). Normally referred to by the abbreviated term Gestapo, the latter was already well known for its brutal interrogation methods. Rumor had it that the Gestapo could be either ruthlessly efficient or bungling idiots.

Working hand in hand with the Germans, and equally detested by the French, was the collaborationist police force called the Milice—composed of Frenchmen who had been enticed to aid and abet the occupation forces. This militia had been created by the Vichy government in January 1943 to assist the German intelligence and security agencies in their campaign against the French resistance, and had become, in essence, a "French Gestapo." Some said that its ranks included convicted criminals whom the Germans had released under the condition that they work faithfully for the occupiers—work which included tracking down members of the resistance and anyone who supported them.

Maps were issued, and the men were briefed on the topography of the area. One map, in a scale of 1:50,000 (meaning one inch on the map represented fifty thousand inches on the ground), covered the area where they were to jump. A series of Michelin road maps, though, would prove best for daily use and for identifying drop zones for Special Force Headquarters in London. Each man also received a map printed on silk, to be tucked away in the bottom of a pocket so that it would be available, if needed, in survival or escape situations.

Finally, the Jeds were shown a list with names and descriptions of Allied agents known to be operating in the area. The names, of course, were pseudonyms, and the list was to be memorized, not carried.[8]

After remaining in the house all afternoon, the men were taken out to dinner by Major Horton. Decked out in their assorted field uniforms, the small group walked through London's eerily quiet streets. Men in a wide variety of military uniforms, so prevalent throughout the city only a few days before, were few in number on this night. The small group of men finally settled on a restaurant that was nearly empty and enjoyed their first good meal of the day.

The night seemed long in coming. With wartime Britain on double daylight saving time (standard time plus two hours) it remained light until half past ten.

*   *   *

Many Londoners who were not on the streets that night were listening to the nine o'clock BBC news broadcast, where they learned that troops of General Mark Clark's Fifth U.S. Army had entered Rome earlier that day. Following the news, as it did every night, the French-language BBC service aired the "personal messages" that provided coded signals to the French resistance.

At nine-thirty, in the library at Southwick House, Group Captain John Stagg of the Royal Air Force, chief meteorologist at Supreme Headquarters, Allied Expeditionary Force (SHAEF), briefed General Eisenhower and his senior commanders on the near-term weather prospects. Brass and braid filled every easy chair and couch in the small room. Outside, the storm had been gathering strength throughout the day and seemed to threaten disaster if the operation proceeded as scheduled. Every man in the room understood the implications of another postponement. If the landings could not take place on the morning of June 6, as then scheduled, the tide and moon conditions—tides coming in at just the right time to aid the landings and moonlight enough to aid the airborne divisions— would not be favorable again for nearly two weeks. Months of planning and training and waiting were taking their toll on troops as well as commanders. The strain was palpable. But Stagg predicted that a break in the storm would arrive in time for the landings scheduled for the morning of June 6. The commanders would meet again at four-fifteen in the morning for a final update and decision on whether the invasion would be launched.

Early on Monday morning, June 5, through gusting winds and a cold, driving rain, Eisenhower drove the mile from his tent to Southwick House. His staff and subordinate commanders were waiting there for him. Group Captain Stagg once again gave the general the latest weather forecast, which continued to call for a slight break in the storm—probably no more than twenty-four hours. Eisenhower asked each of his subordinate commanders for their recommendation. After each had spoken, Ike thought for a moment, surveying the assembled group through brisk blue eyes, and then gave his decision.

"O.K., let's go."[9] Eisenhower had just ordered the launching of history's greatest military invasion.

General Eisenhower would spend the day visiting British and American units as they prepared to depart. As the day progressed, the sky over southern England remained gray, but the wind began to die down. There was still a distinct chill in the air, while only days before it had been hot.

Throughout that Monday, the two Jedburgh teams sequestered in the row house on Devonshire Close pored over maps and worked on memorizing code names and other details. To Sergeant Kehoe, Captain Cyr seemed a bit edgy, constantly asking questions. But it wasn't just Cyr; all of the men were pretty nervous.[10]

Again, that evening, Major Horton escorted the Jeds to a local restaurant. Unknown to the men as they enjoyed their meal that night, five thousand ships and ten thousand airplanes were preparing to carry nearly two hundred thousand troops across the channel to the beaches of Normandy.

In the very early hours of Tuesday, June 6, light sleepers in London and throughout southern England were aware of endless formations of aircraft passing overhead in a southerly direction. Beginning around midnight, the continuous drone of more than ten thousand Allied planes—bombers, fighters, and troop carriers loaded with fifteen thousand American and eight thousand British paratroopers—caused a vibration that could be felt in the buildings below. Some planes circled over London for nearly two hours as groups formed up before heading toward Normandy. The din continued until after dawn—and by then, tens of thousands of Allied soldiers were fighting to gain and hold a sixty-mile-wide beachhead on the coast of Normandy.

At the Devonshire Close house that Tuesday morning, the Jeds woke to a clear, warm day. An hour before noon, the BBC announced that the invasion of occupied France was under way. By day's end, the Allies would have fifty-five thousand men ashore. All that day and into the following morning, the six Jeds kept the radio on, following the latest updates from the Normandy beachhead.

On Wednesday morning, Major Horton arrived in a Dodge truck stenciled with U.S. Army markings. The men had been issued weapons—American .30-caliber carbines and Colt .45-caliber automatic pistols—radios, frequency crystals, and cipher materials. They threw their gear in the truck, boarded, and were off to the SAS camp.

About fifty miles northwest of London, they came to the medieval city of Oxford, and Major Horton stopped long enough for the men to enjoy a stroll through the university grounds. After hours of sitting through briefings and memorizing details of the mission—as if cramming for the greatest of final exams—the pause at Oxford was like stepping into another world. The Americans, especially, seeing it for the first time, were enchanted with the majestic spires, and the medieval residence halls and academic buildings. Bob Kehoe appreciated the peaceful interlude. Strolling through the manicured gardens of an institution in its eighth century of existence, the oldest university in the English-speaking world, took him away from the war for a time. Much information had been thrown at the Jeds over the past few days—code names, order-of-battle data, cipher procedures, danger signals, evasion methods, agent identities. It could be mind-numbing; the brain needed a break from it all. But the respite ended too soon.[11]

Leaving Oxford, the truck wandered along narrow English roads until it came to the quaint old town of Fairford, in Gloucestershire. South of the town, the truck pulled into a camp that was adjacent to an airfield. In May, the SAS brigade had moved here to be close to the airfields used by their transport, the Royal Air Force's No. 38 Group. They ran a secure camp, meaning that it was enclosed by a double barbed-wire fence and no one was allowed to leave without specific orders.

Kehoe's first impression of the French SAS men was that they were itching for action. "Wild" was a word he used to describe them. They certainly appeared fit, and had obviously trained hard and well. Not surprisingly, both the Jeds and the SAS were uncomfortable with the relationship that had been forced upon them. The redundancy in their missions was obvious to the dullest of military minds, and both groups were uneasy with it. The SAS seemed to regard the Jedburghs as interlopers. Who were these six guys, seemingly just along for the ride? The SAS men were confident of their ability to handle the mission at hand, and they could see little of value that the two Jed teams might add. The men joked and made small talk, feeling one another out, as if the Jeds were new kids in a tough school.

That evening, the two Jedburgh teams were taken to meet the leader of the French SAS contingent that was going into Brittany, thirty-six-year-old Commandant (Major) Pierre-Louis Bourgoin. He was a brawny six-foot-three, with a jowly face that featured a long, broad nose and intense, narrow-set eyes. A thick shock of brown hair sprouted from the widow's peak above his forehead. Commandant Bourgoin would be called handsome only by very close family members. But he was clearly not a man to be trifled with, and the absence of an arm did nothing to diminish that impression. An Algerian-born teacher, he had received his lieutenant's commission in a reserve regiment in 1928, had distinguished himself in battle in North Africa early in the war, and the second of two wounds had cost him the arm. He had taken command of the 4th SAS Battalion in England in November 1943.

Bourgoin met each of the Jeds and, upon greeting Bob Kehoe, remarked how young the sergeant looked. He then directed the Jeds to attend a meeting that he planned to hold in the officers' mess at the evening meal. This, unfortunately, caused a stir. How was Sergeant Kehoe to accompany his teammates to a meeting in the officer's mess, an area off limits to enlisted personnel?

Special Force Headquarters had instructed the Jeds to remain together at all times while on the SAS base. But, like all European armies, France's observed many age-old traditions, including that of a distinct class barrier between officers and enlisted men. The Jeds soon found that the French SAS was no different. Irritated at the thought of having to exclude Sergeant Kehoe from the meeting, Captain Wise convinced their hosts to dispense with custom and to allow Kehoe to join them for dinner and to attend the war council. The French radio operator on team George, Kehoe noted, had just been made an officer.

Thursday—which was Captain Cyr's twenty-third birthday—was spent studying maps with the SAS and sitting through more of Commandant Bourgoin's chalk talks. The Algerian spoke and carried himself with authority, and his men loved him. In the evening, the Jed teams mingled with the SAS officers, and the drinks flowed freely, and as the Jeds learned more about these Frenchmen, their respect grew. Many of them had trained and fought with the British SAS in North Africa. Then they had all gone through commando training in Scotland, as well as parachute training. As the hours passed, the frost on the SAS began to thaw.

Some last-minute promotions came through for the Jeds. Wise was raised to the rank of major and Kehoe to technical sergeant, the rank known today as sergeant first class. But Aguirec's promotion to full lieutenant, the equivalent of first lieutenant, wasn't to come until later.

On Friday, the men packed their gear and prepared for the jump. Kehoe, who had the most to carry, was allowed to make use of a container for the two radios, each of which weighed nearly forty pounds. His carbine went into another container, but he kept his pistol with extra loaded magazines on his belt. Adding to his bulky load were eight cipher books, another book-sized box containing his transmission crystals, and extra dry-cell batteries for the receiver.

The officers each carried a carbine and a rucksack which contained all equipment not otherwise worn or strapped to the body. Like Kehoe's, the officers' rucksacks carried ammunition, rations, and a few extra items of clothing. In a canvas money belt, each officer carried the standard Jedburgh issue of one hundred thousand French francs and fifty U.S. dollars; Kehoe carried another fifty thousand francs and fifty dollars. Each man wore the standard grayish-green British parachute smock over his uniform. The smock would be discarded along with the parachute upon landing. Lastly, the parachute was strapped on.

When all equipment had been checked, the Jeds and the SAS men headed out to the airstrip, where a row of majestic four-engine British Stirling bombers awaited them.[12]

2

INTO THE HORNET'S NEST

THE long, blunt-nosed Stirling had a wingspan of ninety-nine feet, which proved barely adequate; the plane was difficult to get off the ground and ponderous once it was airborne. Because it was so inferior in performance to the next generation of bombers—the American B-24s and B-17s, for example—Britain's Bomber Command had stopped using the Stirling in early 1943. The black planes which now stood before the Jeds had been relegated to the shadow war; they belonged to two squadrons from 38 Group, which flew primarily for the SAS.

Both Jed teams prayed that the mission would be a go. So many missions were scrubbed at this stage because of bad weather over the target area or a last-minute message from the field warning that German activity near the drop zone made it too risky. Some unfortunate teams took off and made it nearly to the drop area before the mission was aborted and the team had to turn back.

It was a pleasant enough evening, with only a slight cloud cover. Special operations air missions like these depended on moonlight, both to provide jumpers some ability to see the ground below them and to aid the reception committee in its work. Cloud cover increasing to the point of obstructing the moon could cause a postponement of the mission. This night was near the end of the moon phase—a half-moon lingered low in the sky—so an uncomfortably long delay was possible.

Containers packed with weapons, explosives, and other gear for the maquis were first stowed aboard by the aircrew. These would be dropped after the parachutists had all jumped. Two of the containers held Bob Kehoe's carbine and the team's two radios. The men checked each other's parachutes to ensure that the harnesses were in good condition and fastened correctly.

The aircrews had planned a late-night departure. In early June days were long, and the crews wanted the added security that a takeoff in darkness provided. Brittany was not far away; it would be a relatively short flight. At 2330 hours (or eleven-thirty PM) the heavily laden men of the Samwest SAS party and Jed team Frederick lined up to board three Stirlings from 620 Squadron. Each plane would carry about fifteen jumpers, along with the dispatcher and the crew. All told, the three planes' cargo included fifty men, twenty-three containers, and five smaller parcels.

Not far away, Jed team George and the Dingson SAS detachment began climbing aboard two Stirlings from 299 Squadron. The same load of men and containers that the Samwest group had put into three planes in this case was loaded into only two. The Stirling's fuselage was long but narrow and, with space taken up by the containers, it was a tight fit for the jumpers. They were packed in like travelers on a cheap bus. At twenty-six minutes past midnight, team Frederick's plane lifted off. Nine minutes later, team George was airborne.[1]

On team Frederick's plane, the pilot steered low along a prescribed route, one that would become familiar to the crew in the coming week. The Jeds were seated in the middle of a row—known in paratrooper jargon as a stick—of SAS troopers. Kehoe's position in the stick determined that he would be the fourth man to jump. Four husky Bristol engines pulled the big plane over the Channel at just over two hundred miles per hour. In the bomber's dark interior, the steady grind of the Bristols was oddly comforting—if you let it, it could put you to sleep. At times, the plane bucked or jigged, or suddenly shifted direction ever so slightly, as the pilot sparred with the wind and attempted to dodge antiaircraft fire when they crossed over the French coastline. Slightly more than an hour into the flight, the dispatcher shouted the "Running in!" alert. The plane passed over the drop zone once and circled back; the SAS and Jeds would be ready to drop through the open bomb bay on the second pass.

Any fear of jumping had been forced to the deepest recesses of Bob Kehoe's mind by the thoughts of what might happen once the men left the aircraft. Two of the three possibilities that coursed through his consciousness were not attractive. Machine gun and small-arms fire could greet them as they hung helplessly under canopy. Worse, the Gestapo could be on the ground waiting to police them up as soon as the jumpers touched down. The third prospect, of course, was that all would go as planned. Then the men were standing, with their static lines hooked to the overhead cable, and almost without realizing it, Bob Kehoe found himself reciting the Twenty-third Psalm.[2]

When the dispatcher shouted, "Go!" the Stirling emptied its human load faster than seemed possible. The jump procedure on the Stirling was new to the Jeds. Like commuters hurrying to make a subway connection, the men raced toward the rear of the aircraft, scrambling as fast as their load and the bear-hugging parachute harness would allow. Reaching the gaping bomb bay opening, they spilled through into the moonlit Breton sky.

Kehoe's mind was jolted back to mission awareness by the shock of the parachute opening—but the euphoria that an air-filled canopy evokes in every jumper was followed sooner than expected by a bone-jarring landing. Although the pilot had tried to drop the men at an altitude of between six hundred and eight hundred feet, Kehoe was sure that they must have jumped from less than five hundred feet. There had barely been time for the parachute to open.

Kehoe got up from the ground and began rolling up his chute. He looked around but saw no sign of the other Jeds. Not far away, fires were burning. He was startled at first when two figures approached in the dark from a nearby woods. Kehoe's first reaction was to reach for his pistol, but the two men greeted him warmly and told him that they would take care of his parachute. They told the young American to follow them, and Kehoe was led to one of the fires. Other jumpers filtered in, and soon he was reunited with Major Wise and Lieutenant Aguirec.

The SAS men quickly conducted checks to account for everyone and to determine whether anyone had been injured. One SAS trooper, Kehoe quickly learned, had been killed upon landing because he had ignored standard safety procedure that called for detonators to be packed separately from explosive charges. That accounted for the odd, muffled explosions that the Jeds had heard during their descent. The SAS man had gambled and lost.

The reception committee was large—much larger than it needed to be or should have been with Germans not far away. Normally, reception committees were formed and assigned to mark the site for the pilot and then to quickly clear it of parachutes, containers, and other debris after the drop. Jumpers were to be whisked off to a safer location. All of this was to be done as rapidly as possible—before the Germans could react.

But the Jeds found themselves in the midst of something more like a celebration—a community event. People of all ages crowded around them in the glow of the fire. Excited children scampered about as if they were on a school outing. Women thrust mugs of bitter apple cider into the Jeds' hands, or gave them Brittany's version of Calvados, an apple brandy which has been called the "White Lightning" of Normandy (potent stuff—as much as 140 proof—you could use it for lantern fuel). They also offered the men bread and butter and cheese.

People questioned the French SAS about their families. Where were the men from? How had they gotten to England? The local people were intensely interested in Bob Kehoe, the man in the strange olive-drab uniform. While the French were familiar with the tan British battledress worn by Major Wise and Lieutenant Aguirec (the latter with French insignia), no one from these parts had seen an American uniform in more than twenty years. And he was so young!

Word spread through the crowd that this was the advance party for a major Allied landing to come on the shores of Brittany, and so the Jeds were pumped for details of the presumably imminent operation. And the bonfires—they were enormous. The whole thing had a high school pep rally quality to it.[3]

The team had come down in farmland south of the town of Guingamp in north-central Brittany, amid a patchwork of hedgerow-bordered fields with narrow and often sunken one-lane trails.[4] The scantily populated countryside was rugged and rocky, with traces of forest and scattered farmsteads and grasslands supporting small cattle herds.

The SAS detachment which had jumped in here on the eve of D-Day had organized the reception committee from local resistance workers—but had done a poor job of it. Security on the drop zone was a joke. German troops occupied a town barely two miles away. Seemingly oblivious to the danger, this large crowd of men and women had gathered to watch the spectacle. Cigarettes burned in the night, not that it mattered much with the large bonfires still ablaze, fires which should have been much smaller and should have been extinguished the minute the planes departed. The Jeds were appalled.

In fact, the SAS advance party—the handful of men who had formed the reception committee—could not have done a better job of *violating* security rules if they'd worked from a checklist. Noise and light discipline was nonexistent. And the throng that had gathered to watch indicated that far too many people knew far too much about things that they had no business knowing. There were even reports of the SAS men dining in local restaurants. It all seemed headed toward a bad end. You just didn't carry on like that in the enemy's backyard.

Eventually, the drop zone was cleared, and Sergeant Kehoe found that his carbine had not survived the jump. The container it was in had been smashed on impact. Both radios, however, were all right. Someone handed Kehoe a Sten submachine gun for his personal use.

With the equipment accounted for, the Jeds followed the SAS advance party to the base camp southwest of Guingamp. The camp was well concealed, about a mile into the Forêt de Duault, a modest-sized vestige of the conifer forests that once covered inland Brittany. There were many hardwoods now, and thick growths of a dense, spiny shrub called gorse. The camp was fairly high up on the side of a rather steep hill, where boulders were crowded in amongst a thick stand of trees. It was a good site, difficult for the Germans to spot, even from the air.[5]

Late on their first day in camp, the Jeds stumbled onto an ugly scene. Groups of partisans had been filtering into camp throughout the day, anxious to benefit from the distribution of arms that had accompanied the Jeds and SAS. While walking about the camp late that evening, the Jeds came upon a small crowd gathered around three people in civilian clothes. One of the three, a man, was sprawled on the ground, his face battered to a pulp from numerous beatings. The other two were women. The maquis had accused the trio of spying for the Germans.

The recruiting of resistance fighters, the Jeds had learned back at Milton Hall, was one of the most dangerous of guerrilla activities. Over the past few years, the Germans had become adept at infiltrating Vichy loyalist French into resistance groups to act as spies for the Germans. An alternate, and often more effective, method was to quietly capture a known resistance member and, through the threat of harm to his family, turn him into an informer. And in the spring of 1944, the Germans had stepped-up their efforts to penetrate the maquis in the hope of learning details of the expected invasion.

Ideally, when new recruits joined a maquis group, they underwent a period of probation while background checks were conducted. Candidates were kept under surveillance and did not meet other members of the group until each check had been accomplished. Whether these three people had survived such a vetting was not clear, but something had tipped off the maquis as to their true allegiance.

Questioning was quickly followed by guerrilla justice. The maquis inquisitors shot one of the women and stabbed the man to death. According to author Roger Ford, Captain Leblond later reported that, as a result of the interrogations, two people—a man and woman—were determined to be spies, infiltrators working for the Germans. The man had contradicted himself three times and was found to have a plan of the camp on him, and the woman was carrying a list of nearby villages. Leblond reported that he had ordered that both of them be shot.[6]

Perhaps fear of appearing too soft for the partisan war prevented the Jeds from intervening. Among the things at which special forces men had to be adept was the ability, when the situation called for it, to mind their own business. After all, they were newcomers and had yet to prove their value to the group. Prudently, they accepted that this was not their concern, and they were careful to stay out of it.[7]

Sergeant Kehoe was to make radio contact with London as soon as possible; the operations staff there would be anxiously awaiting word of the team's safe landing and recovery by the maquis. But London would not receive such a message on this day. Try as he might, Kehoe's first attempts at making contact failed. The seriousness of this was not lost on him. Indeed, all of the Jeds knew that the "wireless" man was key to their success and their survival. He was their lifeline, their sole means of gaining and maintaining contact with London. Kehoe would try again the next day.

Britain's Special Operations Executive, which early in the war had depended on the Secret Intelligence Service for radios, had begun developing its own in mid-1942. After a couple of early less-than-adequate models, the SOE introduced the Type B Mark II set, more commonly called the B2, in 1943. This radio proved to be highly effective and popular with users. In the version designed for agents who operated in civilian clothes, the transmitter, receiver, power supply, and accessories were all housed in a common-looking suitcase not much larger than an attaché case. Completely equipped with headset, aerial wire, and other accessories, the set weighed thirty-two pounds and had a range of more than five hundred miles. A modified version of the B2, carried in a compartmented canvas backpack, was developed for use by the Jedburghs and came to be called the Jed Set.

Whereas the B2 was designed to work from the main power supply found in houses or other buildings, or from a six-volt battery, the Jed Set was capable of operating in the countryside, away from main power supplies. It included a receiver which operated on dry-cell batteries and a transmitter powered by a small, tripod-mounted hand-cranked generator. The entire Jed Set was packed in five small canvas-web satchels and weighed thirty-seven pounds.[8]

Radio contacts were to be made according to a pre-arranged schedule. That schedule also determined the frequency to be used, and this varied according to the time of day, because optimum signal propagation varied throughout the day. Setting the frequency was accomplished by inserting the proper crystal, a fragile postage-stamp-size slice of quartz in a small rectangular Bakelite (plastic or resin) housing, with a pair of plug-in prongs. The precisely cut thickness of the quartz determined the signal's wavelength.

The next day, June 11, Sergeant Kehoe moved farther up the hill to make another attempt at sending his message. Finding what appeared to be a good spot, he laid out the hand-cranked generator and his transmitter and sending key and strung up his aerial wire. He then took out the message he had prepared based on Wise's instructions, written out and enciphered for transmission to London. When all was ready, someone turned the generator for him and Kehoe tapped out the message. In its deciphered form back in England, the message read: "ARRIVED SAFELY WITH ALL CONTAINERS AND EQUIPMENT. HAVE CONTACTED LOCAL GROUPS. GREAT POSSIBILITIES COTES DU NORD AREA. SEND JED TEAM AND ARMS FOR THEM. ADVISE SOONEST POSSIBLE DROPPING GROUND."[9] When he was finished, Kehoe destroyed the written message and packed up his radio.

Bob Kehoe had been a nineteen-year-old lab assistant in a chemical plant, with two years of college under his belt and no firm plans for the future, at the time of the bombing of Pearl Harbor. Anxious to enlist in response to that attack, like countless others, Kehoe had first tried joining the air corps with the intent of going to flight school. His nearsightedness, however, had closed that door. He had been taking a course in radio mechanics in civilian life, so he decided to enlist in the army Signal Corps, and was sent to Camp Crowder, Missouri, for basic training and radio operator training.[10] Near the town of Neosho, in the Ozarks of southwest Missouri, Camp Crowder had been established as a U.S. Army Signal Corps Training Center early in 1942. And Neosho, like so many other small communities of the time, saw its population more than double almost overnight with the camp's construction. Averaging a military population of forty thousand, the camp generated something of an economic boom for the town that had been the boyhood home of both Thomas Hart Benton and George Washington Carver.

By the fall of 1943, Kehoe was deep into the Morse code training course at Crowder. The Signal Corps began to strike him as pretty dull, however, and he kept his ears open for an opportunity to get closer to the war. Just such an opportunity arrived at lunchtime one day, with an announcement that came over the camp's loudspeaker. There was to be a briefing for any qualified radioman who spoke a foreign language or was interested in hearing about a special mission offering immediate overseas assignment.

Kehoe attended the talk given by a Captain Al Cox, a stranger to Camp Crowder. As details of the assignment emerged, soldiers began to get up and leave; and the longer Cox spoke, the more the audience thinned out. Men with two years of college were most desired, the captain said. Kehoe had that. It would be helpful if volunteers had some knowledge or training in a European language, particularly French. And then the kicker that sent most men scurrying for the door: Parachute training would be required and the prospects for hazardous duty were very good. Still not deterred, Kehoe volunteered, was interviewed, and was among those selected for the project.

For a time, he heard nothing else of the enigmatic assignment, and Kehoe's friends assured him that he had made a foolish mistake. But he noted a tinge of envy when they said it; such secrecy excited young minds. It also drove domineering first sergeants up a wall. Nothing riled a "top kick" more than having to ship good men off to God-knows-where on secret orders that he couldn't even question. God-knows-where, in this case, turned out to be a high-society country club outside Washington, D.C., and a remote camp in the Maryland mountains, both of which had become training areas for the Office of Strategic Services—the OSS. After nearly two months of training and psychological assessment at those locations, the men selected to remain in the unit boarded a train for Fort Hamilton, New York, a port of embarkation for the European Theater.

During his brief stay at Fort Hamilton, Sergeant Kehoe found time for a quick trip home to New Jersey. Under strict security restrictions, he was only allowed to tell his puzzled family that he was about to go overseas. His parents tried to make sense of the sudden change in Bob's status and of his unexpected embarkation. Why was he shipping out so soon, when his two older brothers, both of whom had served longer than he had, remained stateside?

It just didn't make any sense. But Bob could say nothing of his unit or the nature of his work, and it was all a little unsettling to the family.[11]

After having met some of the local maquis and witnessed the manner in which informers were handled, Major Wise, Lieutenant Aguirec, and Sergeant Kehoe began to settle into their work. They were somewhat disconcerted, though, by the way the SAS was feverishly arming the maquis—with little thought to training or security measures. And, soon, the inevitable happened.

On Sunday evening, June 11—the same day that Bob Kehoe had earlier made his first radio contact with London—a small group of patriots gathered at a farm about two hundred yards from the camp. They were freshly armed young men, but were untrained and untested—combat virgins—as green as week-old apples. Having been invited for supper, they were enjoying their meal when a car pulled up to the farmhouse. Two German officers got out and approached the house, unaware of the danger inside.

Upon entering, the Germans politely asked for directions to the nearby town of Carhaix. One of the officers stepped into the room where the young maquisards were eating. Repeating the request for directions, the German was completely unprepared for the burst of submachine gun bullets that ripped open his abdomen. Miraculously, the officer was able to stagger back to the car, all the time containing his ruptured belly with one hand. One of the Germans then pulled out a hand grenade and threw it at the house.[12]

Men at the SAS camp heard the Sten gunfire and the grenade explosion and prepared for action, but nothing more happened that night. At dawn, trucks delivered forty members of a nearby German parachute division, and the paratroopers burned the farm—in retribution—killing everyone there.[13]

The SAS outposts located nearest to the farm opened up on the Germans with every weapon they had, but a quick radio call by the enemy brought help. By mid-afternoon, reinforcements had arrived and an estimated four hundred enemy paratroopers were attacking the maquis outposts. In June 1944, the parachute divisions were probably the best combat troops Germany had in France—so this was no slouch outfit. The enemy paratroopers fanned out and began a slow but steady advance through the forest, directly toward the SAS base.

Sergeant Kehoe, as he was sending another message to London, became aware of the attack when he heard rifle shots coming from the north and west. He immediately broke off the radio transmission and packed up the radio.

Kehoe attributed the German assault to the reckless manner in which the SAS reception committee had behaved, advertising their presence with large bonfires and crowds. He feared that the trigger-happy maquis would generate a mass uprising, which, he knew, the local resistance was in no way strong enough to carry out. They needed time—time to build up arms and ammunition, time to be trained, time for the Allied armies to draw nearer. The best that the Jeds and SAS could hope to do now was to escape with as many men as possible, kill as many Germans as they could in the process, and regroup to fight another day.

The situation rapidly worsened for the maquis and their Allied benefactors, including the Jeds. The isolation of the guerrilla war struck home to them; the nearest Allied combat division was nearly two hundred miles away, in Normandy. There, American and British forces had just linked up to form a sixty-mile long beach-head, but it would be more than a month before sufficient forces were ashore to launch a breakout toward Brittany. So help would be a long time in coming. In the meantime, the Jeds and the SAS had their wits and little else to see them through.

As the minutes passed, the fighting steadily approached the SAS command post. Although another fifty SAS men had jumped in, as planned, raising the total strength of SAS and Jedburghs in the Duault forest to a hundred and fifteen, they were still badly out-numbered. The SAS, along with a few dozen maquis, put up a ter-rific fight, reportedly killing at least fifty-five Germans and wounding close to twice that number, at a cost of seventeen SAS casualties.[14] But, by late afternoon, the sputtering of British-made Stens and Bren guns steadily gave way to the distinctive belch of German Schmeissers and the occasional jackhammer drill of MG42 machine guns. Kehoe and the others had spent hours famil-iarizing themselves with German weapons at Milton Hall, and the authoritative voice of the precision-engineered guns was unmistakable.

When Captain Leblond of the SAS judged their position untenable, he ordered a withdrawal southward to the SAS Dingson base, some ninety miles away. Sergeant Kehoe thought it a stupid decision but was in no position to argue.[15] The Jeds hurriedly packed up their gear, taking only that which they considered necessary to fight their way out and survive. Weapons and ammunition. Maps. Medical aid kit. A small amount of food. They decided to take one radio and hide the other in hopes of retrieving it later; that would lighten their load by nearly forty pounds. And, because Kehoe expected that the Germans would thoroughly search the command post site, he quickly decided to hide the radio some distance away. Shots cracked over his head as he ran down the hill in the direction that the enemy fire was coming from. He recognized that most of the German fire was concentrated on the SAS positions at the edge of the woods. As soon as Kehoe found a spot in a depression—out of sight of the enemy—he hid the radio under a large boulder, covered it as well as he could, and took careful notice of the trees and rocks nearby, as they would have to serve as landmarks when he was able to return.

By this time, SAS troops were leaving in small groups, and those fighting so hard to hold the perimeter would soon have to bolt as well. Intent on avoiding capture (or worse), the Jeds broke out to the east. They had been joined by a British Royal Air Force officer who was serving in a liaison capacity with the SAS, a squadron leader (major equivalent) named Smith. He was a tall man in his forties with a spidery build, and he had jumped in with the follow-up SAS contingent the previous day.

Kehoe couldn't help but notice how Smith's bright blue RAF uniform stood out. None of the Jeds knew Smith, but it was clear that the man preferred to stick with them. Clearly unprepared for such action, though, he quickly proved to be a hindrance, and the Jeds wondered how anyone could send such an ill-prepared man on a mission behind enemy lines. Kehoe also noticed Smith's obvious lack of ground tactical training when, as the others crept along at ground level, Smith walked along the crest of the hedgerows.

Known as "bocage," these embankments of earth, trees, and

shrubbery—anywhere from three to twelve feet in height—had bordered the fields of Normandy and Brittany for centuries, serving as fences. Moving along the tops of the embankments, Smith was silhouetted like a tin rabbit in an arcade shooting gallery. Worst of all, though, was the slowing effect he had on the team. Determined to keep up, he probably did better than most men his age would, but he was not in shape for this. They were literally running for their lives, and he was like a flat tire on a getaway car. Kehoe would never understand how the man survived.

At first, they headed north, following an old forest road. Then German rifle and machine gun fire from the west forced the men to turn eastward and they scampered into some brush, expecting to shortly be overrun by the enemy. They also expected the Germans to begin pumping mortar rounds at them, but that didn't happen. The Jeds then made a desperate decision. The way ahead of them to the east—the only direction they could go to have any chance of breaking out—was thick with brush and hedgerows. To shed all the weight they possibly could, to make better time and put more distance between themselves and the enemy, the team agreed to hide the remaining radio. Hurriedly, the men placed it behind a boulder near the road, although it was not well hidden.

Breaking through the dense growth of vegetation as quickly as they could, the Jeds eventually came to some cultivated fields. Kehoe noted how speedy Squadron Leader Smith had become since he'd been motivated by German gunfire. The small group continued on, using the cover of the woods and brush as much as possible, until it came to a hard-surfaced road and prepared to cross it.

Just then, a fighter plane roared overhead on a strafing run. Although the Jeds couldn't see what it was firing at, they assumed that the plane was German and that they were its intended targets. But when the fighter rolled around for another pass, the men identified it as a British twin-engine Beaufighter; and then they saw what it was targeting.

A German motorcycle patrol was heading north on the same road the Jeds were about to cross. Sustained bursts of fire from the Beaufighter's wing-mounted .303-caliber machine guns discouraged further pursuit by the patrol, and the Germans abruptly reversed direction and disappeared. Had the Jeds just been lucky?

Kehoe recalled that the attack on the command post had come during his radio contact with London earlier in the day, and that he had been forced to break off right after transmitting the signal for imminent danger. Perhaps this fighter had been dispatched as a result of that call. Whatever the reason, luck seemed to be with team Frederick.

The men pressed on, staying in the forest as much as possible and skirting fields when necessary. They had learned their lesson about avoiding roads. As they made their way, they were occasionally seen by local people. The careful Bretons, though, aware of the assault on the Duault Forest, ignored the small group. Germans had posted notices throughout France, warning of the price to be paid for helping Allied parachutists. Men would be shot, women sent off to concentration camps. One such warning issued by the German high command bluntly explained: "Whoever on French territory outside the zone of legal combat is captured and identified as having participated in sabotage, terrorism, or revolt is and remains a bandit or franc-tireur [guerrilla] and shall consequently be shot, whatever his nationality or uniform."[16]

As dusk approached, the Jeds looked for a place to rest but consciously kept their distance from villages and farmhouses—for the Germans surely would be conducting searches. Finding at last what appeared to be an isolated drainage ditch, well-concealed by a thicket of the dense, spiny gorse, the four men crawled in and collapsed. After eating some bread, they let exhaustion overtake them and slept, with no lookout posted, until dawn. When they awoke the next morning, early rays of sunshine revealed that the drainage ditch they had spent the night in was not as isolated as they had believed. Not fifty yards away was a small farmhouse.

Hungry and chilled to the bone, the men decided, despite the potential danger, to see if anyone was in the house and to try to obtain some food. Lieutenant Aguirec approached the house while the others waited in the ditch. A woman answered the door, but when Aguirec greeted her, she responded in a strange language. Aguirec nearly panicked, thinking she might be speaking German. But then he recalled that many people in the area spoke only Breton. A younger woman, who spoke French, appeared. She told the lieutenant that she had heard of the fight in the forest and that she was willing to help the team. She instructed Aguirec to return to the ditch while she gathered some food to bring to the men. Thirty minutes later, the Jeds were enjoying their first real meal in twenty-four hours—potatoes and gravy and bread and boiled milk.

The young woman introduced herself as Simone Le Göeffic. She explained that she was a schoolteacher from a nearby town called Trémargat, but that school had been suspended at the time of the Allied invasion. Of more importance at the moment, though, was the fact that she was involved in the resistance. A woman of disarming charm, with light-brown neck-length hair and an attractive figure, she now took charge of the situation. She instructed the men to remain where they were. She would be back in the evening with instructions and a guide. Then she was off on a bicycle. All day, the Jeds remained in the ditch, speculating on the trustworthiness of Simone Le Göeffic and bothered only by occasional visits from inquisitive cows.

Simone returned that evening, as promised, and with her was a muscular, ruddy-faced young man with light hair named Marcel Queinnec, who was to be their guide. They would have to wait until dark before moving, however, Simone and Marcel cautioned, because the Germans were on a high state of alert. Patrols had been combing the area all day.

After nightfall, Marcel led the team southward toward a town where the Jeds were to be handed off to another guide. But the guide did not show, and so the men remained hidden in the woods outside of town.

During the night, Simone arrived on her bicycle and told the Jeds of three SAS men, two officers and a corporal, who had been severely wounded in the previous day's battle and who'd been taken to a deserted farm near the forest. Major Wise decided that the team should return and see what they could do for the SAS men.

The farm lay at the end of a winding path, not far from the village of Peumerit-Quintin. When the Jeds arrived, they found Marcel's wife, Louise, and another woman from the village, Madame Le Moigne, attending to the wounded men. The SAS casualties, they learned, had been brought in on stretchers under the direction of an SAS sergeant by the name of Jean Robert, who was also present. A doctor had arrived (by bicycle) from Guingamp and performed life-saving surgery on the two officers under austere conditions.

All three of the wounded men appeared to the Jeds to be near death, although the corporal seemed to be in slightly better condition than the officers. Moving the wounded men obviously was out of the question. The two women would look after the SAS men and shelter them from the Germans until they were fit to rejoin their unit. Louise Queinnec—an attractive, smooth-complexioned woman with long, dark hair—and her husband Marcel were schoolteachers at Peumerit-Quintin and had two small children. For the remainder of this summer of 1944, however, the Queinnec children would be under the care of family friends. Marcel's time largely would be spent with Jed team Frederick, and Louise would be occupied with looking after the wounded SAS men.

After seeing that the wounded men were being taken care of, the Jeds made contact with the departmental resistance chief for the Côtes-du-Nord, a man called Marceau. As it turned out, Marceau was a close friend of Marcel Queinnec, who was quickly becoming a valuable asset to team Frederick, being both resourceful and reliable. Marceau had grown up on Brittany's south coast in a Breton-speaking home, only learning French when he began school. He had fought with a division in northeastern France in June 1940, but when his unit was decimated and demoralized to the point of surrendering, Marcel had left and made his way back to Brittany.

Major Wise was faced with a decision. Would the team continue to make its way to the Dingson SAS base, or instead stay and work with Marceau? When an operation has not worked out as planned, or the situation has changed, as indeed this one had, a good leader will remember the higher commander's intent and adjust the plan in accordance with it. Adrian Wise knew what had to be done. The Jedburghs had been formed and trained for months to carry out guerrilla warfare with the maquis, not to scamper from one SAS base to another. Team Frederick would get on with it from right here.[17]

3

AN ALTERNATIVE FORM OF WARFARE

T HE genesis of the Jedburghs lay in events that unfolded more than four years before the first teams jumped into France. In September 1939 Hitler's army and air force invaded Poland, an unprovoked mauling that brought Britain and France to declare war on Germany. Then, in May 1940, after long months of what journalists called the "sitzkrieg" or "phony war," the Nazi war machine launched a blitzkrieg invasion of the Low Countries (comprised of Belgium, Luxembourg, and the Netherlands). Within forty-eight hours of crossing the Belgian border, German tanks broke through the Ardennes forest and entered France by outflanking the Maginot Line, the expensive string of concrete gun emplacements and fortifications along the republic's eastern frontier. Panzers, as the German tanks were called, brushed aside the sparingly armored French forces in the region, forced the British to evacuate their army from the beaches at Dunkirk, and muscled their way on toward the capital.

By June 10, the streets of Paris were strangely empty and quiet; many of her citizens had joined the pitiful exodus of refugees fleeing the city. Cars and horse-drawn wagons, handcarts and wheelbarrows, bicycles and baby carriages, and people on foot filled all roads leading westward or southward from Paris. All forms of transport were loaded down with family possessions—clothing, mattresses, heirloom furniture—anything that could be salvaged or that could ease the transition to the unknown life and dangers that lay ahead. Among the crowds of refugees were the members of the French government, which was abandoning Paris to regroup in Bordeaux on the Atlantic coast to the southwest.

British Prime Minister Neville Chamberlain—naive champion of a failed policy of appeasement—resigned soon after the Germans entered Belgium, and King George VI asked Winston Churchill, then first lord of the Admiralty, to form a new government. From 1933 until 1939, Churchill had been a lonely voice speaking out against Nazi Germany, decrying the appeasement policies of the governments of Stanley Baldwin and Chamberlain. When war came in 1939, Churchill was returned to the post of first lord of the Admiralty and, as the Germans overran Western Europe, was seen as the one man capable of leading Britain through the crisis.

Even though more than three hundred thousand British and French troops had been saved at Dunkirk, virtually all of their weapons and equipment had to be abandoned on the beaches of France. There were not a hundred tanks left in all of Britain, and it would take months—or even years—to build the war machine needed to liberate the fallen countries of Europe. Until such time, the people of France would simply have to hold on, suffering as best they could the humiliation and hardships of occupation. But there were other ways to continue the fight.

Churchill and a few others in government began to talk of an armed resistance movement within France, and Churchill was hardly unfamiliar with the subject. Thomas Edward "T. E." Lawrence, the "Lawrence of Arabia" who had raised the Arabs in revolt against the Germans and Turks in the First World War, was a friend and had been a frequent visitor to Churchill's home at Chartwell in the inter-war years.[1] As Hitler's armies swept over Western Europe in the early summer of 1940, the new prime minister and others considered such an armed resistance movement as a method by which the occupied countries could continue the fight against Germany while the British army was being rebuilt. Plans also were made for an organized force to conduct guerrilla warfare against the Germans on home soil should Hitler succeed in invading the British Isles.

On June 11, Churchill and his top military advisors flew to France to talk with the leaders of the country, who were then en route to Bordeaux. Churchill urged his plan for guerrilla warfare on the French cabinet and senior military leaders, but such ideas generated little enthusiasm, and the French were angered that this was all the British could offer at a time when they were asking for fighter squadrons. Only one among the French agreed with Churchill, the newly appointed under-secretary of state for national defense, the tall and sensitive Brigadier General Charles Joseph de Gaulle. The day after Churchill's first meeting with the French leaders, the young general departed for Brittany, boarded a plane for London, and a week later delivered a radio address calling for all free Frenchmen to stand together in defiance of the German occupation.

France fell soon after Churchill returned to London. The French declared Paris an open city on June 13, and the following day German soldiers paraded arrogantly and triumphantly down the Champs-Élysées. Two days later, Paul Reynaud resigned as premier and Marshal Philippe Pétain, the aged hero of Verdun, took over direction of the French government and sued for peace.

Under the terms of an armistice signed on June 25, Germany occupied three-fifths of France and annexed the regions of Alsace and Moselle. Pétain and his cohort Pierre Laval established a collaborationist government at the sleepy spa town of Vichy to rule over the unoccupied southeastern portion of the country. French divisions were demobilized, though Vichy France was allowed to keep an "Armistice Army" of limited size and capability, and Hitler hauled more than a million and a half French prisoners of war to Germany to be held as virtual hostages, hoping thereby to ensure French cooperation. Pétain's government broke off diplomatic relations with the British and sentenced de Gaulle, in absentia, to death as a traitor.

Men and women of France, humiliated and angered by German occupation policies that led to the systematic plundering of their country to the Reich's benefit, searched for solace in organized opposition. Almost immediately, small and unrelated pockets of resistance began to emerge throughout France. And as summer gave way to autumn, and the initial shock of defeat wore off, those isolated pockets grew and coalesced, like a nascent cancer in the growing body of the Third Reich.

Several senior British government and military officials had foreseen the likelihood of war with Germany as early as 1938 and, like all the war-scarred people of Britain and France, they were apprehensive of another conflict. Both countries had spent much of their youth and treasure on the war of 1914–18 and were fearful of another such costly ordeal. Aside from the astronomical financial cost of that conflict, Britain had lost nearly a million men dead, more than two million wounded, and almost two hundred thousand missing, leaving Churchill to observe that the victory had been "bought so dear as to be indistinguishable from defeat."[2] In March 1938, the Secret Intelligence Service had formed a new branch whose job it would be to study "alternative forms of warfare,"[3] in an effort to avoid losing another generation to barbarous trench warfare.

Churchill and others believed that the people of occupied Europe, through organized underground resistance movements, should have a large role in their own liberation. And Britain, they agreed, needed an organization capable of nourishing and directing such movements. So, in July 1940, the War Cabinet approved the charter for a new organization to be called the Special Operations Executive, or SOE. To its newly appointed director, Dr. Hugh Dalton, the serving Minister of Economic Warfare, Churchill offered succinct instructions: "And now, set Europe ablaze."[4]

To carry out its work in France, the SOE created F Section, one of a number of country sections to deal with resistance movements in occupied Europe. Soon F Section began parachuting agents throughout France with the mission of organizing "circuits" of trained and equipped saboteurs. These were not to be intelligence networks; rather, the business of the circuits would be special operations, and particularly sabotage. Intelligence would remain the business of the Secret Intelligence Service.

Typically, F Section's circuits were set up and run by three agents—an organizer, a lieutenant, and a radio operator. Some were military people, others civilians, and while most were men there also were some women. All potential agents were put through a lengthy and demanding selection and training regimen that weeded out all but those best suited to the work. All spoke French fluently—most without a foreign accent—and they performed their duties in civilian clothes while carrying forged papers to conceal their true identities. Some agents had lived in France as children, others had lived there for many years before the war for business purposes. All of F Section's agents, though, had to be British citizens, or at least hold dual citizenship. For SOE also supported another section—RF Section—which served General de Gaulle's Free French organization; and, by agreement, all agents of French citizenship were allotted to RF Section. In time, F Section would also employ American agents.

Across the Atlantic, President Franklin D. Roosevelt took the first step in establishing an American special operations capability in the spring of 1941. On May 27, primarily due to an increasing threat from German naval actions in the Atlantic, the president declared a limited state of national emergency in the United States.

One of the many emergency measures that the president invoked was the creation of a service responsible for secret intelligence and special operations. In July, he named fifty-eight-year-old William Joseph Donovan to be director of the office of Coordinator of Information, an organization established for that purpose. The stout, white-haired, blue-eyed Donovan had commanded a New York National Guard cavalry troop that rode with Pershing's 1916 expedition into Mexico in pursuit of Pancho Villa. He later earned the Medal of Honor—as well as the Distinguished Service Cross, the Distinguished Service Medal, and the French Croix de Guerre—while leading a battalion of the famed "Fighting 69th" Infantry Regiment in World War I, then went on to become a successful Wall Street attorney and a millionaire.

Roosevelt had long admired Donovan, whom he had first known as a fellow law student at Columbia, and, in spite of his political affiliation—Donovan was a Hoover Republican—the president put

Donovan's talents to work during the 1930s, sending him around the world on secret fact-finding missions.[5] Donovan met with Benito Mussolini in Rome in 1935 and joined Generalissimo Francisco Franco's army in the field in 1939, during Spain's civil war, to get a firsthand look at new German and Italian weapons. He had even observed German army maneuvers near Nuremberg on behalf of the War Department, and visited France, Belgium, Holland, Germany, and Scandinavia.

Arguably, though, Donovan's most important excursion as an agent for the president came when he visited England in July 1940. There, he met with King George VI and discussed British war preparations with Prime Minister Churchill. He also talked with the War Cabinet, the British chiefs of staff, and their commanders in chief.

The meetings which influenced Donovan most, however, were those with Colonel Stewart Menzies, head of Britain's intelligence service, and with Colonel Colin Gubbins of the newly formed Special Operations Executive. Gubbins, a gifted artillerist who was fluent in French and German, had written two pamphlets on the subject of irregular warfare—*The Art of Guerrilla Warfare* and *Partisan Leaders' Handbook*—and he was to figure prominently in the development and approval of the Jedburgh concept. He brought Donovan up to date on work being done to develop resistance movements in occupied territories. Both Menzies and Gubbins were unusually generous with the sensitive information they shared with Donovan, as Churchill had directed them to be.

Shortly after the December 7, 1941, Japanese attack on Pearl Harbor and Germany's declaration of war on the United States a few days later, Churchill sailed to Washington to confer with Roosevelt on an Anglo-American war strategy. The prime minister wasted no time in presenting his proposals—he introduced them during a White House dinner party, which William Donovan attended, on his first evening in Washington. Churchill envisioned landings in western and southern Europe by the armies of Great Britain and the United States, and a simultaneous uprising by the populations of the occupied countries.[6] Although Roosevelt and Donovan were intrigued by Churchill's plan, the more traditional American chiefs of staff were not.

Donovan, like Gubbins in Britain, was left to advocate an irregular warfare strategy to a General Staff which did not understand it or believe in it. Indeed, many senior army leaders of both countries shunned such unorthodox thinking, considered it distasteful and ungentlemanly, and viewed Donovan and Gubbins as adventuristic mavericks. Fortunately, some of the more open-minded Allied generals would later be in positions to see that irregular warfare did have a part in the grand strategy.

In May 1942, Colin Gubbins, by then a brigadier, met with senior British army officials to discuss Special Operations Executive's potential role in the liberation of Western Europe. The discussion centered around a paper which had been drawn up by SOE's regional director for France and the Low Countries, Robin Brook, and a member his staff, Lieutenant Colonel Peter Wilkinson. Among the concepts outlined in the paper was that of a uniformed special forces unit—purely military—which would work with the French resistance. Wilkinson, principal author of the concept, proposed dropping three-man teams of highly trained soldiers behind enemy lines with the purpose of supporting guerrilla resistance groups and coordinating their operations with those of the Allied ground forces taking part in the cross-channel invasion and liberation of Europe.[7]

In early July, Gubbins wrote the chief of SOE's security office, suggesting that the code name "Jumpers" be applied to the project. But the security chief rejected that name; the new group would be code named "Jedburghs."[8]

In the years since World War II, Jedburgh folklore has produced several explanations for the project's code name. The one most often repeated cites the Scottish town of Jedburgh, where, according to the story, the Jedburgh operatives took their training. There is indeed a Scottish Borders town called Jedburgh, but it sits roughly two hundred and fifty miles north of Milton Hall, near Peterborough, England, the Jedburghs' actual training site. A variation on this story notes that the village of Jedburgh was the scene of guerrilla warfare during twelfth-century border wars between England

and Scotland; hence its appropriateness as a name for special forces. Still another version places Jedburgh in South Africa, where British forces were on the receiving end of guerrilla tactics used by the Boers at the close of the nineteenth century. One explanation claims the name comes from the Jedburgh radio sets used by the teams. And, finally, a French version has it that the code name Jedburghs was chosen because it begins with the letter "J" as in "J-Jour," the French translation of "D-Day."

More likely, the name was simply taken at random from a list of pre-approved code names. All of the above explanations ignore the fact that code names used by the British and Americans throughout the war were, for the sake of security, supposed to have no connection whatsoever with the nature of the operation, project, or unit the names represented. Churchill paid attention to this dictum. He had a fascination, almost an obsession, with code names, and he insisted on personally reviewing and clearing for approval all code names, as he reminded General Sir Hastings Ismay, his military deputy, in early August 1943. After reviewing a list of proposed code names and crossing many of them out, Churchill explained what he considered to be characteristics of suitable code names: that they not be frivolous, boastful, or sentimental and that they not reveal the nature of the operation. He noted that proper names (such as those of towns or cities) made particularly good code names.[9]

All British code names during the war came from an approved list maintained by an office in Whitehall called the Inter-Services Security Board. And in the case of "Jedburgh," it was likely the next name available on the list.[10]

On November 8, 1942, British and American forces landed in North Africa to begin their campaign against Germany's Afrika Korps. In response, German forces marched into unoccupied France and ordered the Vichy Armistice Army disbanded. Many of its officers and noncommissioned officers took their training and experience with them into the resistance.

Germany further, and unwittingly, swelled the ranks of the

French resistance with its next move. In need of workers to provide muscle and sweat for its war industry, Germany, in February 1943, demanded laborers from the Vichy government. To satisfy this injunction, Vichy obligingly passed a compulsory labor service law called the Service du Travail Obligatoire, a program designed to send young Frenchmen into forced labor in Germany. An almost immediate result was that hundreds of young men, to escape the labor draft, took to the mountains and forests to join the resistance. By the end of 1943, they would number in the thousands, but they could hardly be called a fighting force. Compelled to live as outlaws in the most remote rural areas, for these young Frenchmen survival was the main concern. They were sustained through clandestine support from local people or from captured German supplies, but these pockets of potential resistance fighters were unorganized. Weapons were scarce, and most of the men who had them were untrained in their military application. These were the men—many of them only teenagers—who would come to be called the maquis.

Meanwhile, in the United States, Bill Donovan's organization had, in June 1942, assumed a new name—the Office of Strategic Services, or OSS. In December the OSS was activated as a military organization under the direction of the Joint Chiefs of Staff, with responsibility for the conduct of both secret intelligence and special operations. In January 1943, Donovan's staff completed a formal agreement with SOE, gaining access to the SOE's training facilities and giving OSS the opportunity to begin fielding its own language-qualified special forces.

The Americans rushed to catch up to the British in their special operations capability. Personnel authorization increases for OSS were approved by the War Department, and two squadrons of B-24 bombers (later expanded to a full group) were allocated to fly special operations missions. Aircraft modifications were begun, American crews were trained by their experienced British counterparts, and construction began on an airfield at Harrington. An American packing station, where supply canisters and packages would be prepared for air drops to the resistance, was established at Holme, eighty miles north of London and located conveniently near Harrington.

The next step was to find the men who would comprise the Jedburgh teams. For the American contingent, this task fell to Major Franklin Canfield, an OSS special operations staff officer in London, who immediately arranged for a recruiting effort in the United States. Canfield primarily sought volunteers who were physically athletic, and especially any who were familiar with the French language. He hoped to find at least fifty officers and fifty enlisted radio operators who showed a sufficient degree of confidence, self-reliance, maturity, and stability.

Military skills were also important, and so men who already knew how to handle weapons, could apply small unit tactics in the field, were familiar with explosives, and were already parachute qualified would be a step ahead of the rest. The radiomen were required to be capable of sending and receiving Morse code at a speed of at least fifteen words per minute.

OSS headquarters in Washington helped Canfield organize the recruiting effort and provided officers to do the recruiting. In September 1943, the recruiters began drawing a dragnet through an army that was in the middle of unprecedented expansion. Nearly fifty new army camps had been built from scratch across the country, and older installations had been greatly expanded to accommodate the millions of men who had entered the service since the beginning of the war. Jedburgh recruiters were most likely to find the type of officers they sought at camps with large populations of paratroopers: Fort Benning, in Georgia, and Fort Bragg and Camp Mackall in North Carolina. They also would sweep through other camps throughout the South.

Radio operators were to be found at three schools run by the U.S. Army Signal Corps—the High Speed Radio Operator School at Fort Monmouth, New Jersey; the Morse Code School at Camp Crowder, Missouri; and the air force Radio Operator and Mechanics School at Scott Field in Illinois. Radio operators from the U.S. Navy also were trained at these schools, and one sailor volunteered and served on a Jedburgh team.

The routine was the same at each camp. Recruiters began by reviewing personnel records to identify any men who spoke French. Notices appeared on unit bulletin boards announcing a briefing for anyone interested in overseas duty. When those enticed by the notice had assembled, the recruiter explained that the assignment called for volunteers who would undergo parachute training, and that there would be danger involved. Those who were still interested were then individually interviewed by the OSS recruiter. At no time during this process, however, did the recruiters mention OSS or the Jedburgh project by name. Volunteers were simply told that, if they were selected, orders would follow.

Shortly after the recruiters completed their rounds, about one hundred prospective Jedburgh officers and more than sixty radio operators received orders to report to Washington, D.C., in October. Surprisingly few of them spoke or understood French at anything above an elementary level.

Meanwhile, Britain's Special Operations Executive was looking for British Jedburgh candidates, and it was mainly from the armored regiments that the recruiters sought radio operators in September 1943. Before long, more than sixty men had been chosen to undergo testing at a camp near Oxford, and from that screening about fifty men went on to Special Training School No. 54, west of London, in October. The school—which doubled as a receiving station for messages sent by SOE agents already operating throughout Europe—occupied a country house called Fawley Court, just north of the town of Henley-on-Thames. The Jedburgh recruits were housed nearby in a Victorian house called Countess Gardens, and by Christmas their group's number had been cut to forty-five candidates.[11]

In late October, the search for British officers began. Notices on unit bulletin boards throughout England beckoned the curious and the adventurous. Those who responded were sent to a hotel on Northumberland Avenue in London for an interview. Among the interviewers was Wing Commander Forest Yeo-Thomas, an officer who had parachuted into occupied France for SOE in early 1943 to encourage the unification of resistance organizations. He knew what to look for in a man, and he didn't hesitate to turn away those who, in his opinion, failed to display the necessary degree of discipline. Of eight officers he interviewed in one day, Yeo-Thomas rejected six, convinced that a few of them "had volunteered merely in order to obtain a free railway voucher to London."[12]

Following the interviews, the men were told to pack gym shoes and a few other items of clothing, and they were hauled to a country house for two days of physical and psychological testing. There, according to volunteer Stanley Cannicott, they were subjected to strange interviews with a psychiatrist. Cannicott, a future psychiatrist himself, was convinced that "they were crazy."[13] Two weeks later fifty-five selectees were taken to a mansion called Milton Hall, near Peterborough.

The Jedburgh plan also called for French officers and radio operators, and in July 1943 a request for such men was sent to de Gaulle's Free French General Staff in Algiers. French combat arms officers in North Africa at that time were particularly susceptible to the Jedburgh recruiting pitch. Vichy French forces there had thrown in with the Allies after the 1942 Anglo-American invasion of North Africa, and Free French divisions were in the process of being rearmed by the United States.

Many combat units were scheduled to be restructured as service and support units, however, and infantry, armor, and artillery officers in those units were anxious to find a means of joining the war against Germany in more active roles. Even those soldiers who were fortunate enough to remain in the rearmed combat units feared sitting out the rest of the war in North African garrisons. Many of these men decided to volunteer and take a chance with this new offer, and those who did were sent in small groups to Maison Blanche airfield, near Algiers, in November. There they boarded Royal Air Force planes to Great Britain. Most of those selected were regular army—career officers—and most were combat-experienced platoon leaders and company commanders.[14]

Another handful of French officer volunteers came from the French Military Mission in the United States. Among them was seventeen-year-old Lieutenant Michel de Bourbon, the Prince de

Bourbon-Parma, a descendent of the family which once provided France's monarchs. He and the other volunteers from the French Military Mission joined the American Jedburgh candidates who were then gathering in Washington.

The officers and men who had been selected in the stateside recruiting effort began arriving in Washington in October. Most arrived by train at the busy Romanesque Union Station and stepped out into a vibrant city, crowded and full of energy. Radio operators arrived in small groups—one of the larger ones came from Camp Crowder, nine men came from Scott Field, and a few arrived from Fort Monmouth. Officers arrived individually or in twos or threes, most coming off a leave that had been granted en route.

As with any military assignment there was some administrative processing, and then the men found themselves in a taxi or a bus or an army truck (depending on how large a group had reported in) and they were driven off into the Maryland countryside northwest of the city. After about a thirty-minute ride, the vehicle turned left off River Road and followed a long, shaded driveway which eventually curved around to the main entrance of the clubhouse at the Congressional Country Club.

When the club had opened in 1924 it was seen as a place where leaders of government and business could relax in style, and it became known as the Playground of Officialdom. For nearly twenty years it had hosted countless golf tournaments, dinner dances, weddings, tennis matches, horse shows, and other gala events. But the Depression years had had an impact—membership and revenues had fallen, operating costs had risen, and, by early 1943, the club was on the verge of bankruptcy. Then, in March of that year, the Office of Strategic Services had obtained a government lease on the property for use as a training area for the duration, with a guarantee of restoration after the war. Like the rest of wartime Washington, the Congressional Country Club had been called to serve. And to the OSS, the club became known simply as Area F.

In peacetime, the impressive four-story early-Italian clubhouse featured a grand ballroom, a Presidential Suite, an indoor swimming pool, a two-story gymnasium with a basketball court, and bowling alleys. But OSS had transformed the club into something resembling a military installation. The ballroom had become an oversized classroom, complete with folding chairs and blackboards. An army mess hall replaced the main dining room, the bar was now the officers lounge, and the indoor swimming pool had been boarded over to provide office space for the staff.

Dozens of Quonset huts and pyramidal tents with wooden floors littered the lawns and the tennis courts, which had been covered with a layer of crushed cinders. The fairways and greens of the rolling 406-acre golf course had become an obstacle course, a confidence course, and other training areas. And across River Road to the north were pistol and machine gun ranges.

Shortly after their arrival, the newcomers were assembled in the club's ballroom for an orientation. When the men had taken seats on folding chairs, a colonel made some welcoming comments, stressing the secret nature of their assignment, and provided some insight into the purpose of their stay. They had all volunteered for hazardous duty; and this, he said, would entail working with European resistance groups in occupied territory—well behind enemy lines. The staff at Area F was charged with evaluating the candidates to ensure that each met the requirements for the assignment. The men would undergo physical tests and psychological assessments, and those judged to be unsuited for the work would be reassigned to regular duty.

The assessments began at once, and over the next few days the men underwent an endless succession of interviews and completed many questionnaires. An assessment staff of psychologists and psychiatrists hoped to expose the troublesome, the inept, the lazy, the misfit.

Bernard Knox, who'd volunteered for the Jeds from his army air corps station in England, later wrote of what the assessment staff were looking for:

> The problem in choosing men for such an operation, of course, is that once they are landed in enemy territory, you can no longer control them. They may do the obviously sensible thing: go to ground in a safe hiding place, do nothing to attract

attention to themselves, and wait for the arrival of friendly troops. The psychological and psychiatric tests the Jeds were subjected to had one basic objective: to select men psychologically incapable of remaining quiet—troublemakers, in fact; people who could be relied on to upset applecarts.[15]

Knox felt the assessment team "delivered the goods," noting, "I have never known such a bunch of troublemakers in my life."[16]

But the days were not filled with interviews alone. There was a training agenda as well, and the men tackled it with gusto. "When they arrived at Area F," instructor Roger Hall later recalled, "they were a rough-and-tumble gang of two hundred hellions, paratroopers from Fort Benning, for the most part, who had volunteered for secret missions. They didn't know the exact nature of their future assignments, and they couldn't have cared less."[17]

The training, patterned after that of the British commandos, was seldom dull. Training days normally began at the crack of dawn and often lasted until midnight. Mornings would start with physical training, usually with runs as long as five miles, rope climbing, chin-ups, pushups (sometimes while wearing a backpack), and crossing the nearby Cabin John stream on a rope tied between trees on opposite banks.

Sometimes the training would continue long after sunset, with challenging night compass runs which tested a man's stamina and map-reading ability while at the same time giving instructors the chance to teach orienteering skills. Night exercises in raids and ambushes and stealthy infiltration techniques added an element of excitement.

The men also learned to use some new weapons and learned new ways to use old weapons. They learned how to fight empty-handed or with a knife, and they learned a little about explosives. They also made a good impression with the staff at Area F. In the eyes of instructor Roger Hall,

the Jedburghs flew high. Their three prime requisites were guts, brains, and *savoir-faire*. Training them was a breeze, they did all that was expected and more with a nonchalant ease. They also did it with a flourish whenever possible, and usually with a laugh. Most of them had all the basic military stuff down cold, so the instructors were able to concentrate on the specialized hoop-la which dotted the training agenda. The Jeds stayed three hectic weeks, and things were never quite the same after they left.[18]

By early November the roughly one hundred Jedburgh officer candidates had been whittled down by about half. Added to this were the remaining radio operators. After dark one evening, all those selected to remain in the Jedburgh program were loaded onto army trucks, the canvas cargo compartment covers were buttoned down, and the vehicles headed north into the Maryland countryside.

They drove up Highway 15 toward the town of Thurmont, located about sixty miles northwest of Washington in the Catoctin Mountains. Not far from town, the trucks turned onto a dirt road, and moments later stopped just before a wooden sentry box. A Marine guard emerged and raised the log gate which blocked the road. The trucks continued up the narrow road, through a thick forest of chestnut and dogwood, hemlock and red oak and pitch pine, to a place which had been known as Catoctin Mountain Park. They stopped at an area of the park known as Camp Greentop, which had been a camp for handicapped children. It was part of a vast complex built as a Works Progress Administration project in the late '30s, and before the war it had been known as the Catoctin Recreational Demonstration Area, a retreat for federal employees and their families.

But now Greentop had transformed into another training area of the Office of Strategic Services. The park had been closed to civilians in early 1942, and the War Department had moved in and taken over part of it, an old Civilian Conservation Corps camp at a spot called Round Meadow, that summer. Soon after that, OSS had occupied the Greentop site about half a mile to the northeast, and it soon became a training area for specialized instruction in hand-to-hand combat, surreptitious infiltration, specialized shooting, and demolitions. It was christened Area B, with subdivisions called B–1 and B–2. Headquarters was in a large log cabin with a covered porch, surrounded by a log railing. The trucks deposited the Jedburgh trainees at Area B–1.

The army and the OSS, however, were not the only residents at the Catoctin Mountain Park. Farther up the road to the east was another camp—which had been called Hi-Catoctin—often used in the past for Boy Scout and Girl Scout outings. By the time the Jedburgh volunteers arrived in the area, though, a ten-foot fence with a barbed-wire overhang surrounded the compound. There were sentry booths at regular intervals, equipped with telephones, and floodlights and patrolling Marines with guard dogs.

Upon America's entry into the war, President Roosevelt's staff had selected this portion of the park as a weekend retreat for the chief of state, similar to his retreat at Warm Springs, Georgia, but only sixty miles and two hours driving time from Washington. Roosevelt had begun going there in July 1942 and was to spend much time there during the war. He named the site Shangri La, but a later president named Eisenhower would change the name to Camp David. The existence of the presidential retreat was to be kept secret, but just a fortnight before the Jeds arrived in the Catoctin mountains, the *Chicago Daily News* had run an article on Roosevelt's hideaway and given away its location.[19]

At Area B, the Jeds found comfortable, if rustic, quarters and good food. With the growing November chill, the trainees were glad to move out of the tents of Area F into cabins with indoor plumbing and stone fireplaces. Separate buildings housed a mess hall and classrooms.

As at Area F, training days in the mountains began at sunup and continued until after dark, and the hours were filled with classes on explosives and demolitions, communications, first aid, hand-to-hand combat, tradecraft, weapons, map reading, and cross-country navigation.

At Area B the Jeds met one of the most unforgettable instructors they would ever have—a wiry, bespectacled British major named William Ewart Fairbairn. One of the things that made him so unforgettable was the fact that, at five feet ten, one hundred and seventy pounds, and fifty-eight years of age, Fairbairn could throw around any of the Jeds (who were all thirty years or more his junior) with ease. The little man with the craggy features and the horn-rim glasses exuded strength and self-confidence. Under his close-cropped graying hair were a bulbous nose and dark eyes that seemed to look in all directions at once, missing nothing. Fairbairn had spent thirty years as a Shanghai policeman, rising to the level of assistant commissioner. And after years of riding herd over a water-front population of gangsters and pirates and cutthroats, Fairbairn knew how to take care of himself. He had been schooled in the oriental arts of self-defense and silent killing, and he was here to teach what he called the "Fairbairn method" of unarmed combat.[20]

Martial arts, as developed and practiced in the Orient, were not widely known in the United States at that time, and the Jedburgh trainees marveled at Fairbairn's techniques. He introduced the men to the body's nerve centers and pressure points, and he showed them countless ways of using fists and elbows and knees and fingers as weapons to attack those sensitive areas. He taught them the principles of joint manipulation and techniques for silently taking down sentries, and he urged them always to follow every maneuver with a swift kick to the opponent's groin, just for good measure. One student recalled how Fairbairn would hand a stiletto to a trainee and invite him to stick it into the instructor. "You would find yourself looking up at the sky when he got done with you."[21]

Major Fairbairn's curriculum included knife fighting, and he taught the men how to use the Fairbairn-Sykes fighting knife, which he and a colleague named Eric Sykes had designed. It was a foot-long stiletto with a high-grade steel blade, diamond-shaped in cross-section and razor sharp on both edges, making it suitable for both slashing and stabbing. And Fairbairn showed the Jeds all the places on the human body where vital organs or arteries could be most easily reached.

Whenever a weapons class appeared on the day's training schedule, Fairbairn was the instructor. Dressed in his usual coveralls and tan army garrison cap, he taught his instinctive pistol shooting method, quickly stepping forward with one foot to shoot from a semi-crouch position, and he drilled the men in his method of quickly changing magazines in the .45-caliber pistol. Then he would send students with loaded weapons down trails through the woods, and spring-loaded silhouette targets would jump up from behind bushes. He had even had a facility built that came to be called "the mystery house" or "the spook house." Students would enter the darkened building armed with a .45-caliber pistol and two magazines of six rounds each. As the trainee stepped carefully down the narrow passages inside, with Fairbairn following behind whispering instructions, cardboard German soldiers would suddenly pop out from behind a wall or around a corner, and the student would have to react and shoot.

Demolition classes included practical exercises—blowing up trees and walls and old cars. And nights were often spent patrolling through the moist autumn foliage. Physical training continued, with the men setting and breaking personal records in pushups and tearing through the obstacle course. The tough training and the Spartan mountain living had the desired affect, and the men grew hard.

Food was plentiful at Area B and was always well prepared, and for Thanksgiving the men were served a five-course feast with all the trimmings. Afterward cigars were passed around. But entertainment was harder to come by, and after the fourth viewing of a film on the Incan civilization the men had the dialogue memorized. And, from time to time, they had to sit through wearying talks given by officials visiting from Washington.

By most accounts, it was during just such an occasion at Area B that a Jedburgh tradition was born. Its origin was Fort Benning's parachute school, where an officer trainee had reportedly been dropped for fifty pushups, and in counting out the final few repetitions, had said, "forty-eight . . . forty-nine . . . fifty," then jumped to attention and muttered, half under his breath, "Some shit!" Most of the Jedburgh officers, of course, had gone through Fort Benning and had heard the story.

In his autobiography, *Hazardous Duty*, Jedburgh veteran John Singlaub described the origin of the tradition that grew from this incident. A guest speaker's oratory had exceeded the bounds of Jedburgh patience when "a bizarre chant rose in the rear ranks of our formation. 'Forty-eight,' a man called. 'Forty-nine,' two more replied." As the speaker puzzled over the meaningless catcalls and continued his talk, another shouted "Fifty!" Then, in unison, all roared "Some shit!"[22] The target of the outburst was left speechless, and the ritual became a Jedburgh trademark, to be used on many such occasions in the future.

By early December, the days became easier and the men relaxed, enjoyed some passes, and played some football. They were issued .45-caliber pistols, Fairbairn knives, wristwatches, and some special cold-weather clothing.

One night the Jedburgh officers enjoyed a steak dinner and a few drinks and went to bed. They were mustered at two in the morning, told to put on their newly issued cold-weather gear, loaded onto trucks, hauled to a railroad siding, and put aboard a northbound train. The men were told to keep the window curtains in the railroad cars drawn.

They jolted to a stop at New York's Grand Central terminal a couple of hours before noon, but the men were ordered to remain in the cars with the curtains drawn. The cold-weather gear was becoming unbearably hot by the time they were told to fall out, about two hours later, and were warned not to speak to anyone. They marched with packs and full combat gear across to Forty-second Street, where they climbed aboard army "deuce-and-a-halves." The big trucks snaked through Manhattan's urban canyons, crossed a bridge to Brooklyn, and delivered the Jeds to Fort Hamilton in the Bay Ridge section, just across from Staten Island. Fort Hamilton was an embarkation center where troops were prepared for overseas shipment, a place where shots were given, dollars were exchanged for English pounds, and booklets that told of the country and people of Great Britain were issued. The Jedburgh radio operators would arrive about a week later.

On a cold and overcast Monday night, the Jedburgh officers boarded a ferry which took them up the Hudson River to Manhattan's West Side passenger ship terminal, to the Cunard line's berths at Pier 90 at the foot of Fiftieth Street. And the men stared up at the largest ship that any of them had ever seen.

Early in the war, Winston Churchill, as one means of consummating the Atlantic Alliance, had offered up two of the greatest ocean liners in the world—the Cunard-White Star line's *Queen Mary* and *Queen Elizabeth*—for service as troop ships to bring

American servicemen to the British Isles. The giant ships, each more than a thousand feet long, had been stripped of their peacetime splendor, the luxuriant furnishings and carpeting put into storage, though much of the Art Deco styling remained. Each ship still featured an immense map of the North Atlantic on a wall of the First Class Dining Room, where the progress of peacetime voyages had been tracked.

Now every available space, including the drained swimming pools, had been fitted out with rows of wooden or metal bunks stacked three or four high, and more than twelve thousand fold-down canvas bunks called "standee" berths had been installed on each ship. Additional lavatories and showers had been added. Each of the *Queen*s, originally designed to carry slightly more than two thousand passengers and a crew of a thousand during peacetime, could now carry fifteen thousand troops—a full division—even though the lifeboats would barely hold half that. And in the warmer months they carried another two thousand, with additional bunks placed on deck. Portholes and windows, roughly two thousand on each ship, had been blacked out, and the ships had been painted entirely in dreary gray, covering for the war's duration the elegant satin black hulls, the white upper works, the red funnels. Because the *Queen*s made such prestigious targets for the enemy, anti-aircraft guns and cannons, deck guns, and rocket launchers had been installed.

As the Jedburgh officers lined up to board the *Queen Elizabeth*, each was issued a mess card and a card with his berthing assignment. Red Cross volunteers doled out coffee and donuts. And the men, loaded down with field gear and barracks bags, filed up the gangplank from the pier, under an overcast sky, and were met at the top by the British crew, all Cunard employees. The men worked their way through the maze of passages and stairways to find their assigned berths, and soon the Jeds were scattered throughout the ship.

Those in the rank of captain might get a stateroom, which held fewer men but was still crowded. A cabin which in peacetime accommodated two people now held six or eight men in steel cots stacked two high, and barracks bags and other gear consumed most of the remaining space. Other cabins held as many as twelve men, and two Jed lieutenants found themselves sharing a sixteen-bunk cabin with a detachment of army chaplains. Many of the men aboard the ship, the Jeds noticed, were airmen.

It was cold and threatening rain as tugboats pushed the liner back into the Hudson at high tide in the early morning darkness of December 14, 1943. Smoke billowed from her funnels as she turned and crept downstream, past Ellis Island and the Statue of Liberty on the starboard side, through The Narrows and into the Atlantic.

As wartime trans-Atlantic crossings went, this run by the *Queen Elizabeth* was uneventful and, aside from daily evacuation drills, the officers were left to pass their time as they wished. A recreation room remained thick with cigarette smoke and laughter and the clatter of dice. Some men preferred the smaller room which doubled as an officers' lounge and library. But the Jeds were clannish and tended to stay together when not in their quarters; and each night the men set their watches ahead an hour.

Meals on both *Queens* were served almost continuously, with six shifts resulting in two meals a day for each passenger, breakfast in the morning and dinner in the late afternoon. With so many men to feed, the seemingly endless chow lines for one meal often didn't wind down until the next meal was beginning. Even when a soldier finally got his food, he might have to eat it standing up if he couldn't find a spot to sit. The mess cards the Jed officers had been issued told them where and when to eat, such as: "Officers' Dining Room, 'R' Deck Aft, Third Sitting." Officers ate well, under the circumstances, with dinners including such entrees as fillet of haddock, Florentine roast duckling, and Pear Mont Blanc.

The greatest defense for each of the *Queens* against submarine attack was a cruising speed of around twenty-eight knots—more than twice the surface speed of a U-boat and four times its speed submerged—and they were safer traveling alone, rather than in convoy with ships that could average no more than ten knots. The ships steamed in a zigzag pattern as an additional defense, changing course about every eight minutes, and at full cruising speed such a turn could send food trays scurrying off the table. There were no storms during the *Elizabeth*'s crossing, but the North

Atlantic was always rough and the ship rolled and pitched constantly, enormous dark-gray waves showering the deck with salt spray.

As the *Queen Elizabeth* neared the British Isles she picked up a destroyer escort, and those topside spotted Northern Ireland off to the right. She steamed up the Firth of Clyde, and the men, most of whom had never been outside their native land, caught their first glimpses of Scotland. They drifted past rolling pasturelands and thatch-roofed houses and patchwork fields lined with stone fences. Then the great ship slowed to a stop and dropped anchor off the city of Gourock, at the mouth of the great estuary which feeds the port of Glasgow.

On that cold afternoon of December 20, the fifty-five American Jedburgh officers went ashore and found the drab Scottish port town packed with men in a wide variety of uniforms. At first the Jeds were tucked away in a warehouse. Then, when darkness came, two trucks picked them up and hauled them to a railroad station. Three trains and a day later they arrived at a commando training area near Arisaig on the northwestern coast of Scotland, where the men were comfortably billeted in three spacious old homes used by Special Operations Executive to house trainees—Garramoor, Inverie, and Traigh House. The beautiful but barren countryside which surrounded the Americans had more in common with Wyoming than with the lush greenness of England.

Three days after the American Jedburgh officers arrived in Scotland, the American radio operators sailed from New York aboard the *Queen Mary*. War voyage number 30E for the great ship began at dawn on the clear and cold morning of Thursday, December 23, with just under twelve thousand troops and a crew of more than a thousand aboard. Among the troops sharing the cramped ship with the Jed radiomen were those from an anti-aircraft searchlight battalion and a combat engineer battalion, and there was a general service engineer regiment aboard which was composed entirely of black soldiers.

Like those of her sister ship *Elizabeth*, the *Queen Mary*'s twelve decks were divided, for troopship purposes, into three areas—the Red Area, comprising the forward third of the ship; the White Area, the midships; and the Blue Area, the aft third. As troops boarded the ship they were issued colored buttons corresponding to the area in which they would be berthed, and signs on the bulkheads directed the men to their berthing areas with red and white and blue arrows. Most of the sixty-two Jed radio operators were berthed as a group on the promenade deck, in what had been the liner's tobacco shop and gift shop.

Troops on the Boat Deck, seventy-five feet above the waterline, watched as America slipped beyond the horizon. Many of them were seeing it for the last time. Men wandered about the three acres of deck space or leaned on the wooden rails, covered with initials and graffiti carved by troops of earlier shuttles, and watched the great ship's wake as it remained visible in the distance for as much as a mile. Because German U-boats were known to patrol the east coast of the United States, an escort of four or five destroyers stayed alongside the liner throughout the first day, until she was well out to sea.

But the crossing of the *Queen Mary* which brought the American Jedburgh radio operators to England would prove to be nothing like what the officers had experienced on the *Elizabeth*. Shortly after leaving New York a violent storm began, with gale-force winds and giant waves that tossed the ship for the duration of the crossing. It was an absolutely miserable experience for all, with most of the men aboard being on a ship for the first time in their lives; and virtually everyone got seasick at some point, some remaining so throughout the wretched voyage.

The Jed radio operators were appointed military police (MPs) for the duration of the crossing. Some of them guarded prisoners in the ship's brig, but many had to rotate through shifts on an even less pleasant detail. The ship's large First Class Dining Room, with the map of the North Atlantic on one wall, served as the enlisted men's mess hall. And it was the job of the Jed MPs to station themselves at the doors to the mess hall and help men as they tried to make it from the serving line to a table. Bob Kehoe was on the detail, and he later recalled trying to keep men "from being tossed across the deck, which was covered with several inches of seawater, food, and vomit."[23] Once seated, troops tried to eat unappetizing meals of overcooked pork chops, bully beef, boiled cabbage, brussels sprouts, or lamb stew from trays intent on sliding down the long table with each roll or pitch of the ship. Men were then faced with the challenge of retaining the meal on their way back to their bunks. Many failed to do so.

The mess hall was a constant mass of moving lines and unending noise—queues to get food served in army mess kits and eaten at crowded tables, lines to dip the emptied kits in a barrel of greasy water, all to be done at the rate of forty-five minutes per man. Before one group had even cleared the dining area, a loudspeaker summoned the next group from the block-long lines that snaked through the ship. Many men came to find the ship's nine canteens preferable. Here they could buy twenty-five-cent candy bars for a dollar, or live on crackers and Cokes.

Long lines, however, didn't just lead to the mess hall. Men had to stand in line just to get to one of the lavatories, each of which was shared by about sixty men and usually consisted of open rows of urinals and toilets. The floors were continuously awash in an inch-thick mixture of water and vomit, leaving a nearly permanent stain line on the men's boots.

Aisles were jammed full of duffel bags and gear, and men had baggage lost or stolen. There was no place to change clothes, so men stayed in the same uniform during the entire voyage, and the limited supply of fresh water and an overtaxed ventilation system resulted in a ship's interior that was stuffy and rank with the odors of cigarette smoke, vomit, and unwashed men.

Days became an endless routine of boredom and misery. Aside from the daily evacuation drills, troops played poker, tossed dice, tried to read or sleep, or went to see the movies that were shown nightly. But most of the men spent most of their time standing in chow lines. At sunset each night, blackout time was announced over the loudspeakers, the black-painted porthole windows had to be closed, and smoking no longer was allowed on deck.

December on the North Atlantic was cold, and men on the *Queen Mary* sometimes spotted icebergs. And then it was Christmas Day. When writing of the experience later, Bob Kehoe would recall how an effort was made to serve a special dinner, but I am not sure many could enjoy it. Religious services held in the mess hall were well attended; a combination of loneliness, fear, and general misery made men extra-conscious of traditional ties. Standing guard duty, I shared the feelings of fear and separation. The hymns, even at a distance, were reassuring.[24]

On the morning of December 29, the *Queen Mary* arrived in Scotland, though a thick fog prevented the Jeds from seeing much of it.[25] Later, the weather grew clear and warm, and the Jedburgh radio operators debarked and were immediately escorted to a station and put on a southbound train to join the British Jed radiomen at Henley-on-Thames. There, the men were taken to the country house called Fawley Court, where they were billeted in Nissan huts, a British version of the Quonset. The first contingent of French radio operators arrived at about the same time. The men were all introduced to the Jedburgh radio set which they would be using in the field, and they trained with it until reporting to Milton Hall in the first week of February.

The French Jedburgh volunteers had begun arriving in Scotland in November, and those who passed a session of physical and psychological testing had been sent to the offices of General de Gaulle's intelligence organization at 10 Duke Street in London, where each was interviewed by a board of four officers. After a week, those selected were sent to a large house in the country—and if they asked where they were they were told that they didn't need to know.

One of the first instructors to meet the French officers was Captain Bernie Knox, an Englishman who wore an American army uniform and spoke faultless French. So fluent, in fact, that one of the Frenchmen, Lieutenant Paul Aussaresses, was certain that Knox must be French, as he had a trace of accent similar to that of the poor working class in the eastern districts of Paris.

Another of the American instructors was an engineer lieutenant who would eventually join the Jeds, a paratrooper who had twenty-six jumps to his credit and who used one four-letter word so often in the first few minutes that Lieutenant Aussaresses, who understood no English at the time, assumed it to be an English form of punctuation. Aussaresses, who would go on to become a general in the French army, would later claim to have learned 50 percent of the American military vocabulary in his first five minutes at the base.

After about two weeks of physical training and an introduction to explosives, the French officers moved on to a place called Gumley Hall, where they remained until the last week of January. Then they were sent through parachute training and on to Milton Hall.[26]

The training areas and country houses that hosted the Jedburgh trainees were part of an elaborate network of schools that Special Operations Executive had developed since the early years of its existence. Never before and, arguably, not since has such a vast and complex factory for the development of special operators existed. The various country sections, including the French Section, used this machinery of training and assessment to produce the agents it sent to occupied Europe, and at the close of 1943 it was serving the needs of the Jedburghs.

The American officers remained at Arisaig, under constantly dreary and overcast skies, for about two weeks. The short winter days were filled with basic commando training—long cross-country hikes with heavy rucksacks on their backs, obstacle courses, hand-to-hand combat drills, and pistol firing. Then, beginning December 28, the men were sent in three groups through another psychological assessment, this time in the south of England, at a place the men began to call the "booby hatch."

Apparently not satisfied with the results of the American Jedburgh assessment conducted in Washington, the British had insisted that all Jedburgh candidates, Americans included, be evaluated by SOE's Student Assessment Board.[27]

Again, each of the officers sat through a few days of various written psychological tests—intelligence tests, word-association tests, ink blot tests, and more—and interviews with psychiatrists. But they also went to a small training area outside, where they were subjected to hands-on situational exercises designed to reveal an operative's tolerance for frustration, his ability to think quickly and clearly and reasonably in difficult situations. The men might be told to complete a task with materials that were ill-suited to the purpose, or with "assistants" who were purposely more of a hindrance than a help.

Lieutenants with little notebooks followed the Jeds around, occasionally jotting down their findings, noting how a man adapted to a situation, overcame obstacles, improved solutions, and coped with stress and disappointment. There were even ways of measuring the time of hesitation that a candidate showed prior to attempting an obstacle. Other tests determined a man's faculty for memorizing details of a room, a face, or a map or other document. There was much that the assessment personnel needed to learn about a candidate's character in a very short time, and the staff became quite adept at it.

Aside from the obvious requirement for moral and physical courage, the Jeds should display confidence and self-reliance, good judgment, a degree of controlled aggressiveness, and discretion with secret information. The men had to be highly resourceful in order to complete their mission—even when communications and support were disrupted; they had to be able to adapt to rapidly changing situations.

Their work required an alert mind, capable of a quick appreciation of a situation—one that was decisive and inventive. Mental stamina was no less important than physical endurance; and maturity, emotional stability, and self-discipline would be needed for the men to hold up under stressful situations or during periods of prolonged isolation. And because of their international make-up and the nature of their work, their willingness and aptitude for working with other nationalities was an absolute must. As advisors, they needed to be perceptive, persuasive, assertive when necessary, and diplomatic—capable of interacting with others with no thought to class distinctions.

The assessment staff looked for men with an above-average intelligence and a desire for self-improvement. And each man selected would possess all of the physical and mental qualities that would enable him to accomplish his mission alone, if necessary, but which at the same time would make him a cooperative team player.

The last group of American Jedburgh officers completed the assessments in early January 1944. Only thirty-seven of the fifty-five American officers evaluated were selected for further training.[28] French officers experienced a similar rate of attrition.

The upshot, of course, was that all this weeding out resulted in a shortage of American and French officers. So a search for additional American officers from among the thousands of men assigned to U.S. divisions in England, especially the 9th Infantry and the 101st Airborne, began in January and was completed by late February. To make up the shortage in French officers, SOE and OSS each sent an officer on a recruiting mission to the Middle East, where seventy more French officer volunteers were found. They arrived at Milton Hall in late March.

Rather than sending the sixty-two American radio operators to the Student Assessment Board, a team of three psychiatrists visited Special Training School 54 and interviewed each candidate. Forty-six of the sixty-two American radio operators were chosen to continue training.[29]

The buildup of invasion forces in the British Isles was well underway, and American divisions and support units poured in from the States. By the end of May 1944, there would be more than one and a half million American troops in Britain, occupying one hundred thousand buildings in more than eleven hundred locations.[30] All, of course, required billeting, training and medical facilities, supply depots, and airfields. The result was an intense competition for real estate.

The British and American special operations staffs in London had begun searching for a site to serve as the Jedburgh training school and holding area in the fall of 1943. In October they settled on a large country estate known as Milton Hall, located about ninety miles north of London and just west of Peterborough. The property included an expansive Elizabethan brownstone house at the end of a half-mile-long driveway through well-kept grounds, the ancestral family home of the Earl Fitzwilliam. Special Operations Executive gained permission to use the estate and began the necessary renovations. Many of the oak-paneled rooms in the seventeenth-century house were transformed into billeting and classroom space, lecture halls, supply rooms, and administrative offices. The surrounding grounds, including a golf course on the property, became training areas.

The Jedburgh training center was to have been ready for occupation and the commencement of training on New Years' Day, 1944, but material shortages and construction delays prevented occupation until early February. In the interim, temporary arrangements were made. The officers were divided into three groups and sent to three different Special Operations Executive training schools, one at Fairford, Gloucester, another at Gumley Hall, in Lancashire, and the third at Walsingham, in Surrey. At these sites the officers received most of their preliminary training, and in the first days of February they reported to Milton Hall.

On February 5 the radio operators arrived, forty-six Americans, forty-five British, and twenty French.[31] And from the time they arrived, they were included in all general training along with the officers, although they would also continue to receive specialized training in wireless telegraphy.

Prior to the commencement of training at Milton Hall, though, all Jedburgh trainees had to complete an abbreviated SOE parachute training course at Ringway, near Manchester—even those who had completed the parachutist course at Fort Benning. Beginning on the first of February the men were sent for the three-day course in groups of fifty. American paratroopers had been trained to jump from slow twin-engine C-47 cargo planes, exiting the aircraft through a side door. They would now have to learn the SOE method: dropping through a hole in the bottom of the fuselage of a faster, four-engine bomber.

The British cadre at times must have found the Americans a challenge at times. One aspect of the training that was new to the Americans was jumping from a large basket suspended from an airship, a huge football-shaped balloon. Groups of four would be taken up and, one at a time, the men would be given the command to sit at the hole in the floor of the basket and then to jump. On one occasion, while a group was waiting for a man to position himself at the hole, one of the American Jeds, Captain René Dussaq—a former

Hollywood stuntman who had once done a handstand on a ledge at the top of the Empire State Building—stunned the instructor by doing a swan dive over the side of the basket.[32]

The really disconcerting thing about the balloon jump was the amount of time it took for the parachute to open. When jumping from an airplane, a parachute normally opened when the jumper was within sixty to ninety feet of the plane, and the slip-stream helped to rapidly inflate the canopy, usually within a few seconds. But when jumping from an anchored balloon floating some six hundred feet above the ground, a parachutist's body fell uninterrupted for a hundred and fifty to two hundred feet before the parachute opened.

The Fort Benning graduates would jump and then count "one thousand, two thousand, three thousand . . ." as they had been taught to in their Stateside training, but instead of feeling the opening shock as expected, they were still falling—and were sure that they had "bought it." Then the canopy would open with a slight tug. Such feelings of dread were not confined to the Americans. A British Jedburgh officer, James Hutchison, later wrote that he felt a "curious detached feeling" on his first balloon jump. "I became an onlooker on my own fate," he recalled, "as though thinking 'I wonder if that man's parachute is going to open.'"[33]

Shaggy, fat sheep and bored cows still roamed freely about the lawns of Milton Hall, but the dairy barn had become a Morse code classroom, complete with female instructors from the First Aid Nursing Yeomanry. Several huts stood on the grounds, serving as barracks, and the large sunken garden was a weapons training area. The golf course was a demolition range, and the quadrangle behind the mansion had sprouted a boxing ring and other exercise equipment.

Inside the old mansion were many classrooms, and a large room on the ground floor had been fitted with a movie projector and screen. But little of the old house's charm had been lost in the transition. Suits of armor still stood stoically by, and many large portraits hung on ornately furnished walls. British Captain Stanley

Cannicott later described how "eminent, be-wigged gentlemen looked down on us in a faintly disapproving and questioning manner as we trained with our explosives."[34]

The Jedburgh training school at Milton Hall was administered by an Anglo-American staff. The first commandant was British Lieutenant Colonel Frank Spooner—a regular army officer, formerly of the Indian army—who had previously served as commandant of SOE's finishing school at Beaulieu, the final training stop for F Section agents. But Spooner's style of leadership, according to one of the French officers, "had a sense of formal discipline, maybe narrowly minded," and was not best suited for heading a special forces training camp.[35] The staff included twenty-five instructors, seventeen British and eight American.[36]

The first morning at Milton Hall began early, and when British batmen arrived to greet the officers with morning tea they were roundly cursed for their efforts. It was dark and damp and raw outside as the men fell out for muster, taking fifteen minutes to get squared away while a sergeant major barked in vain at men from half a dozen countries. Stanley Cannicott, in his memoir *Journey of a Jed*, described the men's reaction as Colonel Spooner then tried to call the formation to attention: "The dutiful Brits sprang to attention, the French raised their eyes and their hands and said 'We do not understand,' the Americans looked the other way and I will not print what they actually said."[37]

For the next few months, the Jeds followed a training program designed to sharpen old skills and at the same time familiarize the men with techniques and equipment that were totally new to them. As always, days began with calisthenics, but the hikes became more demanding, twenty to twenty-five miles over rough terrain, and there were difficult night compass courses.

Survival training included fieldcraft and how to live off the land—even the fine art of poaching. After one long cross-country march, recalled Captain Cannicott, the trainees bivouacked in a wooded area. Soon, a truck drove up and stopped. A live sheep and a bag of flour were thrown out of the back and someone shouted, "That's your supper."[38]

Just as important was another kind of survival skill, the kind that involved knowledge of Continental customs and mannerisms, ignorance of which would mark one as an outsider. Conditions might call for Jeds to wear civilian clothes and eat in French restaurants. So the men had to learn to dress like Frenchmen, and the Americans had to learn to keep the knife in the right hand and the fork in the left hand when eating, and not switch the fork to the right hand after cutting meat, as they would at home. The Brits had to unlearn the habit of putting milk into a cup before pouring the tea.

Language instruction continued, and there was observation and memory training. And the men were introduced to tradecraft skills—how to establish and operate intelligence networks, use forged papers, and conduct surveillance; how to follow someone without being detected or, more important, how to discern when one is being followed—and what to do about it. They learned of curfews being enforced in occupied territory and of the enforcement methods used by police and security forces. They were introduced to codes and ciphers for clandestine communications, and officers were given limited training on the wireless equipment and Morse code, just in case the radio operator got "knocked off."

From time to time, the men would assemble in the old mansion's Great Hall to hear guest speakers talk of the geography of France, or of the French resistance movement, its history and organization, and its most effective methods. And always, if a speaker began to lose his audience, he would hear the growing chant: "forty-eight . . . forty-nine. . . ." But the speakers who held the Jeds' attention were those who had been to occupied France on a mission with one of F Section's circuits, and the men would listen intently as the agent described what life was really like behind enemy lines.

Additionally, because the Jeds would be living among the enemy they had to know the organizations and uniforms and ranks of not only the German military, but also of the various German and Vichy police units.

In weapons classes, the men became familiar with British, American, French, and German small arms—pistols, rifles, shotguns, submachine guns, and light machine guns—including not only their operation, but also the disassembly and assembly of each weapon. They learned how to employ anti-tank mines and how to neutralize booby traps, and they became proficient with hand grenades. Major Fairbairn was there to drill the men in his "instinctive shooting" technique—firing a pistol from a crouch position with two hands or from the hip with one hand—and he taught them to always fire two shots in rapid succession. The old Shanghai policeman also continued to teach hand-to-hand combat, knife fighting, and silent killing.

Demolition training included learning to use plastic explosives—malleable enough to be molded into any form and stable enough to take considerable abuse without exploding. The stuff was powerful and hot-burning, capable of bringing down trees or cutting through steel. The Jeds also were introduced to primacord (a flexible explosive detonating cord), time pencils (devices used for initiating explosions after pre-determined time delays), and to a variety of other fuses and igniters. Bridge and railway demolition were studied, along with the sabotage of power stations, factories, canals, electrical transformers, high-tension-wire pylons, dams, and reservoirs.

Probably every Jedburgh trainee, no matter what his background, learned new skills at Milton Hall—from driving a motorcycle to picking a lock to paddling a boat without making a sound.

One important detail which remained was the formation of the three-man Jedburgh teams. And, as with everything else, the Jeds found an unconventional way to accomplish it. Around the middle of March, the commandant instructed the Jeds to begin seeking out their own teammates—men with whom they felt they could work best in the field. To operate effectively, the men making up a team had to be physically, emotionally, and temperamentally compatible—matched like a team of horses in harness. The men were more apt to find their own best mates, reasoned the Jedburgh staff, instead of having mates chosen for them. The only criteria was that each team must have a British or an American officer, another officer of French, Belgian, or Dutch nationality (which would determine the country that the team would operate in), and a radio operator of any nationality. By this time, of course, the officers had all gotten to know one another somewhat, and friendships had formed.

Over the next two weeks, officers paired off and began a trial period known as the "engagement." If this "courtship" period proved satisfactory to both parties, the "marriage" was officially recognized by a posting on the bulletin board, and the couple either chose or was assigned a radio operator. Regrettably, some engagements were broken and an occasional marriage would end in divorce, in which case the process was started over again. By the first of April, however, most of the teams had been formed, and the men would go through all remaining training events as teams. And so they gelled—men who, in civilian life, might have met on the street and never taken notice of one another.

The newly formed teams found many opportunities to train together on field exercises called "schemes." These drills, usually forty-eight to seventy-two hours in duration, gave the Jeds a chance to perform under clandestine circumstances. Teams might be dropped by parachute into Scotland or Wales and have to make their way back to Milton Hall without being caught. The men would be armed and in uniform, and police and even the Boy Scouts along the way would be alerted and given descriptions of the men. One team reportedly beat the others back by hijacking a train.

On another survival scheme, the team of Major Wise, Lieutenant Aguirec, and Sergeant Kehoe had been making its way across the Yorkshire moors all day. At day's end, the men—who were supposed to be living off the land—decided to cheat a little by stopping at a farmhouse and asking if they could buy some food and perhaps sleep in the sheepfold. But the farmer and his wife, who had a son in the service, fed the men a hot meal and gave them a warm bed to sleep in. Other schemes might require teams to contact resistance members, tail a subject, or give the slip to someone following them.

In March the Jeds began taking part in a series of major field exercises—the first a six-day affair called Spill Out, then another called Sally, and then one called Levee. In April there was Exercise Spur and, finally, in late May, came the exercise called Lash, which was still ongoing when D-Day arrived.

*　*　*

Formal planning for Operation Overlord, as the cross-channel invasion was called, was, for the most part, completed by the end of March. The assault would take place over a sixty-mile frontage of Normandy beaches. British divisions, coming ashore on the easternmost beaches, would capture Caen as quickly as possible and push south. The Americans would land to the west and at the base of the Cotentin peninsula. The British would thereby be in a position to provide some protection for the U.S. troops as they pushed out to capture the port at Cherbourg and those in Brittany.

The first phase of the operation was the establishment of the beachhead and the subsequent expansion and buildup of a lodgment area as follow-on forces and supplies continued to come ashore. Of critical importance to this plan would be the protection of the area from enemy counterattack. It was projected that it would be weeks before a large enough force could be brought ashore to allow the Allies to break out of the lodgment area and go on the offensive.

Eisenhower himself thought that the first five or six weeks would be critical in getting forces ashore and keeping them ashore. As late as three weeks before the invasion Eisenhower's chief of staff, Lieutenant General Bedell Smith, was only giving fifty-fifty odds that the Allies would be able to stay ashore. Eisenhower's naval aide had his own doubts after sitting through a briefing, held just two weeks before the invasion, and hearing that the latest intelligence estimates numbered the German forces in France at fifty-eight divisions, some three-quarters of a million troops in all.[39] Overlord's success was far from certain.

General Smith, like Eisenhower, recognized how badly the Allies would need support from the French resistance. Smith complained that the American and British chiefs of staff were tying Eisenhower's hands by not allowing him to be more open with the French in planning for the invasion.[40] Because the French were considered a security risk, the supreme commander was not even allowed to share the planned invasion date and landing sites with General de Gaulle.

Even if the initial Allied landings were successful, the plan only called for putting seven divisions ashore in Normandy on the first day. Eisenhower's planners sought every means possible to buy time for the subsequent expansion of the beachhead and the buildup of forces. As it then stood, they calculated, the ratio of landing forces to defending forces in the immediate invasion area would be marginally in the Allies' favor. But this could change dramatically if additional German divisions were hastily moved into the Normandy battlefield as reinforcements.

In their calculations, Overlord planners judged that the Allied landing force could be successful so long as German mobile reserves on D-Day did not exceed twelve divisions. Any more than that and the advantage in forces might go to the Germans. Of the twelve-division reserve, planners further reasoned, no more than three could be allowed to approach within striking range of Caen on D-Day. This number could increase to five on the second day following D-Day (D+2) and to nine by D+8. No more than fifteen German divisions could be allowed to move into the area within sixty days of the landings.[41]

But how many divisions would the Germans be capable of moving to Normandy if they recognized the landings as the main Allied invasion and reacted accordingly? Eisenhower's intelligence staff crunched the numbers and concluded that by D+25, the Germans might be able to move as many as thirty-one divisions, nine of them panzer (tank) divisions, to the Normandy battlefield. Such a force could overwhelm the Allied invaders. Somehow, the Allies needed to prevent this from happening, and the final Overlord plan, along with some highly classified supporting plans, spelled out how it would be done.

Three means were to be used to deter or delay the movement of German divisions to the beachhead area. The first was an elaborate and, in the end, highly successful deception operation called Fortitude. The object of Fortitude was to reinforce Germany's belief that the cross-channel invasion would come in the Pas de Calais area of the French coast near the Belgian border. The deception would prove successful and would accomplish its objective of persuading the German high command to keep the bulk of its highly mobile Fifteenth Army—eighteen divisions strong—tied down between the Seine and Holland, waiting for Allied landings which never came.[42]

A second means of thwarting German troop movement was the Transportation Plan, which called for the bombing of key bridges and rail yards throughout France and the Low Countries by the Allied air forces.

The third instrument to be used in delaying German reinforcements was the French resistance. An early version of the Overlord plan had been completed by an Allied staff in London in 1943, and British and U.S special operations planners had been asked in June of that year for their concept for employment of the French resistance in support of the operation.[43] In April 1944, with the final Overlord plan completed, General Eisenhower's operations officer, Major General Harold R. Bull, asked for an updated and detailed review of the special operations plan.[44]

The plan, laid out in Appendix P of the preliminary Overlord plan, remained essentially unchanged in the final version. In the first phase of Overlord, the resistance would contribute to the Transportation Plan by cutting rail lines and obstructing road movement by ambush and sabotage.[45] The support of the resistance would become crucial in the event of bad weather, which often grounded aircraft in the European theater. Additionally, in areas where civilian populations in the immediate vicinity of targets might be threatened, partisans could be more precise in their attacks. They were, in a sense, the "smart bombs" of their day.

Once the lodgment area was secure, the resistance would shift to a general campaign of guerrilla warfare—sabotaging communications; attacking enemy supply depots, command posts, and road and rail traffic; and, where necessary, preventing enemy demolition of bridges or other structures that were needed by the Allies.

General Eisenhower was convinced by this time that the French resistance would play a key role in supporting Overlord, and he was equally sure that he needed some means of controlling and directing and encouraging them. He and his British counterpart in the Mediterranean, General Sir Henry Maitland Wilson, both recognized that the most important function of the Jedburgh teams would be as a means of providing such direct influence over the resistance fighters.[46]

Eisenhower had known of the Jedburgh concept since September 1942, when he was commander of U.S. troops in Britain. An early draft of the concept had been tabled at a meeting of joint planners in Washington in late August of that year. War Department officials had agreed with the concept, with the proviso that the Jeds be employed under the direct control of the theater commander. Before giving the concept their official endorsement, however, they had decided that they needed Eisenhower's opinion, and in September the concept had been forwarded to him in London for his recommendation.

On September 11, 1942, Sir Charles Hambro, chief of Britain's Special Operations Executive, met with Eisenhower in the general's second-floor corner office at Grosvenor Square. It was not Hambro's first visit to Eisenhower's office. He and General "Pug" Ismay, Churchill's military deputy, and a colonel representing the special operations branch of OSS had met with Eisenhower back in July, shortly after his arrival in London.

Major General Bill Donovan, director of the OSS, was present at Hambro's second meeting with Eisenhower, and Donovan would meet separately with Ike two days later. It was during these meetings that Eisenhower first learned of the Jedburgh project, and immediately after their conclusion Donovan informed the Joint Chiefs of Staff in Washington of the general's recommendation. Eisenhower followed up with his formal and favorable endorsement of the Jedburgh concept in a message to the War Department on September 16, 1942, adding his agreement that the Jeds should operate under the theater commander's control. He also suggested that planners reconsider the idea of the Jeds being dropped in uniform.[47]

Clarification of the chain of command for directing the unconventional warfare campaign in support of Overlord came in May 1944. Special Operations Executive and the Special Operations Branch of the Office of Strategic Services had been working essentially as a combined headquarters in London since January. With D-Day approaching, and in recognition of the role it would be playing, it was decided that the headquarters needed a designation which could be used for open dissemination. In other words, one which did not identify SOE, the name and existence of which was still classified at the time. So, on the first day of May, General Smith, Eisenhower's chief of staff, issued a directive naming the organization Special Force Headquarters (SFHQ). It would be directly subordinate to Eisenhower's Supreme Headquarters Allied Expeditionary Force (SHAEF).[48]

With their formal training program completed, the Jeds continued to participate in field exercises, but they also had more time to relax as they awaited the coming invasion and their deployment to the field. There were games of soccer and rugby and softball. And in the evenings men might catch a ride into Peterborough for drinks at the Bull Hotel or one of the local pubs. Some enjoyed dances held at the Peterborough town hall. But others found Peterborough a bit dull, and preferred a visit to the "Fox & Hound," a pub within walking distance of Milton Hall in the opposite direction from Peterborough.

Music lovers tuned radios in to the Armed Forces Network or to German propaganda stations, which played all the current hit songs along with the equally entertaining propaganda messages of British expatriate Lord Haw Haw.

Weekends often meant passes to London. The Jeds found that, for all the bombings and hardships imposed on Londoners during the war, many of the city's pre-war attractions managed to carry on; some even flourished as a result of the war. Shows at theaters such as the Windmill and the Prince of Wales featured chorines wearing smiles, and perhaps some form of military headgear, and little else.

Streets were a colorful showcase for military garb from all over the world. Even war correspondents were often in uniform. Some of the men found time to visit the more traditional tourist attractions such as Trafalgar Square, Buckingham Palace, the Tower of London, and Westminster Abbey. They could stop by the American PX on South Audley Street and stock up on candy bars, cigarettes, gum, soap, and razor blades, or grab the latest issue of *Yank* for threepence or the *Stars and Stripes* for a penny. The Jeds often frequented the clubs run by the American Red Cross, such as the Eagle on Charing Cross Road and the Washington on Curzon Street. The Red Cross's Rainbow Corner (on Shaftesbury Avenue near Piccadilly Circus) had American flags flying outside and the army, navy, and air corps emblems on the façade, and offered a café with good food, jukeboxes and a game room, a barber shop, a library, and even a bed for the night. Some of the men enjoyed dancing with "nice girls" at the Palladium Ballroom or the International Room, where the dance floor was large enough to accommodate three hundred couples.

The men might rendezvous at Piccadilly Circus, under giant ads strutting from Edwardian buildings: "Wrigley's—for Vim and Vigour"; "Guinness is Good for You—Gives You Strength"; "Bile Beans—for Radiant Health & Lovely Figure." The bustling crowds and the lively commercialism and the big-city grime might have reminded some of the Americans of Times Square, save for the bright red double-decker busses and the colorful horse-drawn ale wagons pushing through the circling traffic. After dark prostitutes would congregate at the Circus. The girls came to be called "Piccadilly Commandos" and "Hyde Park Rangers," the latter known to ply their trade in the open air.

Lieutenant Colonel Spooner remained commandant at Milton Hall until early April, when he was succeeded by another British officer, Lieutenant Colonel G. Richard Musgrave. But operational control of the Jeds transferred at that time to the British and American co-directors of the Jedburgh section at Special Force Headquarters, which was located in the Montagu Mansions near Baker Street in London.

It had been two years since the Jedburgh idea had been conceived. After making it through a rigorous assessment and selection process and months of training, the Jeds were ready and restless—thoroughbreds eager to break from the starting gate. On the third of June, the first teams were alerted for their mission briefings in London.

4

"SITUATION HOT"

"**4** 000 PARTISANS MUST RECEIVE HUNDRED BRENS, 1000 STENS, 1000 BATTLEDRESS. SITUATION HOT WILL EXPLODE IF ARMS NOT RECEIVED."[1] So began the wireless telegraph message informing Special Force Headquarters in London on June 11 that Jedburgh team George was safely on the ground and operating. In a second message later that day, the Jeds added an order for anti-tank weapons, carbines, and equipment for an additional two thousand men.

Before the reception committee had cleared the drop zone of parachutes and bundles from team Frederick's landing near Guingamp, Jed team George had jumped roughly ninety miles to the southeast. The two Stirlings carrying team George and the Dingson SAS party dropped their jumpers from a higher altitude than those carrying the Samwest party had, a little more than eight hundred feet. Captain Paul Cyr, the American member of team George, was anxious to leave the overcrowded bomber, and when the green light glowed the Jeds and the SAS men spilled out as fast as the gaping bomb bay would accommodate them.

Floating under a full parachute canopy, Cyr watched for signs of activity on the ground below. The moonlight, dim as it was, offered just enough illumination to see the field and a few trees. From about a hundred feet above the ground, he noticed a group of fifteen to twenty people running toward the area where he and some near-by jumpers would land. Cyr hit the ground and rolled. Then, as he tried to stand, he was mobbed, people tugging and pulling, grasping at harness buckles, until they had freed him from the parachute. And all the while they were laughing and shouting to one another—they were having a ball.

Cyr was sure that these mad Bretons had no idea of the danger they risked by making such a racket, and he asked them to keep it down. But the people assured him that there was no danger. The closest Germans, they explained, were quite far away—two kilometers away. That was slightly more than a mile, and the news didn't make Cyr feel any safer.

When the parachutes had been gathered up, Cyr and the other jumpers followed the reception committee to the rendezvous point in the middle of a field. There they found about seventy-five more people, apparently local members of the resistance. They waited just long enough for the SAS men to join them and then they were off. Captain Cyr hurried along with the crowd, keeping an eye out for his Jed teammates.

The team and the SAS party had jumped into an area of scattered forests and isolated farms in the southeastern part of the Brittany peninsula. The Jeds and the SAS left the drop zone—a large field surrounded by a high hedge—and walked to a nearby farm, just west of the hamlet of St-Marcel. The farm was called La Nouée, and it was to serve as the Dingson SAS base. La Nouée was the home of an elderly farmer named Pondard, his wife, and their seven children—five daughters (the oldest was twenty-three) and two sons.[2]

Near the farmhouse, Cyr was reunited with his two French teammates, Captain Philippe Erard and Lieutenant Christien Lejeune.* Erard, a twenty-six-year-old Orléans native and the designated leader of team George, was a graduate of Saint-Cyr, France's military academy. He had been mobilized with his infantry regiment in 1939 and had fought in the desperate battles of June 1940 that had ended in France's defeat. But Erard, like others, had refused to capitulate. Rather than lay down his arms, he deserted

* Philippe Erard's real name was Philippe Ragueneau; that of Christien Lejeune was Pierre Gay.

and joined the resistance, organizing sabotage and propaganda work first in Toulouse and later in Lyon. He had been picked up by the Germans in August 1941 and was sent to prison by a Vichy court but, through the efforts of influential resistance leaders, he was released after three months. Erard had then made his way to Algeria, where he was eventually recruited for the Jedburghs in 1943.

It was three in the morning when they reached the farmhouse, a two-story stone affair with a steep gray slate roof and a long, attached barn of similar construction extending from one side. But the partisans of the St-Marcel maquis, who made their headquarters in the barn, were in a festive mood. Girls showered the men with kisses and poured them wine and handed them bouquets of flowers. And everyone—men, women, and children—acted as if liberation had already come. Some laughed, others cried with joy, as though it were a done deal: all that remained was to march down the road, give the Germans a quick thrashing, and send them on their way back to the Fatherland. And these feisty Bretons, from adolescents to old men, were ready, it seemed, to go and do just that—this very night.

But rational heads prevailed, and the people worked through the remaining hours of darkness to bring the containers in from the drop zone. Finally, the Jeds got two hours of sleep.

Cyr was a small-town New Englander from the picturesque Green Mountain town of St. Johnsbury in Vermont, where he had worked on the town newspaper, the *Caledonian-Record*, before the war. Despite his being underage, he had managed to join the National Guard out of high school in June 1938—one week after his seventeenth birthday. His unit, the 172nd Infantry Regiment, had been called up for one year of federal service in late February 1941, but after the attack on Pearl Harbor the one year had been extended to "the duration." So Cyr accompanied his regiment to Camp Blanding, Florida, to undergo initial training. The regiment was assigned to the 43rd Infantry Division, a New England National Guard outfit that would go on to see action in the South Pacific—but which would go there without Paul Cyr.

In April 1942, Cyr had left the regiment to enter Officer Candidate School at Fort Benning, and had received a commission in the infantry in June of that year. He also found himself attracted by the lure of the new airborne force then being created at Fort Benning. Cyr volunteered for parachute training but had the misfortune of breaking a leg on one of his first jumps. His leg had fully healed by September 1943, and he was back training troops at Camp Blanding when the OSS recruiter arrived there in search of Jedburgh candidates. Cyr hadn't hesitated to volunteer.[3] Nearly a year later, Captain Cyr found himself on French ground with the task of putting months of training to good use by forming an effective combat force out of this mob of Breton patriots.

Partisan warfare was particularly effective in certain regions of France, and for somewhat different reasons in each area. In the south, for example—from the Pyrénées that defined the Spanish border, across the great and rugged Central Plateau, to the Alps on the Italian and Swiss frontiers and even on northward into the Jura and Vosges mountain ranges—the terrain was ideal for guerrilla warfare. Steep, heavily wooded mountains provided relatively safe bases from which the maquis could operate, a sanctuary into which they could retreat after dealing a blow to the Germans. Railroads and highways followed the valleys in between—valleys so confining in places that God might have had ambush on his mind when he laid them out.

But in Brittany—a land so rough in character and so damp in climate that the Romans had largely ignored it two thousand years earlier—it was the people that made things work. The clannish Bretons were as sturdy as the land they lived on, and they shared the same rustic charm. Celtic in heritage (their ancestors had emigrated from Britain in the fifth century), many of the Bretons still spoke a language that was closer to the native tongues of Ireland, Scotland, and Wales than to French. The Bretons—fiercely independent, and accustomed to looking out for themselves and living off the land—were barely tolerant of the mainland French and were not at all accommodating to the Germans.

They made their living from the sea and the soil, for the most part. Each year, schooners sailed from Brittany's ports to bring back cod from the Newfoundland banks, often battling brutal North Atlantic storms to do so. The home waters provided rich harvests of sardines and oysters and mussels. The local farmers spent a lifetime breaking the veneer of sod that hid the granite not far below, and were surprisingly adept at coaxing impressive potato and cereal crops from the poor, loamy soil.

Like many country folk, Bretons could initially be as cold and reserved to strangers as the great stone megaliths that have dotted the Morbihan landscape since Neolithic times. But in that same tradition of country folk, they could also warm to an uncommon friendliness. In happier times, their Celtic spirit was evident in their passion for festivals, with bagpipe music and folk dances, and women dressed in traditional costumes that included colorfully embroidered ankle-length aprons and tall, white-lace headdresses known as coiffes. Rarely, though, did their enemies ever see this festive and genial side of the Bretons. And the people of Brittany were not the least bit intimidated by the Wehrmacht units occupying their land. For four years they had waited for the opportunity and the tools with which to fight back. Clearly, team George had much to work with.

On their first day at La Nouée, the Jeds met resistance leaders and got a feel for the local situation. In the daylight they could see that the farm was surrounded by forest. There was a large field, about five hundred yards in length, and other smaller fields, each cleared out of the forest. The large field served as the drop zone where the Jeds had landed the night before. A long lane reached from the main road to the farm buildings, and the SAS had posted a sentry on the lane.

The Jeds also met a young-looking British agent called Fernand, whose real name was André Hue. The product of a British mother and a French father, he worked for the Special Operations Executive and had jumped in with the initial small SAS team on the eve of D-Day to help organize the resistance in the St-Marcel area.[4]

At about two in the afternoon, a farmer arrived in a horse-drawn cart. In the cart were the packages containing the Jed radios, which had been dropped near the farmer's house—nearly two miles from the drop zone. This was a stroke of luck; the Jeds would now be able to get their first message off to London.

Over the coming days, Captain Cyr grew to admire the French SAS. The men were out every night on demolition operations, cutting telecommunications lines, blowing up railroads, ambushing Germans on the roads, and generally making life difficult for the enemy. Every night they mixed it up with the Germans and then returned to camp with their dead and wounded.

And the Jeds marveled at the efficiency of the SAS resupply system. Planes arrived for eight consecutive nights—anywhere from five to thirty per night—dumping arms and ammunition and explosives. Just three nights after team George had arrived, thirteen Stirlings dropped eighty-seven more SAS men and 249 containers.[5] Still more men arrived five nights later, when thirteen planes dumped another forty-eight SAS, nearly two hundred more containers, and a jeep. The local resistance members hustled night after night to clear the drop zone before dawn. Even though the Jeds also arranged arms drops from London, theirs paled in comparison to those of the SAS. Most of the weapons that arrived in the containers for the maquis were Sten submachine guns, and each of them came with a handful of loaded magazines.

In the make-do world of the guerrilla, the Sten was an engineering marvel. To provide the resistance fighters with a dependable submachine gun in the numbers required, the British had developed in the Sten what was arguably the cheapest, simplest weapon of its kind ever made—and the ugliest. But it worked. The seven-pound Sten proved to be uncomplicated to operate, and the gun held up well under the rigors of combat and rustic living conditions. It was a no-frills version of the more sophisticated German MP40—easy to disassemble and assemble and with parts that were easily concealed. Built with the partisan in mind, it was weapons design at its most elementary level. It required little in the way of maintenance and could operate for months without being oiled. The Sten had a simple stamped-metal tubular design with a thirty-two-round box magazine protruding from its left side. It looked more like a bicycle pump than a weapon. And, although ammunition for it could be air dropped, it could also be found in abundance in German stocks or harvested from the battlefield. (It used the same 9mm Parabellum round used in German Lugers.) But the Sten had two drawbacks: it was prone to jam and it had an unwelcome tendency to fire when dropped on the ground, with results that could be hilarious or tragic. From a technological standpoint, though, it was scarcely more complicated than a socket wrench. The dumbest man in France could master the gun in ten minutes.

By the fifteenth of June, SAS Dingson and Jed team George had armed some twenty-three hundred patriots, forming two large battalions—one east of the harbor town of Vannes, located on Brittany's southern coast, and one about thirty miles north of Vannes.[6]

The Dingson base was running magnificently, and with each successful patrol, the SAS men grew more confident, felt more secure—almost invulnerable. Their aggressive, in-your-face approach to behind-the-lines warfare was effective, and the Jeds couldn't help but marvel at their efficiency.[7] But, inevitably, the Germans came to know all about the farm called La Nouée and what went on there. The very success of the Dingson SAS enterprise, with the nightly airdrop activity and the endless radio communications that made it all possible, was, in the end, its undoing.

As the Jeds of team George had been taught back at Milton Hall, a lengthy stay at any one base location was to invite disaster. And the Germans would soon be ready to strike.

Meanwhile, sabotage operations carried out by resistance groups throughout France, organized—and in some cases led—by agents of Special Operations Executive's circuits, were proving more successful than many had thought possible. By D-Day there were more than twenty F Section circuits in operation throughout France, and they had already armed tens of thousands of guerrillas in maquis groups in every region.[8] In the weeks leading up to the invasion, the groups had been attacking their assigned pre-D-Day targets, mostly industries critical to the German war machine.

But the targets which the resistance groups had been most anxious to strike were their D-Day targets—roads and railway lines, telecommunications sites and command posts. These, they had been told, were not to be attacked until pre-arranged signals were received from Special Force Headquarters just before the invasion, signals which would be aired by the British Broadcasting Corporation (BBC) on certain designated nights following its French news program.

On the first day of June, the BBC had broadcast a secret message which served to alert circuit organizers and resistance leaders that the invasion was only days away. Resistance groups had then listened every evening for their second pre-arranged message, which would be their execute order. Plans had called for D-Day targets to be struck forty-eight hours after receipt of this second message.[9]

At nine-fifteen on the evening of June 5, following the BBC's French news broadcast, the seemingly meaningless personal messages, the execute orders—306 in all—had gone out over the air. And out of a planned 1,050 rail cuts all but 100 had been successfully carried out that night.[10]

The British and American air forces, too, had begun their attacks on the transportation system in France, and by the night of the fifth they had destroyed eighteen of the twenty-four bridges over the Seine and knocked out more than five thousand locomotives. This was after the resistance had already destroyed or damaged more than seven hundred locomotives in the four months leading up to D-Day.[11] As a result, on the eve of D-Day rail traffic nationwide in France was running at 30 percent of its January level.[12]

Jedburgh teams were beginning to arrive throughout France to help the growing resistance continue the sabotage campaign and to delay the German reinforcements trying to reach the Normandy battlefields. Major Adrian Wise and his Jedburgh team Frederick were in position in northern Brittany—and were ready to begin.

5

SURVIVAL

L ATER in the campaign for northern France, after the Allies had broken out from Normandy and begun their fairly swift advance toward Germany, some Jedburgh teams were inserted too late to be of much use. A few teams were overrun by the advancing Allied ground forces only days after jumping, having had little time to effectively perform their missions. But that was not the case with the thirteen Jed teams deployed throughout France during the month of June, or even for the dozen more dropped the following month. For these teams, mission completion often came only after weeks of perilous, nerve-racking raids and manhunts conducted by German troops and Gestapo agents.

Several German divisions were on the move toward Normandy as reinforcements, intent on helping defeat the Allied invaders on the beaches. Many more German units remained in place throughout France as reserves, though, and to maintain security in the rear. And until the ground war came to them, these units could devote much of their time and energy to hunting down guerrillas and Allied special forces. Eluding such units was the challenge now facing Jedburgh team Frederick.

★ ★ ★

Major Wise and team Frederick were ready to begin helping the resistance leader Marceau organize and arm his maquis groups throughout the department of Côtes-du-Nord in northern Brittany. At first, all they could do was give Marceau some badly needed cash to use for feeding and paying his maquisards, most of whom still had families to support. Before they could begin arranging air-drops of arms and supplies, the Jeds first had to retrieve the radios which Sergeant Kehoe had hidden in the forest during the attack by German paratroopers four days earlier.

On Friday, June 16, the Jeds enjoyed dinner at a small café in a village a few miles northeast of their campsite. Later, they sat around the table with Robert, the French SAS sergeant who had brought the wounded men to the barn the day of the attack. Sergeant Robert was a seasoned veteran of the French army. Quiet by nature, tall and slim, he carried himself with the dignity and bearing of the professional soldier he was. Bob Kehoe judged him to be in his early thirties. The Jeds were working on a plan for recovering the radios from the Duault forest, and Robert offered to help. The Frenchman indicated that he thought he knew how they could do it.

Sergeant Kehoe's understanding of French, though limited at first, had been improving since his arrival in Brittany. Even when listening to spirited conversation among a group of Frenchmen he was able to follow the gist of the dialogue, while missing some of the detail, rather like listening to a radio program intermittently interrupted by static.

As he listened to Robert's plan, Kehoe grasped enough of the conversation to realize that the plan called for speedy movement. Much more speed, it seemed to him, than men on foot could accomplish. What Kehoe didn't catch was the reason for the urgency. The maquis had learned that the Germans were planning a major operation of some sort in the area; the radios were desperately needed and time was of the essence. In fact, Robert planned to go after them that very night. If all went well, the radios would be safely back in the hands of the Jeds before dawn. Kehoe knew that executing the operation on foot would take at least two days. He soon found out where the necessary speed would come from.

Hidden in a nearby shed was a 1934 automobile which had been up on blocks since the German occupation began. The car belonged to a mechanic who had clandestinely kept it in working order. Employed in a St-Brieuc factory over the past four years, the mechanic had smuggled a considerable amount of fuel out of the factory—one cup at a time. The wheels were re-mounted, the car was pushed from the shed, the hand crank was turned, and the engine roared to life. Kehoe, Robert, and two young maquisards climbed aboard, and they drove off down the road toward the forest some ten or twelve miles away.

With a teenager at the wheel, Sergeants Kehoe and Robert rode with their weapons at the ready. Another teen had come along to help guard the car while Kehoe and Robert searched for the radios. Headlights remained off and the journey was made in complete darkness. They had to avoid detection, and they would be passing through two or three villages which would be observing wartime blackout ordinances. As the car crept along the winding country road, Kehoe and Robert watched for German patrols or for any sign of an enemy roadblock ahead. At the entrance to each village the driver pressed the accelerator, and Kehoe and Robert scanned the buildings and kept their weapons pointed out the windows as they rolled past.

During the German attack four days earlier, team Frederick had hastily abandoned the maquis camp in the forest and, to move faster, had hidden both radios. Sergeant Kehoe had buried one under a boulder in the immediate vicinity of the camp, and the second had been quickly stashed behind a boulder along the forest trail that the Jeds had taken while being chased. Kehoe and Robert planned to search for both sets, but they knew nothing of the current situation at the former campsite. Were there any Germans still in the area? Had the enemy planted mines around the abandoned encampment? Or along the trails leading to it?

Uncertain as to what lay ahead, the two sergeants knew that they had to approach the area using extreme caution. As they neared the forest, they directed the young driver to pull down a side road so that the engine would not be heard from the campsite. Ensuring that the car was well hidden in a thick stand of gorse and guarded by the two teenagers, Kehoe and Robert set out for the camp.

Only a sliver of moon remained in the mid-June sky, and the countryside was quiet and dark. The two men carried flashlights but dared not use them except in an emergency. They made good progress through the woods, even without illumination, and in less than an hour they found the old forest road which led to the camp. Sergeant Kehoe led Robert along the trail until he recognized the spot where he'd stashed the second radio, but when he searched behind the boulder he found no radio there. German patrols had apparently discovered it. Though disappointed, Kehoe was not really surprised; he had not had time during the chase to hide the radio well.

Time was passing quickly and it would soon be daylight. Sergeant Robert had hoped to also be able to look around for remnants of the SAS force in the area—dead or alive—and find out if stockpiles of weapons had survived enemy searches. So he and Kehoe agreed to split up, conduct separate searches, and rendezvous later. Sergeant Kehoe then proceeded directly to the abandoned campsite.

The Samwest camp had been spread out over an area of about five hundred yards by two hundred yards, and Kehoe soon recognized the general area. He had hidden the radio under a boulder not far from the SAS command post and near the center of the camp. Without much trouble, he found the boulder which he had used as a landmark. But, when he crept down the hill to find the boulder under which he had hidden the radio, Kehoe found that, in the darkness, many boulders looked similar to the one that he sought. For nearly an hour he went from one to the next, digging underneath, only to find nothing. Finally, just as dawn approached, his relentless excavating paid off and he uncovered the complete Jed set, unharmed.

Kehoe shouldered the forty-pound radio pack and scrambled up the hill. He found an anxious Sergeant Robert waiting at the rendezvous point, and the two set off for the car at a brisk pace. With the coming daylight, their return drive was relatively quick.

The young American and the experienced Frenchman had gotten a difficult job done under dangerous conditions and, in the process, they developed a new-found respect for one another. The taciturn Robert, despite an occasional show of arrogance, had proved him-

self to be a natural and resourceful leader. He still needled Kehoe
(perhaps a dozen years his junior) about his youthful inexperi-
ence—often chiding that the American surely must have lied about
his age to enter the army—but Kehoe knew that he had passed
muster in the eyes of the older man.[1]

The maquis' sense of urgency for the radio recovery proved well-
founded. On Sunday, barely twenty-four hours after Kehoe and
Robert returned with the radio, an estimated four thousand Germans moved on the Duault forest and the surrounding area. After
throwing a cordon around the area with roadblocks, motorized and
foot patrols ravaged the countryside, raiding farms and torching
homesteads. Civilians were taken into custody for interrogation.
Troops combed every inch of the forest during the well-planned
operation.

With radio in hand, team Frederick could begin arming and
organizing the maquis of the Côtes-du-Nord. First, they moved
south to a more secure area, establishing a camp about five miles
east of the Duault forest, not far from the barn where the wounded
SAS were being cared for. The campsite was in a rugged pasture
where the prickly, yellow-flowered gorse shrubs were particularly
tall and thick, providing good concealment. For added security,
contact with members of the resistance was kept to a bare mini-
mum, and was nearly always made through the network of female
schoolteachers.

The new camp was more than a mile from the nearest paved road
and was reached by following narrow footpaths used by the farmers whose cows grazed throughout the area. The Jeds erected no
tents or shelters of any kind, opting to sleep in a ditch with only
blankets, provided by the French, to give some small measure of
warmth during the wettest of Junes that any of the locals could
remember. It was an animal's existence—damp, cold, dirty—but it
was also a secure one. There was little in such an austere camp that
could be spotted by a German plane flying overhead or by the occasional patrols passing on the nearby roads. Gunfire was heard from
time to time, and the men never doubted the immediacy of the
German presence.

They were also positioned well from a logistical standpoint. They were less than a mile from the old barn where the wounded SAS men lay. Marcel, Simone, and the other local patriots caring for the SAS men would be able to carry food to both the wounded men and the Jeds on the same trip. But the team also knew that, for security reasons, it could not remain at the site for long.

Anxious to get their radio into operation and let London know that they were back in business, Kehoe made his scheduled contact on June 18, the same day the Germans swept through the Duault forest just a few miles away. Kehoe's cryptic message told Special Force Headquarters of the attack on the SAS camp and of the dispersion of the Samwest SAS party, of the care being provided the three wounded SAS men nearby, and of the Jeds' successful contacts with resistance leaders.

Special Force Headquarters had not heard from team Frederick since the twelfth, and it gratefully acknowledged the contact at once. Questions would arise at SFHQ of the authenticity of a transmission from the field after so many days of missing scheduled contacts. Had the team been captured? Was it transmitting under duress to aid the Germans in manipulating London's operations? But Sergeant Kehoe was careful to include his safety signal in the message, as instructed during the briefing back in London, to signify that he was transmitting freely and securely.

Meanwhile, Allied forces continued to come ashore in Normandy—fifteen divisions by June 12, another five by the nineteenth—building up to the day when the Allies would be strong enough to break out of the lodgment area.

On Monday, the nineteenth, SFHQ sent a message to team Frederick confirming the location of drop zones which the Jeds had identified. Headquarters also congratulated Peseta (Bob Kehoe's code name) on his promotion to the rank of first sergeant.[2] It was his second promotion in ten days, and it put him, at age twenty-two, at a rank typically held by older and much more seasoned veterans. It also meant that, in less than two weeks, his monthly pay had gone up from ninety-six dollars to one hundred and thirty-eight dollars. Virtually all of the Jedburgh radio operators were enjoying the same accelerated advancement, and many of the Americans became first sergeants by the time their missions were completed.[3]

With the team separated from the SAS and on its own in a relatively secure location, Kehoe could begin following a standard communications routine. Both SFHQ and the field operators took every precaution possible to limit transmission times to reduce the likelihood of enemy detection by radio direction-finders. For its part, SFHQ sent messages to the field in one-way broadcasts during the late-night hours, typically during the first few hours after midnight. These nightly broadcasts began with a list of stations, or operators, that were the intended recipients of the messages. Once all of the messages had been broadcast the entire series was repeated. If Kehoe received a message, he copied it down and then deciphered it—all by flashlight.

Operators in the field sent messages to London during scheduled contact times, usually during the day. And, whenever possible, they would move some distance from the camp to transmit, thereby reducing the chance of radio direction-finders locating the campsite. The Jed set could receive messages with power provided by the dry cell battery, but the hand-cranked generator was needed when transmitting, and local maquisards would often assist by turning it. Such a schedule was tiring, and enemy signal jamming or inclement weather only made it more demanding. Luckily for Kehoe, the Germans' enthusiasm for patrolling and radio direction-finding searches was dampened by the rainy weather.

Marceau, the resistance leader with whom team Frederick was working, turned out to be a key man in this part of Brittany. His real name was Yves Le Hegarad, and he was the FFI chief for all of the Côtes-du-Nord. The FFI had been created by General de Gaulle in early 1944 and was intended to accomplish a merger of all indigenous resistance movements in France, including the maquis. The organization was called the Forces Françaises de l'Intérieur (French Forces of the Interior), and was nearly always referred to as the FFI.

One of the most active elements of the French resistance, though, was the leftist Francs-Tireurs et Partisans (Irregulars and Partisans), or FTP, and it was particularly strong in Brittany. The FTP was the paramilitary arm of France's Front National political movement, which was dominated by socialists and communists and often, at least early in the war, took its directions from Moscow. As was the case throughout France, maquis leaders at all levels in Brittany shared the common military goal of driving the Germans from their country. But they also had political agendas, and these were not always the same. Quite naturally, in a country which had been occupied for four years, resistance leaders were concerned with the form of government France would adopt upon liberation. And while FTP leaders were socialist-oriented, most of the FFI supported de Gaulle, who was intent on keeping the socialists and communists from gaining power in post-war France.

The FTP had agreed to fight under de Gaulle's FFI organization, but the relationship was always tense and tenuous. Some FTP leaders in other parts of France flatly refused to recognize de Gaulle as their leader, but in Brittany they cooperated with the Gaullists. It was because of leaders such as Marceau that they did so.

Marceau's real authority over the many small maquis groups was limited, with each group primarily loyal to its immediate leader. Although Marceau was nominally the departmental chief of the FFI he also had strong links with the FTP. His leadership qualities enabled him to maintain the support and cooperation of maquis groups throughout the department, regardless of political ideology. He also maintained daily contact with the Jeds, normally by courier, and visited the camp as often as possible.

To be effective in their work, it was important for the Jedburghs to distance themselves from the internal politics of the resistance, and Sergeant Kehoe was finding that this was perhaps easiest for him to do. As an American, he was more inclined to be viewed by the locals as truly unbiased when it came to French politics. But such was not the case with the French Jedburgh team members, and remaining wholly impartial was not always easy for them to do. At times, Major Wise fretted that Lieutenant Aguirec engaged in too many political discussions with resistance people.[4]

Once contact with London had been re-established, the Jeds began arranging air drops, bringing in the arms and supplies and money so desperately needed in the area. On the night of June 23, sixty containers floated under parachute to a field northwest of Guingamp, about twenty-one miles north of team Frederick's camp. In the process of arranging a reception committee and marking the field to be used as a drop zone, the Jeds were careful to train the guerrillas to perform such work on their own.[5]

Team Frederick found the maquis to be not only willing but enthusiastic fighters, often erring on the side of rashness in their eagerness to take the fight to the enemy. And no matter how risky a planned operation was, the Jeds were never short of volunteers.

Sometimes the enemy responded with reprisals and atrocities visited on the local people, usually in the form of burning houses and other buildings. The Germans were aided in this by the Milice, the collaborationist Vichy constabulary whose members betrayed their own countrymen for a pat on the back and a fistful of francs from the occupier. If the maquis loathed the Germans, it was nothing compared to what they felt for the Milice. Major Wise would later report, "I personally witnessed the ill treatment and execution of five Milice and none of us felt the least pity for them."[6]

The last half of June was a busy time for the Jeds. Supply drops continued and more German targets were struck, including an ammunition dump. Sometimes, though, Bob Kehoe would have to hastily send a message asking London to postpone a drop because of enemy activity near the planned drop zone. On June 24, however, he was able to report: "REGION HUMMING WITH ENEMY ACTIVITY. SUCCESSFULLY CARRIED OUT ATTACK ON COMMUNICATIONS. BOCHE* COMMUNICATIONS IN BRITTANY IN CHAOS. WILL TRY AGAIN [to receive another parachute drop] AFTER AMMUNITION DUMP. OUR MORALE TERRIFIC." And on the following day the Jeds asked that their next drop include: "BATTLEDRESS AND CIGARETTES, SOAP, TOBACCO, PIPE AND RATION FOR TWO WEEKS FOR JED TEAM ALSO BATTERIES FOR RECEIVERS."[7] On the twenty-eighth the Jeds confirmed their ability to accept another Jedburgh team, but warned that two days advance notice would be prudent because the area was crawling with Germans. They also asked London to send one million francs for team Frederick, to be carried in by the new arrivals.

More arms and supplies arrived on the night of June 29, when

---

* Pronounced "Bosh," a contemptuous term used by the French in referring to the German occupiers.

four Halifaxes—British bombers converted for special operations use—dropped thirty containers and sixteen packages to a field ten miles south of Guingamp.

Things were heating up. The Germans were stepping up efforts to search out and destroy the maquis. They also were making it clear that parachutists who gave material support and encouragement to the maquis were considered outlaws, just like the guerrillas, whom the Germans called "terrorists." In the last week of June, Germans began posting notices on buildings and fences throughout Brittany. The handbills warned citizens that Allied parachutists were nothing but spies and terrorists, and if captured such men would be shot immediately, along with anyone found to be helping them.

But such threats had little effect on maquis operations, and the tempo of team Frederick's work continued to accelerate. On July 6, Kehoe sent another message requesting delivery of weapons, grenades, and explosives, as well as for boots for a hundred men. Boots were especially important for the men of the maquis, many of whom came from rural France, where people often wore wooden shoes because they provided much better insulation from the dampness and the mud than did leather shoes. But wooden clogs—called *sabots* by the French—were ill-suited for guerrilla warfare, where one had to be prepared to run.

Kehoe's message also told of an attack on a maquis group near Guingamp a few days earlier, a fight which had cost the lives of seventy German soldiers and ten maquisards.

The Germans, however, were not the only ones turning up the heat. Special Force Headquarters began pushing to rapidly expand operations in Brittany in preparation for an Allied breakout from Normandy. By the second day of July the Allies had slightly less than a million men in France. That day, London radioed team Frederick that arms and supplies, as well as additional Jedburgh teams, were to be dropped as fast as the men on the ground could accept them and arrange for their security and dispersal. Headquarters asked the Jeds to identify as many dropping grounds as possible.

Reinforcements coming from London would find plenty of work waiting for them. Maquis groups were growing constantly and were critically short of weapons, explosives, and equipment. As the arms arrived and stockpiles grew, though, Wise's team found it impossible to keep up with the necessary training. There were simply too many small groups scattered far and wide across the department, and so maquis leaders with military experience had to pitch in and conduct most of the weapons and tactics instruction. It was still necessary, however, for the Jeds to train the maquis on the use of specialized explosives and demolition equipment sent from England.

Relief began arriving on the night of July 8, when Jedburgh team Felix jumped and was met by a reception committee arranged by team Frederick. Team Felix would take over responsibility for the eastern half of the Côtes-du-Nord department, leaving the western half to team Frederick.

That same night, Captain Bernie Knox's Jedburgh team Giles parachuted in to the rough department of Finistère at the westernmost tip of Brittany, where the peninsula's most important port, Brest, lay. On the following night two more teams were dropped to the southern Finistère, and another two arrived a week later. In the northeast corner of Brittany, two teams dropped to the Ille-et-Vilaine department on the night of the eleventh.

For a fortnight, team Frederick and the maquis ambushed German patrols and truck convoys, attacked enemy fuel dumps, and blew rail lines. They sabotaged German communications by blowing high-tension power lines and transformers and cutting the underground cable connecting Brest with Paris. Map coordinates for a German general headquarters and for infantry and artillery unit locations were radioed to SFHQ for handoff to the air force for bombing missions. Although the Jeds and Marceau tried to maintain control of all maquis operations by designating or approving targets and tactical plans, they were not able to prevent some FFI bands from acting on their own. These uncoordinated attacks, while usually successful, were risky and often resulted in costly enemy counterattacks or reprisals. German commanders were increasing their efforts to move eastward to help check the swelling Allied lodgment area in Normandy, but German units remaining in Brittany continued their ruthless counter-guerrilla campaign.

Three times in one week the Germans had fired on maquis elements on the road just behind the Jeds' camp, and so Major Wise decided it was time to move. The Jeds struck camp on July 9 and relocated about nine miles to the east.

On a rocky, wooded hillside just above the hamlet of Canihuel stood a deserted one-room cottage. It was on a rough, single-lane country road which appeared to be used only for livestock and horse-drawn vehicles. The Jeds decided to set up their command post in the cottage. Accessibility to the place was good enough to facilitate the direction of FFI operations throughout their area of responsibility. Clearly, though, it would not be as secure as their previous camp. Here they would be in a building, out in the open, with some major roads not far away, and the tiny cottage would be crowded. But at least they would be out of the weather.

Sergeant Kehoe reported the team's new location to London that same day, and in the message he also passed on Major Wise's recommendation for a promotion to captain for Lieutenant Aguirec. Special Force Headquarters would signal back two days later that Aguirec had been made an acting captain.[8]

Team Frederick's new camp soon became a fully functional command post. The Jeds and Marceau, who had become a fairly permanent part of the team, established a courier system to maintain contact with maquis groups throughout the region. Their stable of couriers included two gendarmes, in their official blue and black uniforms, who were sympathetic to the resistance, and five local girls who got around by bicycle. In the case of the gendarmes, travel throughout the area on bicycle or moped was part of their everyday job, providing a convenient cover for their courier work. Greater risk was involved for the girls, but women of all ages typically enjoyed much more success in getting through German checkpoints than did men. They naturally seemed more innocent and they didn't have to explain why they hadn't been conscripted for labor.

Simone Le Göeffic, the attractive young schoolteacher who had given food to the Jeds that first night after the German raid on the SAS camp in the Duault forest, came to help out at the new command post. Her chores included preparing meals, and she cooked using the cottage's ancient fireplace. The Jeds soon found themselves eating well. Simone was assisted by a petite woman in her mid-twenties named Aimée Pouhaër. Although Aimée was quiet by nature, Bob Kehoe found her easy to talk to, and he enjoyed listening to her describe what life in Brittany was like before the Germans came.

A young man named Josef Forestier acted as the camp's supply officer and proved himself resourceful in quite unexpected ways. One day he arrived at camp with a supply of women's underwear that he had managed to find. The Jeds, still in the unwashed clothing they had left England in a month before, were not too proud to accept a pair each and wear them.

Kehoe found the Canihuel camp ideal for radio communications. By this time, Kehoe had grown confident that the reliable Jed set would never let him down. It had worked perfectly so far, even when making a scheduled contact while German troops were nearby—even in the next field—which often happened. He spent most nights sitting at a table in the small cottage, listening for broadcasts and encoding or decoding messages by the glow of a flashlight while the others, both men and women, slept in the single room.

A week had passed at the new camp when Wise and Kehoe were interrupted one morning during a scheduled radio contact with London. An excited maquisard arrived warning of "Boche and Russian cavalry" searching the woods nearby for maquis. (Some of the Wehrmacht—or German army—units in Brittany were composed of East European volunteers in German uniform, and among them was a squadron of Ukrainian horse cavalry.) There were also reports from nearby farmers of unusually heavy movement of Germans on the roads, including slow-moving vehicles—a sure indicator of radio direction-finding activity.

At this point, the Jeds should have been on the alert. Only a few days earlier, one of the young female couriers had arrived suddenly on bicycle as the Jeds were having dinner. The young woman was visibly shaken and told of a raid on a farmhouse to the east. A group of men had gathered there to prepare for the reception of an airdrop which team Frederick had arranged. While the men were sitting at dinner in the farmhouse, German soldiers kicked in the door and came in shooting, killing everyone present and then burning the house down. Major Wise was concerned enough by the woman's story to send Simone and Aimée elsewhere as a cautionary measure.

The Jeds should have thought out a procedure for hastily abandoning the command post in an emergency situation, but they had been busy with other things. Wise and Kehoe had been working hard to keep up with the radio messages required by the increasing operational tempo. The demand for airdrops was growing daily, and reports of impending danger had become somewhat commonplace, so the men were not overly concerned with this morning's development. Still, they had posted a sentry as a precaution.

Shots rang out, and they weren't far off. Both rifle and machine gun fire, and Bob Kehoe judged it to be no more than a few hundred yards away. With only five or six men in the cottage, fighting it out with a German raiding party was out of the question. There was nothing to do but run, only taking time to grab weapons, hand grenades, radio crystals, cipher books, and the already enciphered messages. German bullets chipped at the stone walls of the cottage as the men quickly gathered what they could and bolted out the door and down the hill opposite the fast approaching enemy. The radio was left behind, but the Jeds were more concerned with their own survival, and got away from the building only seconds before the Germans closed in.

Maquisards who had been in the command post had scattered to nearby farms. But the Jeds were conspicuous in their uniforms. They ran into a wooded area about a hundred and fifty yards downhill from the cottage and followed a small stream to a spot from which they could observe the enemy soldiers. This was more than a mere probe; it was later estimated that six hundred to eight hundred enemy troops were scouring the area. Most appeared to be infantrymen, but there were also troops on horseback.

Then a German officer noticed the aerial strung between two trees next to the cottage, and he sent troops to search the small house. Soon they discovered the radio and they almost certainly found a map, which had been inadvertently left behind, showing dropping grounds throughout the department. It was a devastating loss and one that had to be reported to England as soon as possible to enable cancellation of all planned air operations. But the urgent need was for the Jeds to get away.

The Germans, however, seemed in no hurry to leave. Enemy troops were spread far and wide, and the Jeds knew that the entire area would be thoroughly searched. Already, they could tell by the voices of men shouting directions and by the occasional gunfire that they were completely surrounded.

Major Wise decided to lead the team out of the trap that had closed around them. After luckily crossing three fairly open fields without being noticed, the team crawled into a thirty-yard-square patch of gorse next to a trail. Once the men had dug deep into the brush, they remained still, waiting for darkness before going any farther. And they prayed that the Germans would not bring search dogs.

Only thirty minutes passed before the first German patrol stalked by, just a few yards away, on the trail. The Jeds froze. Again and again people walked by. The Jeds could tell which ones were German soldiers by their boots, and while the Germans sometimes fired shots they never thought to shoot into the brush. The three Jeds remained motionless all afternoon, only moving onto their sides when necessary to relieve themselves.

One group of perhaps a dozen soldiers came strolling down the trail and stopped right next to the gorse. Only a few feet separated the Jeds from the men in the hobnailed boots. By this time, the Jeds had agreed that they would not be taken alive. Their weapons were charged and ready, and if they were discovered they would come out shooting and make a break for it, knowing that they would probably be cut down before getting far. Lying on the ground under the gorse, First Sergeant Kehoe kept his .45-caliber pistol held at arm's length, aimed toward the trail a few feet away. Curiously, he noticed that his hands, which moments before had been trembling uncontrollably, were now still.

The enemy soldiers were carrying on a lively conversation and the Jeds feared that if the talking stopped the Germans might hear them breathing. None knew enough German to understand what the conversation was about. After a while the soldiers left, firing a few random shots as they continued down the trail.

When dusk came, the Jeds sensed that the immediate danger was passing. Gunfire had become intermittent and it eventually stopped altogether. The men crawled backward out of their hiding place and looked around. They saw no Germans, but they did spot a farm boy tending to some cows. The men questioned the boy and learned that the Germans had been patrolling nearby all day but had left shortly before dusk, apparently not wanting to remain in the area after dark.

Wise, Aguirec, and Kehoe moved out to the east, keeping under the cover of the woods as much as possible, and crossed the road which ran into Canihuel. It had been down this road that the German troops had come. Darkness had settled in by the time the men reached a farm owned by a resistance sympathizer. The farmer fed the men, and the team then continued on for a few miles before finding a spot in a wooded area where they might get some sleep.

In the days to follow, word passed quickly throughout the resistance to avoid the small cottage which had been team Frederick's command post. The Jeds heard that people in the area feared reprisals from the Germans if they made any contact with the Jeds or with the maquis. They also learned that several members of nearby maquis groups had been killed during the attack or as a result of the subsequent searches. Most of the maquisards, however, had been able to melt away into the surrounding forests and farms.

The Jeds had learned a hard lesson about the risks involved in operating from a farmhouse, abandoned or otherwise. From here on, the men decided, they would stick to the woods and the fields and ditches of the countryside, avoiding villages and hard-surfaced roads. And, for the time being, they would have to be extra careful. The Gestapo by now had learned much about team Frederick's operations and would be redoubling efforts to track the men down.

Sergeant Kehoe even thought that the team should change into civilian clothes. One reason the Jedburghs operated in uniform was to be accepted by the resistance as representatives of Eisenhower's command. That, Kehoe felt, had already been accomplished. The Gestapo probably had descriptions of the three men and was hunting them—their uniforms only made them easier to spot. But the Jeds remained in uniform, and in the days that followed, the team would, from time to time, encounter a German patrol and come under fire. The Germans would always break contact, however, as soon as the Jeds retreated into the woods. That was where they were safest.

Reestablishing radio communication with London was Major Wise's first concern. With the loss of the radio, the Jeds, for the time being, would have to relay messages through another team's radio operator. They had been able to get word of their situation to Jedburgh team Giles in the Finistère almost immediately, for Giles reported the attack and the loss of Frederick's radio to Special Force Headquarters on July 18. Thus alerted, SFHQ avoided using any drop zones already identified by team Frederick, because the Germans undoubtedly now were aware of them.

On the nineteenth, Jedburgh team Felix, located about forty miles east of Canihuel, also reported team Frederick's situation to London and asked that a new radio for Frederick be dropped as soon as possible to one of team Felix's drop zones. SFHQ complied, but when the new radio was dropped a couple of nights later, its parachute failed to open and the package crashed to the ground, destroying its contents.[9]

Another set was dropped and this time the precious cargo survived. For delivery to team Frederick, the radio set was broken down into three parts, each to be carried by a separate bicycle courier. Carrying such cargo was highly risky for the couriers; discovery of the radio parts at a German checkpoint would almost certainly result in death for the carrier. All went well, though, and less than ten days after abandoning their Canihuel command post, the Jeds had their new radio and were back in business.

They quickly went about rebuilding their network of contacts. Marceau soon rejoined them, arriving on bicycle one day after passing through a German checkpoint on the main road and sweating out a close inspection of his false papers. The schoolteacher couriers courageously continued to deliver food to the men, and someone provided small pieces of canvas that the men could use as makeshift tents under the thick cover of gorse the Jeds had found and were using as their base.

Once again, the Jeds had been lucky. It had been a close call, but they had kept their wits about them and they had survived. Life in the brush, with the damp nights and the occasional rain, was not comfortable, but the men were still alive. Because of this their morale remained high. Bob Kehoe couldn't help but think, "We beat them again."[10]

By late July, the Jeds were on the move once again, first to a spot about six miles to the north, then on to another area even farther north. Near this site they were pleased to find a maquis force of three well-disciplined guerrilla units, which the Jeds inspected on Sunday, July 30. The maquisards were all in uniform, looked sharp, and were armed. They also had been active enough in the area to become targeted by the Germans. Commanding the best of them was Sergeant Kehoe's comrade Robert, the French SAS sergeant who had saved the wounded SAS men after the raid on the Forêt de Duault, and who later had helped Kehoe recover the Jeds' radio. But Robert was now a lieutenant.

Early Monday morning, while most of the partisans were engaged in physical training, a German force numbering several hundred attacked the maquis camp. At first, only the gate sentry, armed with a Bren light machine gun, was able to put up a fight, and he killed thirty Germans before they could dismount from their trucks. Although the sentry was killed shortly thereafter, the rest of the maquis rallied and put up a stiff fight. Major Wise estimated that German casualties (killed and wounded) numbered about five hundred, while twenty-seven patriots had been killed. Wise also learned that the Germans had paid dearly for attacking another maquis camp farther to the east just two days earlier. That assault had kicked off a fifteen-hour firefight which resulted in a withdrawal by the Germans—after suffering high losses. Only two maquisards were reported killed in that engagement.

But the Germans were not finished yet; that afternoon, they attacked team Frederick's camp. Once again, the Jeds gathered up their gear and got away in the nick of time. When the men thought that they'd moved far enough away so as to be out of immediate danger they established a new camp, well concealed in a gorse thicket on top of a hill. Once again, the Jeds had avoided capture or worse. Major Wise and his teammates had not only been sticking to the woods and the gorse but also had limited the size of their immediate group to include just the Jeds and a few others. The men could only hope that the increased efforts of the Germans to hunt them down were not the result of betrayal by an informant.

The large-scale raids such as those that team Frederick had survived through June and July, however, were not likely to continue—for the Germans had a greater threat to confront. The Allied ground forces in Normandy had been continually building up since the first landings on June 6 and, by the middle of July, the force in the lodgment area had grown to thirty divisions, seven of those armored. The Germans had feared that Eisenhower's forces would soon be strong enough to break out, and that time had come. Although the Jedburghs in Brittany did not know it, help was on the way.

6

THE MAQUIS DE SAFFRÉ

IKE Jedburgh team Frederick in the north, team George, operating from the Dingson SAS base in southern Brittany, would experience a harrowing survival ordeal in the weeks to come. But the team's immediate difficulty upon landing was in communicating with London.

Part of team George's problem was the result of damage their radios had received on the parachute jump. To make matters worse, the Germans were jamming the team's assigned frequency and the Jeds had been unsuccessful in getting London to assign them an alternate. As a result, team George was forced to use a frequency that was reserved for emergency use by all Jed teams. Team George also faced an increasing threat from German radio-locating cars.

After four years of tracking down underground intelligence and sabotage agents, the Germans had become skilled at locating clandestine radio transmitters. Intercept stations, usually located in the larger cities, would pick up a signal originating from within occupied territory and would take bearings on the direction of the source. The intersection of bearings taken from two or more intercept stations identified the general area from which a radio was transmitting. Radio direction-finding cars, stationed throughout the country, were then quickly dispatched to the area. Such cars or vans were equipped with circular, rotating antennae mounted on top, and they would circle the area until they had determined the site of the transmitter. The work of these radio direction-finders was not a problem easily overcome, and it was one which endangered not only Jed team George, but the Dingson SAS base as well.

The early success enjoyed by the Dingson base near the commune of St-Marcel in southern Brittany was due to the energetic and efficient men of the 4th (French) SAS Battalion. Their commander, Pierre-Louis Bourgoin, perhaps by then a lieutenant colonel, had jumped in to take control by the middle of June.[1] Under his aggressive and capable leadership, the battalion's railroad sabotage campaign had virtually shut down all rail traffic between Brittany and Normandy. German units were forced to use road transport as they tried to reach the Normandy battlefield. Scarce gasoline supplies were further depleted as a result, and many units had to resort to horse-drawn vehicles and foot movement. This also slowed the Germans' progress and increased their vulnerability to ambush by the maquis and to merciless strafing and bombing by Allied planes. By June 15, the only functioning rail line in Brittany was a single north-south track running between Rennes and Nantes, on the Loire River to the south—and the SAS planned to attack it that night.[2]

The French SAS operating out of the Dingson base had been tremendously successful in arranging airdrops of arms for the resistance. Five thousand patriots had been armed and newly arrived weapons for another five thousand were stockpiled at the camp, awaiting distribution. The coordination of so many drops, however, meant many radio transmissions and a huge amount of air time. Radio locating cars were often seen within a mile of the farm called La Nouée; and often, when Lieutenant Lejeune, the radio operator on Jedburgh team George, tried to send a message, the cars would arrive in the area within ten minutes.[3]

Radio traffic wasn't the only threat to the Dingson base, though. Flagrant disregard for security had reached the point that members of the St-Marcel maquis, after meetings at their headquarters in the barn at the Pondard farm, had been seen walking back to their homes in Malestroit (a mile and a half to the east) with their weapons in full view. German police had many sources for information. Everyone in small St-Marcel and in nearby Malestroit knew about the maquis and the camp at La Nouée, and too many people had been talking. There also had been some recent arrests. On June 17, team George radioed London with news that the Germans had captured a French parachutist and taken him away in handcuffs.[4] Would the Germans get any information out of him?

Bourgoin's SAS base had been successful, but that success came at a price and the bill was coming due.

Aside from the radio problem, Jed team George soon began to feel like a fifth wheel at La Nouée, suspecting that they might be more useful elsewhere. They had heard from a resistance leader familiar with the region that maquis groups in the department of Loire-Inférieure, just to the southeast, were badly in need of help. According to him, the maquis of the Loire-Inférieure were the worst in the region in terms of organization, training, and leadership; and arms were in very short supply. The resistance leader was especially familiar with a large group near the village of Saffré.

So Captains Cyr and Erard of team George met with Colonel Bourgoin and resistance leaders and proposed that their Jedburgh team, because it did not appear to be needed at the SAS base, move to the Loire-Inférieure and see what it could do to help the situation there. Bourgoin approved and the Jeds made preparations for the move. They planned to depart the following morning, Sunday, June 18, in civilian clothes.

At about eight-thirty the next morning, the men were awakened by an explosion. Then they heard machine gun and rifle fire, and realized that the base was under attack. They scrambled to burn sensitive papers, and hid their radios and code books. Plans for a rendezvous point, in case the men became separated, were quickly made. But then the shooting stopped, almost as suddenly as it had begun.

As they learned later, two carloads of German feldgendarmes (military police) had come down the narrow road toward the farm that morning, stopping from time to time as if searching for something. When the cars reached the point where the SAS had posted sentries a maquisard had fired a Piat anti-tank weapon at the lead car. It was a direct hit and the car had blown up, killing everyone inside. The sentries had then fired up the second car with a machine gun and put another Piat round into the engine of that car. When the shooting stopped they found three Germans unconscious and one badly wounded in the second car. One German had gotten away.

The SAS had brought the Germans who had been knocked unconscious back to the command post for questioning once they came around. The wounded German had been taken to a farm building where a maquis doctor treated him.

As soon as the prisoners regained consciousness they were interrogated. A large airdrop, some thirty planes in all, had been received at the farm the previous night, and one of the prisoners told the SAS that they had been sent out to investigate.

About an hour later, a force of at least a hundred Germans approached the camp behind a screen of about two dozen civilians from nearby St-Marcel. The civilians had been rounded up at random and forced to walk in front of the Germans. The enemy came quite close to the camp before being spotted; and then a fierce firefight erupted, and the civilians scattered. SAS machine guns ripped into the Germans, who quickly fell back to the outskirts of St-Marcel. More wounded, including Germans, were brought in for the maquis doctor and nurses to treat.[5]

Then German machine guns opened up with tracer rounds that ignited a fire in the woods next to the SAS camp. Thick smoke began rolling across the camp, making it difficult for the SAS and maquis to see their targets and, at the same time, masking the movement of the Germans. Four jeeps with mounted light machine guns had arrived for the SAS in the previous night's parachute drop, and they were now put into action. When the Germans saw these vehicles they were convinced that an Allied airborne division had landed—which is what they told their higher headquarters.

As a result, in the early afternoon German paratroopers arrived and launched an all-out assault on the camp—the SAS had a whole new fight on their hands. Making skilled use of machine guns and mortars, the enemy paratroopers advanced steadily on the camp—

even though they were taking heavy losses. German snipers, too, were taking their toll on the maquis and SAS defending the camp, who numbered between six hundred and a thousand.

Meanwhile, the Pondard sisters bravely remained at work in the farmhouse kitchen, preparing sandwiches for the men fighting outside. During the first lull in the battle, however, Bourgoin made sure that they were evacuated to another farm.

The only reason the SAS stubbornly fought to hold the farm was to avoid losing the five thousand weapons stockpiled there. The SAS shot off a radio message to London requesting air support, and by late afternoon a squadron of American P-47 Thunderbolts arrived overhead. The planes stayed as long as their fuel allowed, strafing and bombing those troops that could be identified positively as German.

Bourgoin and his officers had done a masterful job of leading the men in the defense of the farm, but the colonel realized that they could not hold out much longer. Many of the SAS men had been killed or wounded. Germans had approached to within five hundred yards of the camp on three sides by eight that evening. The camp was not quite surrounded; an opening remained to the northwest, through the drop zone. Bourgoin decided they would have to make a break for it. The remaining men were organized for the attempt, and Captain Erard and Captain Cyr were each assigned a company of maquisards to lead.

First, at nine that evening, Bourgoin ordered a counterattack which drove the Germans back about a thousand yards. But the fighting was fierce, and Cyr lost eighty-five of the two hundred men in his company. Bourgoin decided they would wait for dark and attempt to move through the German lines in small groups, and he gave leaders the location of a rendezvous point about fifteen miles away. Explosives were set to blow up the stockpile of arms and ammunition at the camp and men began to form into small teams. The Jeds of team George found each other and were determined to break out as a group.

Once darkness came, the Jeds carefully crept through the German perimeter and headed toward the established rendezvous point. Rifles and automatic weapons bickered with one another in every direction through most of the night. Sometimes the firing was very heavy, other times sporadic. The Jeds were slowed somewhat by the weight of their rucksacks and radios. At times they had to lie still in tall grass next to a road while small German patrols—and even battalion-sized formations of enemy paratroopers—marched by not more than five yards from them. Late that night they lay down to sleep in the middle of a wheat field, only to awaken in the morning to the sound of German-uniformed Russians on horseback searching for them. Eventually they made it to the rendezvous point.

The Jeds learned that Bourgoin had decided to move farther west and establish a new camp. Those maquis fighters who had been able to get away from the farm were scattered through the surrounding forests. Jedburgh team George was to continue on to the Loire-Inférieure accompanied by two resistance leaders. Working under the code names Hauteur and Fonction, these men were operating jointly as General de Gaulle's military delegates for the Brittany region.[6] The group set out on foot with a long journey ahead of it.

André Hue, the SOE man at La Nouée, would later learn that the Germans had had two spies among the maquis at the farm. He also learned that the attack on the farm had been made by several parachute and infantry battalions—in all, it had been a force estimated at four thousand to five thousand men. Nearly six hundred Germans had been killed, as were some fifty SAS and as many as two hundred maquisards. The Pondard family and the wounded had been safely hidden at other farms.

In retaliation, and in an attempt to find members of the maquis or the SAS, Germans had questioned and beaten many people in the surrounding area, and had burned several farms and buildings in St-Marcel.[7]

Jedburgh team George, along with traveling companions Hauteur and Fonction, arrived at their destination in the Loire-Inférieure department at two o'clock on the afternoon of June 27, nine days after the attack on the Dingson SAS base. The men were now about a hundred and fifty miles southeast of team Frederick and about the same distance straight south of the nearest Allied ground forces back at the Normandy beachhead.

For the final leg of their journey through the undulating pastoral countryside of eastern Brittany, the men were able to ride in the back of a French farmer's pickup truck. But they had to share the space with a couple of hogs, and the driver covered the back of the truck with a tarp to conceal his cargo. Twice along the way the driver was stopped by Germans who wanted to see his papers. When the soldiers asked the driver what he was hauling the Frenchman lifted a corner of the tarp on the back of the truck just enough to reveal the pigs, and the Germans had opted not to make a more thorough search.

There were other close calls along the way, too, and the small group had narrowly avoided capture. One farm where the men had briefly taken shelter had been raided by the Germans shortly after the team got out, having been tipped off that danger was on the way. The farmer who had sheltered them was reportedly tortured and then killed by having his head pulled off, and his wife and children were then bayoneted to death. On another occasion, the team's guide found himself needing directions in an unfamiliar area. Although it was three in the morning and well past the ten o'clock curfew for civilians, the guide decided to wake the occupants of a house. When a German officer answered, the men had to run for it.

Lying at the mouth of the Loire River on France's Atlantic coast, the Loire-Inférieure department encompassed the port city of St-Nazaire, one of the ports the Allies hoped to capture and use. (Today the department is called the Loire-Atlantique.) The maquis group to which Hauteur took Jedburgh team George was located on a farm about forty miles northeast of St-Nazaire, north of the river town of Nantes. The group called itself the Maquis de Saffré, after the nearby village bearing the same name.

Right from the start, the Jeds could see that there was much work to be done. Of the two hundred or so men in the maquis, only about twenty-five were armed, and many of them carried .22-

caliber rifles and old shotguns. Some, though, had Stens which they had gotten from one of the drops at the Dingson SAS base. The Jeds learned that there were at least two thousand partisans scattered throughout the area who were awaiting weapons, so the first priority was to get arms sent from England. To their credit, the men of the Maquis de Saffré were enthusiastic, and the camp was thrilled at the arrival of the Jeds (who had changed back into uniform). What the Jeds didn't know was that a Gestapo agent lurked among the elated maquisards.

At supper that evening, plans were made to disperse the men in the morning for the sake of security. Later that night, the man who was secretly working for the Gestapo left camp with information to share about the important new arrivals. Because of him, the Germans had known about the maquis camp for some time. But they had not considered the group a threat and had decided just to keep an eye on it. The arrival of the Jedburghs and the two resistance leaders changed all that. The Gestapo was fully aware of the intent of these men—to arm and train the maquis—and they did not intend to let that happen.

At six in the morning the Jeds awoke to news that German trucks had been spotted closing in on the camp from all directions. Lieutenant Lejeune, team George's radio operator, was three hundred yards away in the middle of receiving a message from London. By the time he got his radio broken down and packed up, German troops were within a hundred yards of him.

The attack came suddenly, and German bullets tore into the camp before any kind of defense could be organized. The untrained maquis recruits had no idea what they should do. Automatic weapons fire raked the camp, and men were hit; some were killed. Hauteur and Fonction coolly gave orders for establishing a hasty defense, but it quickly became obvious that this would soon turn into something like a seal clubbing if they didn't make a break for it. Again, small groups were formed for a breakout. The Jeds took a group of forty to fifty men, along with the farmer and his family, and ran for a position just outside the farm. A maquisard with an automatic rifle was shot dead and Captain Cyr grabbed his weapon. Just as the men reached the position some German trucks pulled up, not more than fifteen yards away, and Cyr and the others emptied their magazines into the trucks before the enemy troops could dismount. They continued on but soon met a maquisard coming from the opposite direction who told Cyr that the group was heading toward some Germans that were approaching the farm.

Cyr's group needed to move fast. While the man they had just met fired at the approaching Germans to keep them at bay, Cyr and the others took off. But they were slowed by the farmer's wife, who could not keep up. So they hid her in a thicket and hurried on.

Suddenly, a German machine gun opened up on them, killing three or four of the men in Cyr's group. The rest took cover in some brush, and the leaders quickly gathered and decided that they should break up into even smaller units of no more than two or three people each. Among the group were five pilots, three Americans and two Brits, who had been shot down over France and had been under the care of the maquis. Before they split up, the pilots and the Jeds quickly exchanged names and addresses so that anyone who made it out could provide information about what had happened to the others.

The Jeds took off to the east. They didn't get more than twenty-five yards when the German machine gun opened up again, but it apparently was firing at the group of pilots, who had gone in a different direction. The Jeds stopped and threw a grenade in the direction of the machine gun and then ducked into some bushes. German soldiers were shouting to each other all around them. Hauteur was still with the Jeds, but Fonction had become separated from the group and was nowhere to be seen.

An odd sort of standoff began. There were others besides the Jeds and Hauteur hidden in the stand of thick brush, which extended over a wide area. The Germans knew they were in there somewhere; they just didn't know exactly where. For the next seventeen hours the men remained as still as they could. The bushes were about five feet tall, and German soldiers climbed trees in an attempt to spot the hidden men. And from time to time they threw hand grenades into the brush at randomly chosen locations. Dogs were even brought in to help pinpoint the hidden maquisards, but they proved useless because too many people had been moving about the area.

Hours seemed like days as the men lay motionless, wondering

how they would get out of the fix they were in. At times, softly and among themselves, the Jeds and the unflappable Hauteur even laughed at their predicament.

After dark, the four men decided it was time to get out. Not far away they found two of the pilots hiding in the brush. The Jeds told the airmen that they were going to attempt to sneak out and head east, and that the pilots should follow in an hour's time if they didn't hear any shots fired. Before leaving, and just in case they were unable to link up with them again, the Jeds gave the pilots eight thousand francs.

Shortly before midnight, the Jeds moved out, slowly and quietly. The only German they saw was a sentry on a road, and they were able to sneak past him. Soon they approached a farm, but when a dog began barking someone blindly fired shots in their general direction, so the men skirted the farm and ran across a field and into some woods. Then they came to another road guarded by another sentry. As the German paced back and forth the small group made it across the road, one man at a time.

Another five hundred yards into the woods they were suddenly startled by the sound of people jumping through some brush nearby. Assuming them to be a German patrol, the Jeds pulled out hand grenades and got ready to use them. But just then they heard members of the group speaking to one another in French. The Jeds whispered to them in French to get their attention, and when the two groups met the Jeds were happily surprised to find Fonction among the others. After spending the remainder of the night in the woods, the men continued walking until they felt they were well away from the area where the Germans continued to search.

Lejeune had gotten a message off to London on the day the Jeds had arrived at the camp of the Maquis de Saffré. The message had reported the team's arrival and expressed the urgent need for arms: "BEGIN TOMORROW 28 DROPPING FOR 2,000 IN SLICES OF 500. RECEPTION COMMITTEE STANDING BY EVERY NIGHT FROM 28TH."[8] It was three days before Lejeune could get off another message informing SFHQ of the attack on the morning of the twenty-eighth and advising that all air operations be suspended. In the meantime, on the night of June 29, four aircraft dropped forty-three containers and eight packages to a field near the abandoned Saffré camp.[9]

In a later message, Lieutenant Lejeune was able to give London an update: "SITUATION LOIRE INFERIEURE BOILING. PATRIOT IS ENEMY AGENT. ALL LOST EXCEPT LIFE AND SET. HUNTED BY GESTAPO. DESPITE STORM ATTEMPTED UNSUCCESSFULLY TO CONTACT YOU. EVERYTHING HAS TO BE DONE AGAIN. REMAINING AND DOING OUR BEST."[10]

Jedburgh team George moved about the area, staying briefly in a small town on the north bank of the Loire River, and then spent a few days in a large château as guests of the count and countess of Landemont, who were supporters of the resistance. The count set up quarters for the men in the library and, for the first time since their arrival in France, the Jeds slept in beds. But they had to be quiet and remain out of sight, because the château also housed many children who had been evacuated from Nantes.

Within a few days, however, the count received a phone call from the Germans, informing him that they were coming to inspect the house with an eye toward occupying it. The Jeds and the resistance leaders (Hauteur and Fonction) were forced to leave the château and hide in a wooded area nearby. When it was safe to move they continued to search for a place to set up camp and begin rounding up the scattered maquisards.

Hauteur and Fonction had been trying to persuade Captain Erard to accept the position of délégué militaire, or military representative for de Gaulle's provisional French government, for the Loire-Inférieure department. Erard had demurred because he felt that, by accepting the position, he would be unjustly expanding the mission of the Jedburgh team. But Hauteur and Fonction argued that there was no one else in the department qualified to fill the role, and so, after a meeting on the night of July 4, Erard agreed.

Hauteur and Fonction left the following morning, confident that they had found someone capable of organizing the resistance in the Loire-Inférieure. Resistance in the department had struggled to organize itself from the very beginning, with seemingly every group of patriots riddled with traitors and informers. Every new leader who appeared capable of creating a viable resistance in the department soon found himself in the hands of the Gestapo in their torture cells in Nantes. Periodic waves of arrests had stifled any further development and even the Jeds, as newcomers, were viewed with suspicion by some. Terror and deception and distrust and fear of one's own neighbor had become the dominating features of life in the Loire-Inférieure. Much work lay ahead of team George if the men were to turn all that around.

The Jeds at once drew up a plan and began work. Probably the most difficult step, but one which had to be taken first, was to identify leaders. Nearly every potential leader they talked to implicated the others as traitors. But, eventually, the right men were found and work proceeded. All leaders had to agree to put political differences aside and commit to the common task of ridding the area of Germans, and agree that all operations were to be conducted in accordance with orders issued by the Allied high command.

Maquis battalions were to be formed, each with its own dropping ground for the delivery of arms. A disciplined system of recruitment was established with security overriding all other concerns— every person recruited was to be vetted by at least two trusted maquisards before being accepted. Instructors were trained and set up to rotate from battalion to battalion to train recruits, and a roving reception committee cadre would likewise help prepare for parachute drops.

Strict adherence to the plan was demanded of all. Maquis groups that failed to comply with orders would receive no pay, no arms, no ammunition, and no supplies. Leaders who were found to be working for the Germans or for individual gain would be dealt with harshly—killed, if necessary.

Shelter for team George continued to be a problem, and the men moved frequently from one safe house to the next. Then a place was found for them, an unoccupied two-room house in a dusty, deadpan one-story village about five miles north of the Loire. The men remained there for eight days. But after a few close calls, including a Gestapo car parking just outside the front door on one occasion, the Jeds packed up and moved on. After hiding out in a ruined chapel for a couple of days, the men were taken by a member of the resistance to another abandoned house. This house was near a village on the north bank of the Loire River, about thirty miles northeast of Nantes. Jed team George rented the house and began to set up a command post.

General Eisenhower got the time that he'd said was needed to prepare for a breakout from the lodgment area in Normandy. The Transportation Plan had been brilliantly executed by the air force; key bridges and some major rail centers had been destroyed. And the French resistance fighters, aided by ever increasing numbers of Jedburghs and other special forces, had done much damage and continued to do more. By the end of June, they had made nearly five hundred more railway cuts, ambushed untold numbers of German convoys, and rendered the enemy's telecommunications almost completely ineffective.[11]

The combined efforts of the air forces and the resistance had succeeded in delaying the movement of several German divisions to Normandy. Eisenhower would later be able to report to the Combined Chiefs of Staff that the enemy had committed some of its nearest divisions—four panzer and six infantry—by June 19, but that "it was not until the beginning of July, when the scale of the Allied effort was no longer in any doubt, that reinforcements began to arrive from more distant locations."[12]

Later estimates would conclude that the actions of the FFI resulted in an average delay of two days for all German units moving toward Normandy, although some units fared much worse. One of the first units ordered to Normandy in response to the landings was the 2nd "Das Reich" SS Panzer Division, which at the time was near Toulouse in southern France. Expected to arrive at the invasion area by June 9, it was two weeks after that date before the demoralized remnants of the division staggered into Normandy.[13] The 1st SS Panzer Division had taken seven days to travel one hundred and eighty-six miles by rail from Louvain, Belgium, to Paris— normally a one-day journey. Even then, the division was still ninety miles from the fighting, and it had to make the remainder of the journey by road.[14] After reaching the Rhine from the Eastern Front in one week, the 11th Panzer Division had needed another three weeks to reach Caen.[15] And it had taken the 276th Infantry Division nineteen days to get from Nice to Normandy.[16]

Two panzer divisions of the II SS Panzer Corps had been sent by rail to Normandy on June 12, each division requiring more than one hundred trains for the movement. Attacks by the resistance had caused their trip to take five days rather than the planned two and a half. And in the end, damaged locomotives and railways had forced the divisions' tracked vehicles to drive under their own power for the final leg of the journey, nearly two hundred punishing miles which reduced vehicle service life by half at a critical time.[17]

Even units much closer to Normandy had found just getting there to be difficult. Germany's 275th Division had been less than a hundred and thirty miles southwest of the battlefield, in Redon, when it was ordered to Normandy. Six rail cuts, a number of maquis ambushes, and strikes by the air force combined to delay the division's arrival at St-Lô until June 11.[18]

All of this bought precious time for the Allies at a stage in the operation when thousands of troops and tons of material were being brought ashore every twenty-four hours. In addition to the delays in troop movements, the enemy's ability to resupply its divisions fighting in Normandy was devastated by the destruction of the transportation network—and maquis and air force attacks on fuel and ammunition supply dumps only compounded the problem.

But just as important were the FFI's attacks on German communications. By destroying landline communications facilities—telephone exchanges, switchboards, junction boxes—and cutting telephone lines and underground cables, the maquis forced the Germans to make greater use of radio, which was much easier for the Allies to intercept. And Allied success in breaking the German Enigma code made such interceptions invaluable in learning of enemy movements and intentions.

Eisenhower took action to reinforce success. On June 15 he wrote to General Sir Henry Maitland Wilson, the British supreme commander of the Mediterranean Theater, and informed him that he was ordering significant increases in air-dropped supplies to the resistance, "which at the moment is giving unexpected results."

Eisenhower's plans included massive daylight supply drops by Eighth Air Force bombers as far into France as they could reach. He asked Wilson if he could do likewise in southern France. Wilson responded two days later that he was "delighted by Eisenhower's proposal" and that he had already made preparations for such drops into the Rhône Valley of southern France.[19] On June 25, 180 bombers dropped 300 tons of supplies to the resistance in four locations, and another major drop would come on July 14, Bastille Day.[20]

The resistance and the special forces had done their parts in helping Eisenhower build up an Allied force on the Continent, and the time had come for that force to go on the offensive.

7

BRITTANY LIBERATED

BRITTANY was all about the ports. Normandy had attracted Overlord planners as an invasion site for a number of reasons, not the least of them its proximity to the port at Cherbourg and those on the Brittany peninsula—mainly Brest, Lorient and nearby Quiberon Bay, and St-Nazaire. Although the Allies planned to rely heavily on an artificial harbor called Mulberry in the initial stage of the invasion, fixed ports soon would be needed for supplying the growing armies in France. They would also be needed for unloading troops that would be arriving from the United States at the rate of three to five divisions per month.

Opening the ports of Brittany, it was hoped, could be accomplished before rough weather had a chance to knock out the temporary facilities at the Normandy beaches. Plans, therefore, called for the rapid capture of Brest, Lorient, Quiberon Bay, and St-Nazaire. To help Allied ground forces rapidly reach these objectives, Supreme Headquarters Allied Expeditionary Force (SHAEF) intended to develop a resistance force of more than thirty thousand armed men throughout Brittany by August 1.[1]

In the six weeks since D-Day, fifteen U.S. divisions and fifteen British and Canadian divisions had come ashore in Normandy. On July 18, U.S. forces captured the key crossroads town of St-Lô in

Normandy, allowing final preparations for a breakout from the lodgment area west of that town. Facing the Americans in the immediate area were twenty-seven German divisions. But, of the 540,000 men that the enemy had committed to the Normandy battle, at least 160,000 already had been lost, along with 30 percent of the 1200 German tanks which had taken part in the fighting.[2] And, thanks to the air force and the French resistance, the Germans were not receiving sufficient reinforcements. Following a heavy air bombardment of enemy positions on the morning of July 25, the First U.S. Army launched operation Cobra with an attack from the Allies' extreme right flank. By the thirtieth, American forces had reached Avranches, near the base of the Brittany peninsula.

On the first day of August, General Eisenhower launched the newly operational Third U.S. Army, commanded by Lieutenant General George S. Patton, Jr., to force the breakout from the Allied lines at Avranches and drive south and west into Brittany. This gave the Americans two armies in the field—the First and the Third. On that same day, Twelfth Army Group headquarters was activated under the command of Lieutenant General Omar N. Bradley to direct the operations of the two armies. Bradley turned over command of his First Army to Lieutenant General Courtney H. Hodges.

After clearing Avranches, Third Army forces were to enter the northeast corner of the Brittany peninsula. From there, Patton planned to have an armored division strike out for Brest, one hundred and fifty miles to the west. He would send another armored division straight south to isolate the peninsula and capture ports on the south coast.

As an added measure, Third Army was given power to direct the activity of resistance forces throughout Brittany.[3] In exercising this authority General Patton set a precedent which would later be followed by other army commanders. According to early SHAEF plans, when Allied ground forces overran FFI elements the guerrillas were to be relieved of their arms and their mission was to be considered as ended. Patton, however, soon ordered that some of the maquis be allowed to keep their arms and remain with the advancing Allied forces, fighting alongside while serving as guides and carrying out reconnaissance patrols. Others would remain armed to continue mopping up by-passed German pockets and to guard roads, bridges, pipelines, and supply dumps.[4]

With the breakout about to begin, Special Force Headquarters radioed new orders to the field, alerting all Jedburghs and other special forces in Brittany that Allied ground forces would soon be approaching their region. It was imperative, the message said, that everything be done to help speed the advance of the ground troops. Jedburgh teams throughout Brittany should take action to prevent the demolition of bridges and installations by the Germans. Team Frederick was assigned responsibility for the main east-west highway which ran along the north coast of Brittany. They were specifically responsible for the central portion of that highway, a stretch running westward from Lamballe through St-Brieuc and Guingamp and on to Morlaix, although the brief message from London did not explain to the Jeds the importance of the road to the Allies.[5]

Route Nationale 12 was the main highway connecting the port city of Brest, at the western tip of Brittany, with Rennes, the Breton capital located at the base of the peninsula, some one hundred and fifty miles to the east. Running parallel to the highway—sometimes north of the road, sometimes south of it—ran the main rail line inland from Brest, a double-track railway extending all the way to Paris. General Patton's staff realized that, if the Allies ever hoped to supply their armies in France from the port at Brest, this rail line would be needed to rapidly move cargo inland.

Patton's chief of staff, Major General Hugh Gaffey, directed his special forces advisor to coordinate with Special Force Headquarters for the FFI to protect the rail line from demolition by the Germans.[6] Special Force Headquarters sent messages to Jedburgh teams in Brittany to arrange this. Cuts which the FFI had made in the railway to impede the movement of German reinforcements to Normandy could easily be repaired by Allied engineers. Some large railway bridges along the route, however, if destroyed by the Germans could not be repaired so easily or quickly. Some of the largest were at St-Brieuc, Guingamp, and Morlaix. The Germans had to be prevented from destroying these bridges, and the immediate task of protecting them and the highway which provided rapid access to them went to Jedburgh team Frederick and the FFI. Their job was to guard the bridges and hold the road until American forces arrived.

The job of capturing the bridges went to Task Force A, a Third Army provisional unit made up of armored cavalry, tank destroyers, and combat engineers. This unit was to race westward on the highway which team Frederick would be protecting and, if all went well, seize the railway bridges intact. Leading the task force was Brigadier General Herbert L. Earnest, commander of a tank destroyer brigade. Earnest planned to move fast, bypassing any pockets of German resistance and securing the railroad bridges as quickly as possible.[7]

To support team Frederick, the FFI called two thousand armed patriots into action to guard the road, and the Jeds increased the number of airdrops to be able to arm the expanding guerrilla force.

Patton wasted no time. He launched a corps with two armored divisions south from Avranches on Tuesday, August 1, and by evening the 6th Armored Division had turned west and had taken the first town on the road toward Brest. Next day, the division tore off in two columns through the center of the peninsula, straight for Brest, without accompanying infantry support. Plans had called for an infantry division to follow each of the armored divisions, but the infantry which was to follow the 6th Armored Division had been committed to defending the Avranches area. Villagers waved as their liberators passed through in a cloud of dust. No forces were left to even guard rear areas and supply routes. Whenever the division ran into German resistance, it relied on the local FFI for infantry support, and when it moved on the FFI guarded the roads and bridges and ensured that supply lines remained open.[8]

By this time, eleven Jedburgh teams were active throughout Brittany and three more would arrive by week's end. As the 6th Armored Division closed in on Brest, Jed teams in western Brittany linked up with forward elements, attaching themselves to the headquarters of American combat units. They provided up-to-date information on the enemy situation, organized FFI support to the armored units, and served as guides and interpreters. By the end of the first week in August, Third Army was even supplying jeeps to some Jedburghs and FFI chiefs.

*   *   *

Meanwhile, tanks of the 4th Armored Division struck out from Avranches on Tuesday and, by evening, had reached the outskirts of the Breton capital of Rennes, a city of about a hundred thousand some fifty miles to the south. But the division ran into strong German resistance at Rennes, and the division commander decided to bypass the city the next day and continue on southward, leaving the follow-on 8th Infantry Division to clean the Germans out of Rennes. Late that night, a series of explosions shook the area. Colonel Bruce Clarke, commander of one of 4th Armored's combat commands, called around on the radio to determine the source of the mysterious explosions. He eventually learned that the midnight eruptions had resulted from the FFI blowing up an enormous German ammunition dump. After skirting around Rennes to the west, the division continued its dash toward Brittany's south coast.

By the time the 4th Armored Division reached Vannes, on Brittany's south coast, the American tankers were working hand in hand with the FFI. One division officer, who characterized the maquis as "bloodthirsty," later recalled having as many as two hundred of the FFI fighters riding on his tanks.[9] The division captured the town of Vannes on Brittany's south coast on August 5; and six thousand maquisards helped by taking the high ground north of the town, a mission which again had been assigned to the FFI by Patton's chief of staff, General Gaffey. This attack by the FFI, judged one Third Army historian, prevented the Germans from making a fortress stand in the Quiberon Bay area as they would do at Brittany's other ports.[10]

On Sunday night, August 6, an armored cavalry patrol from General Ernest's Task Force A entered Lamballe. When no Germans were met, the patrol continued west on Route Nationale 12 until it reached St-Brieuc. There, the soldiers found all three railroad bridges in the town safely in the hands of the FFI. When the main body of the American task force arrived, an engineer company was assigned to help guard the St-Brieuc bridges while the rest of the task force moved on.

On Monday the task force approached Guingamp, where the Germans had a large supply base. After fighting through some weak roadblocks, the Americans pushed into the town and, with supporting attacks conducted by the FFI, captured it by midnight. About four hundred German prisoners were bagged in the process.

General Earnest then dispatched a small force to race ahead to Morlaix, where the largest railroad bridge in all of France stood. A thousand feet in length, the monumental granite structure spanned the Dossen valley, a deep ravine at the head of an estuary. Built eighty-three years earlier to support the Paris-Brest railway, the massive two-story viaduct (the lower level a pedestrian bridge) featured more than a dozen arches and, at two hundred feet tall, towered over the medieval town below. Standing atop the bridge, one could look down over the old town, once an important Channel port, which rose narrow street by narrow street up the steep slopes. To help the FFI secure the bridge until the American forces arrived, an SAS party had jumped in on the night of August 5.[11]

At about this time, a new development required the attention of Major Wise's Jed team and General Earnest's task force. As American tanks swept across Brittany, kicking up clouds of hot August dust, many German units retreated to towns and cities along the coast, hoping to dig in and hold out. A group of nearly three thousand heavily armed Germans had taken shelter on a peninsula on the coast due north of Guingamp. The Germans had started causing trouble for the inhabitants of some small fishing villages on the peninsula and, because they were in position to threaten the flank of Task Force A, Major Wise was able to persuade General Earnest to send help. With tanks provided by Earnest, a little air support, and the FFI fighting as infantry, the threat was eliminated.

General Earnest's task force finally reached the Morlaix viaduct and secured the bridge in force. The Americans had found fairly clear sailing all along Route Nationale 12, and all the railroad bridges had been captured intact—most of them already in the hands of the FFI when the Americans arrived. Aside from the skirmish in Guingamp, the only fighting took place when lead elements of the task force ran up on the tail end of a large German convoy near Morlaix. A brief firefight resulted in the capture of many more enemy soldiers. Task Force A's mission was successfully completed and, by August 9, it was ready to move on to help the armored division which by then was closing in on Brest.

With much of the region under Allied control and the Germans only putting up sporadic resistance, Major Wise began to feel that team Frederick's work in Brittany was finished. Ambushes of any German columns venturing out on the roads had long since become routine. Task Force A had passed down its road clear to Morlaix and had not found a single bridge destroyed.

The ease with which Jed team Frederick had secured this route might give a false impression of both the criticality of the task and the difficulty of organizing and executing a mission over such extended ranges with nothing more than resistance forces. It was accomplished so painlessly only because Jed team Frederick had been on the ground long enough to have properly prepared the maquis groups throughout the department. The men had had weeks to develop effective working relationships with resistance leaders and to earn their trust. They had learned the strengths and weaknesses of the various FFI leaders, and about their dependability and leadership capabilities. The team also had facilitated the arming and training of a considerable number of maquis fighters.

But much more had been accomplished than securing Route Nationale 12. By one historian's later estimate, the maquis groups of the Côtes-du-Nord, during the last month of Jedburgh team Frederick's mission, had put twenty-five hundred Germans out of action, cut three hundred telephone and high-tension power lines, sabotaged many railroads and derailed at least forty trains, captured two hundred vehicles in the process of ambushing some fifty German convoys, burned ten thousand gallons of fuel stockpiled by the enemy, and freed thirty-two condemned Frenchmen from prison.[12]

On Saturday, August 19, the men of team Frederick attended a party at a St-Brieuc hotel, where Marceau, decked out in his uniform as a major in the French army reserves, served as master of ceremonies.

Almost immediately, Captain Aguirec departed for Paris. Once American forces had broken out from the lodgment area in Normandy on August 1 their advance had been fairly rapid. While one corps of Patton's Third Army had been liberating Brittany, the rest of his army had wheeled eastward and, by August 19, some elements had advanced to within fifteen miles of Paris. The Paris FFI rose up that same day and began battling the city's German garrison. The City of Light would be liberated within a week. Bob Kehoe thought their French officer was making the trip just to be there for the liberation and the celebrating which was sure to follow. But Paul Aguirec had a far better reason for going to Paris. His father had lived in the city through the entire war, all the while successfully hiding from the Germans the fact that he was a Jew. Captain Aguirec was anxious to see how his father had come through the occupation and the war. He would join his teammates in England a few weeks later.

Major Wise and First Sergeant Kehoe drove to an airfield north of St-Lô on Sunday and boarded a plane to England. Back in London, the two men underwent debriefings before returning to Milton Hall.

At a two-story flat on Devonshire Mews, Major Wise sat down to write his report of the mission. By his estimation, through airdrops of arms from England and the distribution of captured German weapons, the Jed team had armed forty-two hundred men in its sector of the Côtes-du-Nord. They had done much damage to the Germans through sabotage and ambush, and they had arranged for maquis forces to protect Route Nationale 12 and the railway bridges along the way until the American ground forces had arrived. The team had every right to be proud of its contribution. As for the admiration and respect Wise's team held for the FFI, he wrote, "We have found real pleasure in assisting the French patriots in the liberation of their country, and their splendid spirit of defiance to the Boche has repaid our work a hundredfold."[13]

Jedburgh team George had transplanted itself from southern Brittany to the north bank of the Loire—a wide, shallow, and sluggish river. It was the longest river in France, and its six-hundred-mile course reached its estuary on the Atlantic at St-Nazaire, not far downstream to the west. The area was one of lakes and woodlands to the north, with occasional cultivated flatlands and, more to the south, gently rolling terrain with vineyards where the Muscadet grape thrived.

Jed team Frederick's final mission had involved enabling Allied forces to speed westward, but team George was now in a position to aid the eastward advance of Patton's army. But team George's operation in the Loire-Inférieure would largely be one of frustration, as the men struggled to accomplish the mission with no support from London until the final days. Team Frederick, at least, had received fairly good service from London as far as response to the Jeds' requests for airdrops.

Team George's earlier radio difficulties would prove to be minor compared with the communications problem they were soon to have with London, and which nearly caused the mission to be a complete failure. That the team succeeded, in the end, in overcoming the handicap and completing its mission was a direct result of two things that the Allied special operations enterprise had done right. One was ensuring, through a demanding assessment and selection process, that Jedburgh teams were composed of men who were innovative and persevering—men who would tenaciously seek some alternative way to accomplish their missions rather than accept failure. The other thing that special operations planners did right was the providing of a special forces detachment at each field army headquarters, a team which advised the army commander and his staff, and which also was there to help elements—such as Jedburgh team George—to overcome difficulties and continue the mission.

In their cottage on the Loire River, Jedburgh team George lived in constant danger. German soldiers often bathed in the river right in front of the house. And people continually walked along the river, making radio transmissions risky because of the low whine usually made by the hand-cranked generator.

A girl named Paulette Peltier delivered food to the Jeds by boat each day, but the men had to do their own cooking. Lejeune prepared most of the meals. The team's main worry was a bothersome man, a refugee from Nantes—the historic port city nineteen miles down river—whose job it was to watch some cows nearby. He often came by to talk with the Jeds and he was very inquisitive, which naturally made the men nervous. Captain Cyr stammered as he spoke French in order to hide his accent, but the nosy man from Nantes was a natural stammerer, and the Jeds found conversations between the two amusing, even though they were troubled by the man's many questions.

Some days Paulette was unable to bring food, and then the men would have to cross to the south bank of the river to get something to eat in the village there. They went to the same little restaurant in the village many times, and it was usually crowded with German soldiers. But the Germans usually didn't bother the Jeds, who wore civilian clothes and appeared to be harmless. After a while, people became accustomed to seeing the men in the area.

One day, however, Captain Cyr got into an argument with a Luftwaffe lieutenant, and the men again worried about the American's accent. After that, Cyr wore a bandage over his mouth and the two French Jeds told everyone that he had been wounded. This kept people from trying to get Cyr to talk, but it also made it difficult for him to eat.

One person who often showed up at the restaurant when the Jeds were there always seemed to get a table right next to them. He was a Gestapo man, and the Jeds thought he had a Chinese look to him. Every time he came in and sat next to them he would smile and greet them, and to Captain Erard the Oriental-looking man seemed to be thinking, "Just wait a moment and I'll get you and all your gang."[14]

Erard, Cyr, and Lejeune had made great progress in putting their plan for the Loire-Inférieure into practice. The maquis battalions were shaping up nicely, and the Jeds traveled constantly to meet with the various leaders. Sometimes they bicycled thirty or forty miles in a day, and they had held as many as nine meetings at various camps in a single day.

The Jeds had also begun a sabotage campaign, although it was limited because they were short of explosives. The team had been sending messages continually asking London to drop arms and ammunition and explosives, but nothing ever came. They had to make do with some old French demolition materials which the locals had hidden away, and with explosives stolen from the Ger-

mans. Some demolition jobs were carried out by the Jeds themselves, but others were done by sabotage teams which the Jeds had
organized and trained.

Targets for sabotage were found mostly in the area's extensive
network of canals, which were an important form of commercial
transportation in France. In late July, team George sabotaged the
narrow Nantes-to-Brest Canal by blowing up two locks, stranding
twenty boatloads of German munitions which were caught
between the locks. The team lost two maquisards during the
attack. The sabotage work was not confined to canals; the Jeds also
cut rail lines and burned a key bridge, ambushed German convoys,
and destroyed an enemy fuel dump.

But soon the men of team George agreed that it was time for
them to leave their cottage on the Loire. They had been in the village long enough—there had been some close calls and too many
people were trying to learn what the team was up to. So they
packed up and moved to a farm about eight miles to the northeast.

The maquis battalions were growing and the Jeds liked the way
they were progressing, but ammunition supplies were limited and
thousands of men still needed weapons. Still the Jeds could not get
London to send planes. Five more drop zones were found, and their
locations were radioed to Special Force Headquarters along with
the continued pleas for air drops. Captains Erard and Cyr were
growing increasingly frustrated and angry, and knew that if this
continued they would lose the confidence of the resistance leaders
and their men.

Weapons and explosives were not the only things needed—the
Jeds had long since run out of money to pay the maquis. Brave
Frenchmen were leaving their jobs and families to join the maquis,
but they and their families still had to eat. There was no money to
pay them, and some maquisards had taken to stealing food.

Back in London, Special Force Headquarters had been receiving
team George's messages. But after the message reporting the attack
on the maquis camp at Saffré, at the end of June, they had heard
nothing from the team for more than two weeks. And such gaps in
radio contact always raised suspicions at the London headquarters.

They could not be certain that the Jeds had not been captured. The Germans had proved themselves quite capable of making Allied radio operators transmit while in captivity, requesting that arms and agents be dropped, only to have them fall into the hands of the Gestapo. The staff in London suspected that this might be the case with Jedburgh team George. Erard and Cyr did not know it, but no more parachute drops would come their way until the team's safety was verified.

Then, in late July, the Jeds obtained some important documents which the resistance had stolen from the Germans. They were copies of the German defense plans for the coast of the Loire-Inférieure, including the port and U-boat base at St-Nazaire. French engineers working for Todt, the German construction organization responsible for building military fortifications in France, were also working for the resistance. They had been working on the plans with the Germans, and had been able to take a copy from the Todt offices and bring it to the Jeds.

So far, the Allies had not captured one Breton port. St-Nazaire had always been one of the key targets. If an operation was to be launched to capture it, the detailed German defense plans which the Jeds now had in their hands would be priceless. But they would only be helpful if they were delivered to Allied ground forces soon. On July 29 the Jeds sent a message to London reporting the windfall and suggesting that a Lysander, a small single-engine plane, be sent to pick Captain Cyr up. Cyr would then deliver the plans to Special Force Headquarters. Of course, no Lysander came.

Then, at one o'clock on the afternoon of August 5, word reached the Jeds that American ground forces were rapidly approaching their area. In fact, they were told, the Americans could arrive within hours. The men decided Cyr should take the plans and head toward the approaching American force and hand them over to the first intelligence officer he could find. But first, Erard had to retrieve the plans from a château where the men had hidden them. He was able to do so, but on his way to rendezvous with Cyr at an agreed-upon spot, Erard was captured by a German tank crew. After being disarmed by the Germans, Erard boldly began yelling at the tank commander. The Frenchman claimed to be with the Milice, working for the Germans, and he warned that the tank commander would surely make trouble for himself by interfering with him. The German went back to his tank and spoke with his men, and soon they all climbed back into their tank and drove off, leaving Erard with the plans but without his weapon.

Erard made it to the rendezvous point and gave the plans to Paul Cyr. Soon, more German tanks rolled by after coming under fire by American armored cars. Captain Cyr took a man from the resistance named Colonel Felix with him, and they stopped the first Americans they could find. Cyr explained to the GIs, who were from a mechanized cavalry squadron, who he was and that he had important documents to get to the division or corps intelligence officer. The soldiers took Cyr and Felix to their squadron commander, who agreed to get them back to VIII Corps headquarters. Cyr and Felix were put in an armored car for the journey, and they were accompanied by a tank and a half-track.

Along the way back to the corps command post, the three vehicles were shot at a few times by scattered German forces, but at eight the next morning they arrived at corps headquarters. Cyr briefed the corps intelligence officer on the enemy situation ahead while the staff made photostat copies of the St-Nazaire defense plans. Then the intelligence officer sent Cyr and Felix on to deliver the plans to Third Army headquarters, located in a woods near Beauchamps, a dozen miles north of Avranches in Normandy.[15]

Upon arrival at Third Army headquarters, the two men were directed toward the war room, the nerve center of the command post and the place where they were most likely to find the intelligence officer and the operations officer. Before they could find either of those two men, however, Cyr and Felix were approached by a fit-looking man in his mid-forties, with receding hair and a conservatively clipped mustache, who introduced himself as Lieutenant Colonel Bob Powell.

Robert Powell, a Princeton-educated Manhattan architect with a pre-war commission in the National Guard, spent most of his time around the war room at the Third Army command post, where large situation maps showed the location of every division, Allied and German, on both the Eastern and Western Fronts. Another map displayed only Third Army's area of operations, with the position of all units down to battalion level depicted. Here, the staff brought General Patton up to date on the strategic and tactical situation twice daily, in twenty-minute briefings at nine in the morning and at five in the afternoon.[16]

But Powell wasn't so concerned with the locations of battalions or the combat strength of divisions. He tried to keep track of small teams of men who were trying to stay alive deep in enemy territory, out in front of Third Army. He also looked for ways that the French resistance might be able to help the regiments and the divisions and the corps which came under Patton's command. Lieutenant Colonel Powell was the special forces representative on Patton's staff, the link to Special Force Headquarters, and when the Third Army commander or his operations or intelligence officer wanted something done by the FFI, they came to Powell.

When the Allies began working on the Jedburgh plan back in 1942, they had foreseen the need for special forces staff representatives to be assigned to each field army headquarters to advise the army commander and his operations staff on special forces and resistance matters. Personnel for this purpose were recruited at the same time as for the Jedburghs, and they were put through a training program. Small groups, called special force detachments, were provided to each army and army group headquarters in the spring of 1944. Special Force Detachment 11 was attached to Third Army headquarters, while Special Force Detachment 12 served General Bradley at Twelfth Army Group headquarters. Even at SHAEF, General Eisenhower had an attached special forces team headed by Colonel Robin Brook of Special Operations Executive, who advised the general on special forces and FFI capabilities and helped to coordinate special operations.[17]

Powell was the commander of Special Force Detachment 11, which was composed of thirteen officers and twenty enlisted soldiers working under the direction of the Third Army operations officer. Some of Powell's men were further detached to forward corps and division headquarters.[18]

Paul Cyr had never met Powell before, but Powell recognized Cyr for what he was as soon as he arrived. Cyr was in civilian clothes, but he was wearing an army field jacket and the patch on the jacket's sleeve told Powell that this man was a Jed. Powell introduced himself and Cyr explained the purpose of his visit. Cyr turned the German plans over to Powell, who took them in and showed them to General Patton, Patton's operations officer, Colonel Maddox, and the intelligence officer, Colonel Koch.

Maddox told Powell that he wanted the FFI to help protect the army's right flank, generally along the Loire River, as the army advanced toward Paris and the Seine. He also wanted the FFI to protect certain bridges that Third Army planned to use in its advance, and if they found that those bridges already were blown then they were to locate alternate routes. Maddox also wanted the FFI to protect the army's resupply routes and to mop up pockets of German troops which were bypassed along the way. Colonel Felix left at once to begin making all the arrangements, but Captain Cyr was asked to remain with Powell.

Colonel Powell now would take action that would enable Jedburgh team George to complete its mission and contribute to Third Army's operations along the Loire. Paul Cyr explained to Powell the trouble team George had been having in getting arms and supplies and money from London. Powell immediately radioed Special Force Headquarters and, with Third Army's backing, was able to arrange an airdrop large enough to allow Team George to arm the thousands of maquisards that were still awaiting weapons. Special Force Headquarters was only too glad to hear that team George had not been captured after all, and they promised to send twenty-four plane-loads of arms within the next few days. Cyr then arranged for FFI guides to be attached to one of Third Army's corps headquarters as it prepared to attack toward the Seine. The FFI men knew the Germans' positions and where the enemy had laid minefields.

Captain Cyr then returned to the Loire-Inférieure to help get the FFI started on the tasks which Third Army had assigned it. The maquis battalions still were meagerly armed, mostly with weapons stolen from the Germans, but they established defensive positions along the north bank of the Loire. On some days the Germans hit them hard with mortars and artillery, and the maquis responded with nighttime forays across the river to attack the German positions.

On Friday night, August 11, the parachute drop from London came. Twenty-five bombers arrived over the Loire Inférieure and dropped nearly six hundred containers filled with seventy-one tons of arms and supplies.[19] Overnight, the maquis battalions organized by Jedburgh team George became much stronger. By the third week in August twenty-five hundred men had been armed and four thousand were standing by to receive weapons as soon as more arrived. Captured arms continued to come in as well. As the fighting continued, the maquis would capture German prisoners almost every day and send them back to the American units, but they would keep the German weapons for FFI units. Third Army also helped by sending the FFI German mortars and heavy machine guns captured in Normandy.[20]

Third Army units continued to ply the FFI every day for up-to-date information on the enemy—where the Germans were, in what strength, and what they were doing. Jed team George responded by organizing teams of men to collect the information and dispatched couriers to get it back to the Americans.

When it came time for the 4th Armored Division to attack the Loire River town of Nantes, the maquis groups working for team George played a big role. Nantes lies about thirty miles upriver from St Nazaire and had itself once been a busy port. The maquis provided the Americans with information on all German positions in the Nantes area and then, when the division began its assault, the FFI attacked the enemy positions from the rear. The division captured the town easily.

General Patton had declared as early as the first week in August that the maquis were proving to be an important factor in the Brittany campaign.[21] General Bradley agreed, calling them a "valuable ally." Bradley also recognized the contributions of the Jedburghs and the SAS, however, when he later wrote, "With the aid of specially trained Allied detachments that had been parachuted into their hide-outs, the French underground blocked the Brittany roads and drove the Germans into their fortified forts."[22]

Eisenhower, too, had recognized how the maquis had helped the Allied effort by cutting communications, delaying the movement of German reinforcements to Normandy, and serving as infantry and guides to the American divisions liberating Brittany. But he also saw that they did much more than that. "Not least in importance," the supreme commander later wrote, "they had, by their ceaseless harassing activities, surrounded the Germans with a terrible atmosphere of danger and hatred which ate into the confidence of the leaders and the courage of the soldiers."[23]

The besieged ports of Brittany, however, were becoming less important to the Allied high command. The 6th Armored Division had reached Brest by August 10, and the city and its immense natural harbor and seventeenth-century port were encircled by American troops, the FFI, and a handful of Jedburgh teams. The Germans held Brest with a thirty-thousand-man garrison which included the remnants of an infantry division and the elite 2nd Parachute Division, which just had arrived from the fighting in Normandy.[24] German garrisons at St-Malo, Lorient, and St-Nazaire also held out. Hitler, understanding their importance to the Allies, had ordered the ports to be held to the last man. It would be forty-six days before Brest fell, and by then it was no longer needed.[25]

Cherbourg had been captured and its port facilities repaired, and supplies had begun unloading there on July 19. There was hope that the ports of Le Havre and Antwerp could be reached before too long. The Allied invasion of southern France, planned for the middle of August, also offered the prospect of opening the port of Marseilles.

This led Eisenhower to decide that the priority should be pushing eastward rather than spending time and forces capturing the ports of Brittany. Instead of devoting additional forces to that purpose, especially when the Germans were sure to leave the ports heavily damaged, Eisenhower decided they could best be used elsewhere. He saw an opportunity to strike eastward with the bulk of Patton's army, leaving only a corps to hold the Breton port cities under siege. With any luck, the Allies might be able to encircle much of the German army in Normandy.

Bradley had approved Patton's plan to attack eastward from Brittany on August 6, and Third Army had begun to move. Then, the next day, two German panzer divisions spearheaded a German counterattack toward Avranches in an attempt to slice through Third Army's rear. Fierce fighting took place around Mortain until the Germans began withdrawing on the twelfth. Over the next eight days the Allies fought to trap some nineteen German divisions in the pocket which had formed as a result of the German attacks and Patton's breakout from Brittany. By the time the Falaise-Argentan gap, as the jaws of the trap came to be known, was closed, however, much of the German force had escaped to the east.

Farther to the south, Patton also was driving to the east with two corps, and by August 19 Third Army had captured Chartres and Orléans and was reaching for the Seine River.

Meanwhile, other Jedburgh teams had been jumping into the French countryside ahead of Third Army. One team, which had dropped directly in the path of Patton's army, was headed by a skinny American captain who, twenty-nine years later, would become head of the Central Intelligence Agency.

8

"JUST IGNORE 'EM!"

NOTHING about Bill Colby suggested that the bespectacled twenty-four-year-old was a member of an elite special forces outfit. He was as thin as a teenager, about five foot eight, and had a studious look. People would more likely take him for the man who handles new accounts down at the bank. Although he qualified as an army brat—his father was a colonel—he didn't seem to fit that mold either. There was much more to Bill Colby, though, than met the eye.*

His father, Elbridge Colby, taught English literature at Columbia and then at the University of Minnesota. He met and married an Irish Catholic girl from St. Paul named Margaret Mary Egan, and in 1920 their first child was born, a boy named William Egan Colby. Elbridge Colby had served in Panama during the First World War and, by the time his son was born, he'd decided to make a career of the army. He would retire as a colonel in 1948.

Like all army brats, Bill Colby grew up on the move—Panama, China, Minnesota, Georgia. He was just sixteen when he graduated from Burlington High School in Vermont, and he went on to Princeton, where he was elected to membership in Phi Beta Kappa. After his junior year, he traveled to France and spent the summer

---

* William E. Colby would serve as head of the Central Intelligence Agency during the Nixon and Ford administrations, from 1973 to 1976.

with a French family in the Loire valley. When war broke out late that summer of 1939, Colby returned to the United States on an armed British ship. He graduated the following year; and when France fell shortly thereafter, he hoped to immediately enter the army. At Princeton, he had excelled as a member of ROTC, the Reserve Officer Training Corps. He had made cadet captain and had attended the Citizens Military Training Camp at Fort Devens, Massachusetts. He then awaited the commission which should come with his graduation. But there was a catch.

To be commissioned as an officer in the United States Army you had to be twenty-one years old, and Colby's twenty-first birthday wasn't until January 1941. He had thought about one day becoming a labor lawyer, and so, to make the best use of his time while he waited for his commission, Colby applied at Columbia Law School, was accepted, and entered in the fall of 1940.

By the following summer, America's involvement in the war seemed more likely with every passing month. Colby was by then old enough to accept his commission, and he entered the army in August and was sent to Fort Bragg, North Carolina. He was there when the Japanese attacked Pearl Harbor and when Hitler declared war on the United States.

Soon afterward, Colby moved on to the Field Artillery School at Fort Sill, Oklahoma. After completion of his training as an artillery officer, Colby was held at Fort Sill to teach tactics at the artillery Officer Candidate School. This was a disappointment to him, as he was anxious to get to a combat outfit. Six months later, when a notice appeared on the unit bulletin board calling for volunteers for the new parachute battalions, he signed up at once.

Back when Colby had graduated from high school he at first wanted to go to West Point, but his nearsightedness had kept him from competing for an opening. As he prepared to undergo the physical exam for jump school, he was determined not to let his eyesight get in the way again. He made a point of standing near the eye chart while he undressed for the physical, and memorized the 20/40 line. When time came for the eye exam, his performance was less than convincing, but an understanding doctor passed him anyway. Parachute training at Fort Benning, Georgia, began for him in the fall of 1942, but he broke an ankle on his second jump and it would be the following March before he got his silver jump wings and proceeded to an airborne unit.

Soon Colby was in an officer replacement unit at Camp Mackall, just outside Fort Bragg, where he watched with envy as hundreds of men left the replacement unit, all having been assigned to one of the new airborne divisions. Then, in September 1943, a major from Washington, D.C., arrived at Camp Mackall. Although he didn't announce it at the briefing he gave, the officer was from the Office of Strategic Services and he was looking for officers for the Jedburgh project. He asked for volunteers to jump into enemy-occupied territory, and to Bill Colby this sounded like a good opportunity to get into the war. So he volunteered.[1]

By December Colby had made it through the demanding selection process at the Congressional Country Club and the training in the hills of northern Maryland, and was sharing a cabin with twelve other men aboard the *Queen Elizabeth*, bound for Britain. During the voyage, he had even had the opportunity to dine with an old friend whom he had run into on the ship, an officer who was then serving as an aide to Major General Matthew Ridgway, commander of the 82nd Airborne Division.

When the Jeds began forming into teams at Milton Hall in the spring, Colby linked up with two likable French lieutenants named Jacques Favel and Louis Giry.*

Favel was a particularly lively and fun-loving sort, and already had earned a reputation among the Jeds as a skirt chaser. He was about Colby's height and of medium build, had brown hair, thick and untamed, and had rascally brown eyes. Favel also had a mustache which had been with him since he was a corporal, when he had grown it out of necessity because, without it, he appeared to be no more than fifteen years old.

Favel and Colby got along well despite some differences in how they liked to spend their free time. Favel enjoyed sitting in on the poker games which always seemed to be in progress at Milton Hall when training was done for the day, but Colby would never play. Colby was more likely to be found with his nose in a book, and one in which he was particularly absorbed was T. E. Lawrence's *Seven*

---

* Jacques Favel's real name was Camille Lelong; that of Louis Giry was Roger Villebois.

Pillars of Wisdom, which he had picked up in a London bookstore and was reading for anything it might offer a novice guerrilla leader. But often, on free weekends, Colby would join his two French teammates on a pass to London, where they would chase girls, visit the nightclubs, and go to the dog races, which Colby particularly enjoyed.[2]

It was Saturday, August 12, when Colby, Favel, and Giry were alerted for a mission. At their briefing in London the men learned that their team would be known as Bruce. Their work would involve helping a man named Henri Frager train and equip maquis groups in the Yonne department of central France. The broad valley of the Yonne, roughly sixty miles southeast of Paris, consisted mostly of rolling farmlands and pastures and vineyards. It was a landscape of gentle hills crowned in groves of pine, birch, and oak, where the old provinces of Orléanais, Burgundy, and Champagne converge.

The Jedburgh teams which had been sent to Brittany had worked at a disadvantage, having to start from scratch because F Section had never been successful in establishing a strong circuit there. Team Bruce, however, would be joining one of the largest circuits in France, one which had been active in the Yonne Valley since early 1943. The circuit was called Donkeyman.

Henri Frager was the organizer of the F Section circuit called Donkeyman.* The soft-spoken Alsatian with the hazel eyes and the prematurely gray hair and the slight limp had first gone to war against the Germans in 1914 at the age of seventeen. After that war he had become a successful architect. He had re-entered the army as a captain in 1939 and had joined the resistance when France fell a year later. By 1942 he had begun cooperating with Britain's Special Operations Executive and, by the summer of 1944, Frager

---

* Frager's case can be used to illustrate the security measures taken in referring to F Section agents. Henri Frager was his real name, but SOE and Special Force Headquarters would refer to him in message traffic by his code name Louba. In France, he was known by other agents and by special forces personnel by his field name Jean-Marie, yet if the Germans checked his false identification documents, they would see the name Henri Dupré. What name you knew him by depended on what your relationship to him was.

would head a circuit with nearly five thousand maquis fighters. But, from the very start, the Donkeyman circuit had experienced bad luck.

In May 1943, Frager had been joined by a radio operator named Marcel Clech, a forty-year-old courier named Vera Leigh, who had been a dress designer before the war, and a British captain named Sidney Jones. Special Operations Executive had hoped that these three eventually would be able to re-form a circuit next to Donkeyman which had been destroyed through arrests by the Germans.[3] Then, at the end of October 1943, Vera Leigh was arrested in Paris; she would later be executed at Natzweiler concentration camp.[4] Three weeks later Captain Jones was arrested. More bad luck followed on December 19, when radio direction-finders tracked down a transmission signal from Marcel Clech's set. Agents from the Sicherheitsdienst (SD)—the German Security Service—burst into Clech's room and captured him while he was in the middle of tapping out a message.[5]

But it was more than simple bad luck that had been at work in Henri Frager's circuit. He had been working under a serious handicap of which he was not yet aware. Frager's adjutant, a man named Roger Bardet, was a traitor and had been feeding information about the circuit to an agent of the Abwehr, Germany's military intelligence service, for more than a year. Bardet's Abwehr contact was a sergeant named Hugo Bleicher. Bardet and Bleicher had been responsible for the arrests of Vera Leigh and Captain Sidney Jones (with Bleicher making the actual arrests), and almost certainly had been involved in the arrest of Marcel Clech, with whom the two men had met on two occasions.

Forty-four-year-old Hugo Bleicher was one of Germany's most effective agents in France, and his work in 1943 and 1944 had been devastating to some F Section circuits. The former clerk from Hamburg had the appearance and demeanor of a schoolteacher. He had a gift for languages and an even greater gift for manipulating and betraying those who so easily trusted him. The Abwehr had recruited him early in the war.

Bleicher's history with Henri Frager and Roger Bardet dated back to the beginning of 1943. Bardet had become Frager's right-hand man during their early resistance work in the south of France in late 1942. While Frager had been absent on a visit to SOE in London in March 1943, Bardet had fallen into a trap set by the wily Sergeant Bleicher and found himself behind bars. When Bleicher first visited him in his cell to question him, Bardet offered to work for the German and immediately gave the Abwehr man many names of key resistance and SOE people. Bardet had then been released in such a way that it appeared to his fellow resistance members that he had escaped. Frager, of course, was unaware of Bardet's treachery, and when he returned from England to establish the Donkeyman circuit southeast of Paris, he kept Bardet with him.

Many resistance and SOE operatives in southern France were arrested as a result of the information Bardet had given Bleicher. By early 1944, probably as a result of information which interrogators had gained from Leigh, Jones, and Clech, the Germans had caught many more Donkeyman members and had seized a number of the circuit's arms dumps. Frager himself had survived that wave of arrests only because he had been absent on another trip to London at the time.[6]

Unfortunately, the staff at Special Force Headquarters in London knew none of this.

The Donkeyman circuit had survived nonetheless, and had actually grown in spite of Bardet and Bleicher, mostly due to the work of talented people such as Lieutenant Colonel Jacques Adam, Frager's deputy, and Ensign Peggy Knight, a courier. By the summer of 1944, the circuit was operating over an area reaching from Normandy to the Ardennes on the Belgian border. And, in the course of their work, Jacques Adam and Peggy Knight had grown leery of Roger Bardet. Knight, an attractive English girl who had been recruited by SOE after being overheard speaking fluent French in a London restaurant, had arrived by parachute in early May with an OSS radio operator, an American civilian named Henry Bouchard. Frager had warned the two newcomers to be alert because of the recent arrests, and he had put them to work organizing maquis groups in the valley of the Yonne River.

The twenty-one-year-old Knight excelled in the role of courier. She routinely passed through German checkpoints to deliver information to other FFI camps and several times, after the D-Day landings in June, to Allied army commanders. She also carried her weight in tactical operations, though, taking an active part in ambushes of German convoys as the FFI worked to delay the movement of enemy divisions to the Normandy battlefield.

When Frager had returned to France in February 1944, Roger Bardet had boldly arranged a series of meetings between Frager and the German agent Bleicher, whom he introduced as an anti-Nazi Luftwaffe officer interested in working for the British. Frager, taken in by the genial Bleicher, had come to trust the German so much that he had told him of his plans to build up the maquis of the Yonne department. So when Bleicher arrested Frager on the second day of July, as the Frenchman stepped off a train at the Montparnasse station in Paris, Frager was stunned. Three months later he was hanged at Buchenwald concentration camp.[7]

In London, as the briefer gave the men of Jedburgh team Bruce the final details of their mission, he told them that they were to meet Henri Frager in the drop zone, unaware that the circuit leader had already been arrested.

"What should we do if we fail to make contact with Frager or his men?" asked Colby. Any number of things could go wrong, Colby reasoned, and having an alternate plan just seemed prudent. For one thing, the contact plan the team had just heard was based completely on the premise that the team would be dropped precisely where it was supposed to be dropped. The briefer was speechless, however, and it was clear that no one had asked the question before and no one on the staff had apparently bothered to plan for such a contingency. At the last minute, the team was given the address of a safe house to which the Jeds should make their way if they had any problems finding their contacts.[8]

The men were then told that they would be departing for France that night. But bad weather moved in and the mission was scrapped for the night. The next day there was another development. Special Force Headquarters had just received word of Frager's arrest, but still was unaware of how he had been betrayed by his own adjutant. Consequently, a last-minute change was made to Jedburgh team

Bruce's mission: The team's contact would now be the man named Roger Bardet.

Bill Colby had been promoted to major five days before D-Day. But, according to Colby's autobiographical *Honorable Men*, Lieutenant Favel was designated team leader for the mission. Jacques Favel had been born in southern France, in the listless Catalan town of Perpignan—a coastal palm-tree town at the foothills of the Pyrénées, not far from the Spanish frontier. His mother had died when he was five years old, and his father emigrated to the United States in 1919 to join relatives who had been in the New Orleans area since the late nineteenth century. Favel had remained in France but had gone to the States as a teenager in 1931 to live with his father, who by then was the owner of an eight-thousand-acre plantation, raising corn, cotton, and cattle. Favel attended high school in New Orleans, but in 1934 returned to France, and in September of that year he joined the army, serving until 1937.

As the war approached, Favel was drafted back into the army in 1939, and he fought the German invaders in 1940 as a member of a reconnaissance platoon. He was discharged at the time of the armistice and lived for a time in unoccupied France. He then went to French North Africa and, on the day after the Allies landed there, he re-joined the French Army. Because he spoke English so well he had been sent to work in the intelligence section of a French army headquarters near the Kasserine Pass. It was there that the Jedburgh recruiters had found him in late 1943.[9]

As they drifted earthward in their parachute harnesses shortly after midnight on August 15, the men of Jedburgh team Bruce heard the Liberator from which they had jumped trail off into the night. But they soon realized that something was wrong. Hundreds of feet below them they saw a long fire, definitely not the drop zone bonfires they expected. Favel thought it looked like a village that had been torched by the Germans. It turned out to be the burning remains of a train which had been destroyed by an Allied air raid.

The three men came down in a large town, landing roughly among gardens and houses along the main street. Major Colby landed in someone's backyard. "In a burst of feathers," he later wrote, "chickens scattered hysterically; dogs began to bark; people, startled from their sleep, flung open their shutters and excitedly asked each other about the sudden racket."[10]

Indeed, the clamor caused by the metal containers falling on tiled rooftops and cobblestone streets aroused many of the local civilians, and a small crowd soon gathered around the Jeds. The townspeople informed the men that they had dropped into the town of Montargis in the Loiret department, east of Orléans, and had landed near the headquarters of the town's German garrison. Favel estimated that their intended drop zone was about twenty-five miles to the east. Sure that the growing crowd of townspeople would soon arouse the Germans, the men judged it too risky to take the time to retrieve their ten containers with radios and other equipment. They immediately set out to put some distance between them and the town, following a railroad track for a time and then crossing some wooded fields to the southeast.

Colby, Favel, and Giry walked until the first hint of daylight made further movement too dangerous, then found a ditch near a wooded area and crawled in. Only fifty to a hundred yards from the road into Montargis, the team watched all that day as German soldiers and armored cars converged on the town in an effort to locate the parachutists. Troops searched not only every house in Montargis, but surrounding villages and farms as well. As he lay in the grass throughout that long, hot August day, Bill Colby couldn't help wondering how he had gotten himself into such a fix.

When the lazy heat of summer had passed and darkness had returned, the men moved out again, this time following a compass azimuth calculated to deliver them to the safe house where they were to make their alternate contact. Then a thunderstorm hit, making their movement considerably more difficult. Rain beat down on the men, and the ground quickly became a slippery mire. A dreadful darkness made compass navigation nearly impossible. The men tied their pistol lanyards to one another to keep from being separated and struggled on through the pitch-black night, through the rain and the mud, until they heard voices directly ahead. It was nearly two in the morning, much too late for farmers to be up and about. Was it the resistance, or was it the enemy?

Lightning flashed and the men could see a single farmhouse in a clearing ahead of them. The team decided to take a chance and make contact with the occupants. While Colby and Giry covered him with their pistols, Favel approached the house and knocked on the door. At once the voices inside became silent, then one of them called out, "Qui est là?" ("Who is there?") Favel answered, "Un français."[11] Again there was silence from within. Then the door opened and Favel was admitted, and he soon opened the door and told Colby and Giry to come in; everything was all right. By a stroke of luck, the house was being used as a radio station by the resistance, and the men met a radio operator who had only arrived from London eight days earlier. The man quickly sent a message to London reporting Jed team Bruce's status.

Other maquis men arrived the next day and took the Jeds in a battered Citroën to the safe house which the briefer back in London had told them to use in just such a situation as this. The old car in which the Jeds were transported was gasogene-powered, which meant it was rigged with a wood- or charcoal-burning engine. Gasogenes had been around since the nineteenth century, but had come into widespread use among civilians in occupied France, where nearly all gasoline was reserved for military use. Rather than burning gasoline, they used a combustible gas generated by a charcoal- or wood-burning boiler mounted on the rear of the vehicle. Many maquis groups, of course, still used gasoline-powered cars, but these cars were either stolen from the Germans or had been hidden by civilians at the beginning of the war and now were operated on stolen gasoline.

From the safe house, Favel sent word through the local maquis to arrange for a meeting with someone from Roger Bardet's circuit. Within a few days the Jeds were taken to meet Bardet himself at a café in a village farther to the southeast, in the department of the Yonne. When they entered the café, they were met by the silent stares of a roomful of armed resistance men, and a man in his early thirties with coal-black hair, sitting at a table with food and wine, studied them with dark, deep-set eyes. After a moment, the man, tall and thin, stood and introduced himself as Roger Bardet, and he shook hands with each of the Jeds.

The resistance leader invited the men to sit down, and called for food to be brought. He asked the Jeds what had happened to them and where they had been, explaining that he and his men had waited at the drop zone with the fires lit, but no one had come. So Favel and Colby related the events of the past few days and Bardet seemed satisfied. Then he gave the Jeds a rundown on the local situation, and said that his scattered FFI groups currently totaled about five hundred armed men. But he could tell the Jeds nothing about the number of Germans in the area or where they were.

Colby described the meeting with Bardet in his 1978 autobiography *Honorable Men*, and wrote of the uneasy feeling he had about Roger Bardet from the very start. He did not yet know—or even suspect—that the Frenchman sitting before him was a traitor. Clearly, none of the maquisards in the café knew either, or Bardet would not still be alive. Something about the man, though, just didn't measure up to Colby's expectations of a guerrilla chief. In his book, Colby wrote that the uninspiring Bardet "had the look of a minor civil servant, a petty functionary, going through the motions instead of leading." He found Bardet, as head of a five-hundred-man resistance group, to be "anything but energetic, let alone daring."[12]

Luckily, Lieutenant Giry had kept his radio crystals with him on the jump, so, for the next few days, he was able to send team Bruce's messages to London on Bardet's radio. Giry had been a laborer in the city of Nancy before the war, and had been a sergeant in the Free French forces when he joined the Jedburghs. Like the other French radio operators, Giry also had received a lieutenant's commission prior to deploying. Now he was without a radio, however, as team Bruce's two Jed sets had been lost on the jump when the canisters came down in Montargis and been abandoned, and by then they were surely in German hands. But having to rely on Bardet's radio was tying the Jeds down. The cumbersome set could not be moved far, and its batteries continually required recharging.

As Giry busied himself with communications, Colby and Favel set about their work. They began by organizing Bardet's men into companies. Then they set up a training program, concentrating initially on the use of the weapons the maquis groups had already received from air drops. As the fighters began to show mastery of their individual weapons, the instruction advanced to small unit tactics. Before long, patrols were going on limited combat operations against the Germans, with the Jeds continually coaching, advising, and assisting the guerrilla leaders.

One day they attacked a German plane which had been grounded for lack of fuel, and there was a sizable enemy security force which put up a good fight. But in the end, the Germans had to burn the badly shot-up plane after the maquis force withdrew.

There were German garrisons of about five hundred men each in the larger towns of the Yonne, and many enemy convoys were passing through the area as German units retreated eastward. All of them appeared to be lightly guarded. These were tempting targets, but Bardet would not allow the maquis to attack them. He told the Jeds that he had received orders from London not to take any offensive action for the time being. London, he said, would send orders calling for direct action whenever it best supported Allied operations. To the Jeds, however, it simply seemed that Bardet, for whatever reason, wanted to avoid antagonizing the Germans. If they had at first believed Bardet to simply be incompetent, they now grew increasingly suspicious of his loyalties.

Favel and Colby began to look elsewhere for an effective resistance leader and, as soon as they could, they made contact with other groups. And in doing so, the men found that they could rely on Peggy Knight, the competent and energetic young courier of the Donkeyman circuit.

Soon the Jeds met a sixty-year-old resistance chief called Colonel Chevrier, a peacetime lawyer and reserve army officer whose real name was Adrien Sadoul. Chevrier challenged Bardet's authority over the FFI of the Yonne and told the Jeds that he had been appointed as their commander. The old man's immediate group only numbered about twenty men, but Major Colby judged him to be much more of a leader than the enigmatic Bardet. "He was flamboyant, charismatic, constantly on the move,"[13] Colby would later recall, and he was on good terms with other chiefs throughout the Yonne who commanded some two thousand fighters in all, perhaps more. This was the sort of man the Jeds were seeking.

Chevrier told the Jeds what he knew of the Yonne resistance. He told of another maquis chief named Georges, who had about four hundred armed men operating in the area southeast of Auxerre. And of a popular young leader named Vernouil, who commanded another six hundred. Additionally, communist FTP groups totaling about three hundred men, under the overall command of a man named Yvon, were scattered throughout the area. But all of these groups had one thing in common—their size was limited by the number of weapons they had available. If more arms were sent from England, Chevrier explained, they all could expand.

The Jeds immediately began making arrangements for parachute drops. They asked Chevrier for drop zone locations, and the old chief gathered information from all the groups in the department on fields which could be used and gave the information to the Jeds. Lieutenant Giry radioed the information to London along with a request for thousands of rifles, carbines, machine guns, bazookas, and mortars.

By this time, American forces were closing in on the Seine, and one of General Patton's corps began crossing the river south of Paris on Saturday, August 19. With Allied forces so close to Paris, the city's resistance groups began an uprising that same day, seizing newspaper offices, government buildings, and the city hall. Although the resistance in Paris was estimated to number as many as twenty thousand, few of them were armed. They were just strong enough to be a real threat to the German occupation force in the city, but not strong enough to take control of the city by themselves. So a truce was soon called between the resistance and the Germans, with Swedish consul general Raoul Nordling acting as intermediary.

Commanding the German garrison was the bulky Prussian Lieutenant General Deitrich von Choltitz. Hitler had given von Choltitz orders to leave Paris in rubble by way of pre-planted demolitions if the Allies tried to take it, and the city's landmarks had already been primed with tons of explosives. Choltitz, however, did not relish the thought of being remembered in history as the man who destroyed the City of Light, so he decided to put up only a limited fight for the city. The Parisian resistance leaders were unaware of this, though, and they were sure that the city would be destroyed if Allied forces didn't move in soon.

On Monday, an emissary from the Paris resistance, named Lefevre, drove to the Yonne, found Jedburgh team Bruce, and appealed to Lieutenant Favel and Major Colby for help. Lefevre, a city police official, explained the situation in the capital and asked the Jeds to help by arranging for arms and supplies, including anti-tank weapons, to be dropped to the Ile-de-la-Cité, the island in the middle of the Seine where the Palace of Justice and Notre Dame cathedral stood. Favel and Colby agreed to see what they could do and immediately sent off the request to London.

What neither the Paris resistance nor the Jeds knew, though, was that the Allies had planned to bypass Paris. Anxious to maintain the momentum of their drive toward the German border, they wanted to avoid having to commit a large number of troops to costly and time-consuming street fighting in the capital. The German garrison in the city, it was thought, would be compelled to capitulate, at any rate, once their supply lines were cut. Eisenhower, however, had another reason for wanting to defer the liberation of Paris. As the Allied armies advanced farther from the Normandy coast, maintaining an adequate flow of supplies to the front lines was becoming a real challenge. And the supreme commander was in no hurry to add to this burden the responsibility for supplying food and coal to the entire population of the city.

On August 21, Special Force Headquarters received Jedburgh team Bruce's message requesting a parachute drop of arms and ammunition to the Paris resistance, and began at once to prepare to make the drop. But on the twenty-second, General Pierre Joseph Koenig, de Gaulle's London-based commander of the FFI, postponed the operation for a day in hopes that the arrival of Allied forces in the city would preclude the need to further arm the Paris resistance. Koenig, like de Gaulle, was in no rush to provide more weapons to the Paris resistance, because it was predominantly communist. Both men were anxious to install a provisional non-communist government in the city as soon as it was freed.[14]

While the Paris policeman was meeting with the Jeds of team Bruce, another emissary named Roger Gallois drove to General Patton's forward command post. Gallois pleaded with Patton to send a force at once to liberate the city. But Patton refused, citing General Eisenhower's plan to bypass the city, and so Lieutenant Colonel Powell, Patton's special forces advisor, drove Gallois to General Bradley's command post. They met with Bradley and with the commander of the French 2nd Armored Division, which was under Bradley's command. Paris, Gallois assured the army group commander, could easily be taken if the Allies moved at once. The truce with General Choltitz, he feared, might end at any time. Bradley quickly phoned General Eisenhower.[15]

By this time, General de Gaulle was also pressuring Eisenhower to reconsider and to send forces to liberate the city at once rather than bypass it. Eager to see the capital freed of its German occupiers, de Gaulle was equally intent on preventing the communists from taking over the city. Finally, Eisenhower relented—partly, he was to say later, as a reward to the resistance for their contribution in the French campaign. He told Bradley to order First Army to move in.

An FFI group of eight hundred men in Chartres made plans to enter the city with the Allied divisions, but an officer from Colonel Powell's special forces detachment was able to dissuade them, explaining that the group would only get in the way.[16]

Eisenhower wanted French forces to be the first to enter the city, so the French 2nd Armored Division drove on Paris from the west while an American infantry division made a supporting attack from the south. The attacks began in gloomy weather on the morning of the twenty-third and soon ran into stiff resistance by Germans on the city's outskirts. French tanks were also slowed by crowds of Parisians swarming around the vehicles. But, by the morning of the twenty-fifth, the sun was out and the city was liberated, and de Gaulle and his supporters wasted no time in occupying government buildings and establishing political control.

London soon began responding to Jed team Bruce's calls for arms drops to the Yonne, and the maquis throughout the department flourished. Within the first two weeks the Jeds arranged at least a dozen drops, and almost overnight maquis groups grew as farmers and townspeople alike joined the fight. Thousands of weapons ranging from rifles, carbines, and Stens, to bazookas and mortars and machine guns fell from Allied planes onto fields throughout the Yonne. Anticipation of victory and liberation caused many fence-sitters to join the side of the resistance. And with the arms and explosives which London provided, the maquis of the Yonne also began ambushing German columns, attacking German garrisons, and blowing up enemy supply depots.

The Germans were reeling from the onslaught of Patton's Third Army. And as difficult as it was for them to deal with Patton's tanks and with punishing Allied air strikes, they also had to contend with countless hit-and-run attacks by the maquis.

But while Third Army was advancing toward Germany north of the Loire River, tens of thousands of German troops from southwestern France were trying to withdraw to the homeland south of the Loire. Some of Patton's staff officers were becoming concerned about the security of the army's right flank, and because Third Army was the southernmost of Twelfth Army Group's forces, General Bradley had charged it with protecting the army group's flank. Only a shallow river lay between the Americans and as many as a hundred thousand Wehrmacht troops. Patton's own intelligence officer, on August 22, had become so concerned about heavy German traffic south of Orléans that he feared a counterattack by the enemy into Third Army's flank.[17]

On that same day, a U.S. infantry division attacked the Germans holding Montargis, the town where Jedburgh team Bruce had landed just a week earlier. The town fell to the Americans late the next day after a difficult fight. Then the Jeds heard that an American armored unit had reached a town fifteen miles east of Montargis and just north of team Bruce's camp. Colby and Favel decided that they should try to make contact, and they would take with them an American fighter pilot whose P-38 had been shot down some time earlier. The pilot had been taken in by the FFI, outfitted with civilian clothes and false papers, and kept hidden until just such an opportunity arrived.

The U.S. forces east of Montargis turned out to be from the 4th Armored Division. Making it through the Allied lines, the Jeds found their way to the division headquarters and were able to talk with the intelligence officer and the operations officer. They provided the division staff with all the information they had about what lay ahead.

Then, at the request of the division, team Bruce sent maquisards on information-gathering missions to towns throughout the area immediately ahead of the Americans. Primarily, they were to look for German concentrations and report back. The maquis did so, and some of the best information came back from Peggy Knight and from a French woman, each of whom moved alone through some of the most heavily occupied towns.

The Allies did not pause, even briefly, after the capture of Paris, but pushed on, taking full advantage of their momentum. The 4th Armored Division, spearheading Patton's army, swept through the northern part of the Yonne and pressed on for Troyes, in the department of the Aube, where the Seine passed through the old provincial capital of Champagne. And the division made good use of the FFI. On August 24, as the division's leading combat command prepared for its assault on Troyes, the operations officer ordered the FFI to protect all roads leading into the city. They were also to block all side roads that could be used by the Germans in launching counterattacks against the Americans. While the division was making final preparations for the attack scheduled for the following morning, an FFI commander arrived to report that his men had all roads blocked as ordered and that he had several more companies standing by in reserve.

Shortly after the attack kicked off, a jeep carrying a lieutenant from Colonel Powell's Third Army special forces detachment caught up with the commander of the 4th Armored Division's lead element, Colonel Bruce Clarke. The lieutenant, who was accompanied by a French major, asked if there was anything else the FFI could do for him. Clarke said that he wanted the FFI to help secure another bridge downriver from Troyes. The lieutenant and the Frenchman set off at once to make it happen, and Clarke sent a reconnaissance platoon along with them.

Upon arriving at the bridge the FFI found that it had been damaged, but the men secured the area while division engineers brought up a temporary Bailey bridge and installed it. Meanwhile, another maquis group secured a bridge site within the city of

Troyes, and the lead tank battalion from the 4th Armored Division, led by Lieutenant Colonel Creighton Abrams, crossed the Seine there on the twenty-fifth.* The maquis then assisted an infantry division in securing the bridgehead on the far side.

On Saturday, August 26, Chevrier's FFI group occupied Auxerre, the old capital city of the Yonne, with its timbered houses and cobbled streets, and the old resistance leader established his command post there. Jacques Favel and Bill Colby had been keeping an eye out for an airstrip capable of handling C-47 transport planes to bring in more supplies. On Sunday they inspected the airfield at Auxerre, measured the runway, and signaled London that it was suitable.

Meanwhile, back at his command post northeast of Orléans, General Patton continued to be pressured by General Bradley's headquarters to commit forces to the flank protection mission. Grudgingly, the Third Army commander complied by committing an infantry division to the task in the area immediately east of Orléans. But, for the most part, Patton purposely left his right flank essentially open from St-Nazaire on the Atlantic to Troyes, a distance of more than three hundred miles. In his postwar memoir, Patton wrote that he felt confident that the tactical air force unit supporting his army could warn him of any impending attack from the Germans south of the Loire.[18]

Patton couldn't assuage the worriers on Bradley's staff, but to his own staff he was blunt: "Forget this goddamned business of worrying about our flanks. . . . Some goddamned fool once said that flanks must be secured, and since then sons-of-bitches all over the world have been going crazy guarding their flanks."[19] And when his southernmost corps commander, whose flank it was to be left open, expressed concern about the tens of thousands of Germans south of the Loire, Patton replied, "Just ignore 'em!"[20]

But there was more to Patton's cavalier attitude toward flank

* Bruce Clarke and Creighton Abrams would both later rise to the rank of four-star general. General Clarke would retire as the commander in chief of United States Army Europe in 1962. General Abrams would command all U.S. forces in Vietnam from 1968 to 1972 and would serve as army chief of staff from 1972 until his death in 1974.

security than faith in the air force. As a recipient of top secret "Ultra" message traffic, Patton had a fairly accurate picture not only of what German forces lay ahead of him, but also of the intentions of the German forces south of the Loire. The Allies had been intercepting and reading German messages sent by means of the Enigma cipher machine ever since they had broken the code early in the war, and Ultra was the designation applied to intelligence gained as a result of this work. Through Ultra message traffic, Patton knew he could afford to commit only a token guard force on his right flank because the German forces south of the river were under orders to withdraw to the east. They had little interest in crossing the Loire to attack his flank. The FFI, of course, already occupied the entire flank area clear to the German border, including the southern bank of the Loire. Thus, flank protection had become, de facto, a mission perfectly suited to the resistance on the ground while the air force kept watch over the area from above. As an officer on Bradley's staff later quipped, "Patton, as usual, trusted his flank to God, the air force and the maquis."[21]

That was the situation at the Third Army command post on Sunday, August 27, when Major Colby and Lieutenant Favel drove there in search of a new mission for the FFI of the Yonne department. Upon arrival at Patton's headquarters, the Jeds met with Colonel Powell and his special forces staff. One of the first things the men learned was that Chevrier had been officially named chief of the FFI of the entire Yonne department. London had notified Powell's staff of this but had failed to inform Jedburgh team Bruce. Then Powell told the Jeds that General Patton wanted the FFI to guard Third Army's right flank during its advance eastward. To help the Jeds in executing the new mission, Powell requested London to place top priority on arms drops to team Bruce's area. Powell's men also gave Favel and Colby a radio to replace the two they had lost on their jump.

Third Army published a written order to the FFI on Monday. It was addressed to both Chevrier and Roger Bardet in the Yonne, as well as to the FFI leaders of two adjacent departments, and it directed them to ensure the protection of the army's right flank.[22]

As soon as Favel and Colby returned to Chevrier's command post, they began helping the chief and his men draw up a plan for the new mission. To better organize the FFI for the task they divided Chevrier's department into area commands, and they distributed the communist Francs-Tireurs et Partisans (FTP) groups throughout the department so that they were interspersed with Chevrier's units. By the last day of August, Chevrier's guerrillas were occupying positions along a line which ran straight through the center of the Yonne department. Each town along the line was occupied by an FFI company whose commander reported to his parent resistance organization which, in turn, reported to Chevrier.

Jed team Bruce returned to the northern Yonne on Thursday and went over the details of the plan with Colonel Powell and his staff. As an added measure, Powell directed that the FFI blow as many of the Loire bridges as possible. The river approaches the town of Briare from the south before gently curving toward the west and then running in a westerly direction to St-Nazaire on the Atlantic coast, and Powell gave Chevrier's FFI the responsibility for blowing all bridges south of Briare. As soon as the Jeds returned to Chevrier's command post, Major Colby accompanied the maquis chief on a reconnaissance of all the bridges in their assigned stretch of the river, and they found that some had already been destroyed. They issued orders for the demolition of those that remained.

More and more Germans withdrew eastward through the department, their goal simply to reach the German border. Seldom did they halt long enough to engage Chevrier's FFI in any pitched battles, but the FFI attacked enemy columns at every opportunity. Small, isolated German elements became easy targets for the maquis and were quickly found and destroyed. To better protect themselves, the Germans began moving only in large formations along main routes, with security patrols guarding the columns. Such large convoys were easy targets for the air force, however, and soon the Germans learned that they could only move that way at night.

Since crossing the Seine, Patton's army had been in relentless pursuit of the retreating Germans. Caution was thrown largely to the wind in the interest of moving as far and as fast as possible, keeping the enemy off balance and unable to establish a defense.

Small pockets of enemy resistance were bypassed. Infantry kept up with armor the only way possible—by riding along. Tanks often had eight to ten infantrymen riding on top. Tank destroyers could carry a dozen or more foot soldiers and jeeps carried four or five. Other men found every means of transport available—artillery prime movers, quartermaster trucks, and engineer and medical vehicles. Men rested their heads on an arm as they rolled along, trying to grab a few minutes of sleep whenever possible. More infantry followed in two-and-a-half-ton trucks, dismounting to move on foot only when necessary.

Units moved so fast that they ran off their maps almost daily, through grassy plains and wooded hills, through crowds of cheering men, women, and children in every village and town. Church bells rang as the red, white, and blue French tricolor was raised for the first time in four years. And people showered the troops with flowers and fruit and kisses, and rewarded the liberators with bottles of wine, cognac, and calvados. In return, the Americans shared chocolate and gum with the French kids to shouts of "Vive l'Amérique." But, always, the troops kept on rolling.[23]

At this time the FFI was given an additional job. As the Germans departed French towns and cities, FFI units were to immediately occupy them. Roadblocks were built and strongpoints established, forcing any following German units to circumvent the town, further slowing their movement and making them vulnerable to harassing attacks in the surrounding countryside. Hasty occupation would also, it was hoped, prevent demolition by the retreating Germans.

When German forces vacated the town of Monéteau, three miles north of Auxerre, in late August, an FFI company of about a hundred and fifty men occupied the town to protect a large supply of gasoline located there. Later that day, a German force numbering more than two hundred returned to either retrieve or destroy the gasoline, and attacked the FFI with small arms, mortars, and machine guns. Even though they had nothing larger than Bren light machine guns, the FFI fighters held off the enemy and saved the gasoline, which supplied the FFI throughout the Yonne for the next month.[24]

*   *   *

At the end of August, General Eisenhower sent a message to his senior commanders outlining the next phase of operations. Montgomery's army group was to continue attacking to the northeast to seize the Pas de Calais area, capture airfields in Belgium, and take the port of Antwerp. Bradley's army group was to continue attacking in a northeasterly direction in support of Montgomery's assault, but it was also to prepare to attack to the east towards the Saar Valley. The FFI, the message added, "will continue to provide direct support to the operations of the Army Groups by harassing, sabotage, counter-scorching (and mopping-up action), and by protecting important installations of value to Allied lines of communication."[25]

The next day, in a cable to his superiors, the Combined Chiefs of Staff, Eisenhower provided an update on the progress of the campaign in Europe, noting that the FFI had "done much valuable work."[26] He echoed these sentiments when talking to the British press the next day, when he proclaimed that the maquis "had been far more effective than many doubting Thomases thought before D-Day."[27]

By September 15, Third Army had advanced to the Moselle, the last river obstacle before the Rhine. Patton's forces had now advanced beyond Jed team Bruce's area of operation, and other maquis groups and other Jedburgh teams would pick up the work team Bruce had been doing. Team Bruce's work was finished, and Special Force Headquarters signaled for the men to return to London.

The Jeds made their way to Paris, where OSS had established a headquarters soon after the city's liberation and taken over a hotel for the use of agents returning from the field. There Colby, Giry, and Favel met and celebrated with other Jeds, OSS Operational Groups, and circuit personnel also en route to England.

Among those who came to Paris at about that time to catch a plane back to London was an American woman named Virginia Hall. Under the code name Diana, she had just completed her second mission to France. She had conducted her first as an SOE agent, before OSS had become established in Europe, then had switched to the American organization and was deployed to run a circuit named Wrestler with the assistance of a Jedburgh team. Despite having lost a leg in a pre-war hunting accident, Hall had proved herself a most capable circuit organizer and had caused so much trouble for the Germans that they had put a price on her head. But she had been out of contact with SFHQ for several days. Upon her arrival in Paris, she apologized for her tardiness, explaining that she had been hiding from a Gestapo search party. As one OSS officer who was there observed, "One might have thought she was apologizing for having missed a train connection and deplored the inconvenience it might have caused those waiting for her."[28]

One Jedburgh team arrived in a black Cadillac which had reportedly belonged to Vichy Premier Pierre Laval, and when the team boarded a plane for England they relinquished the car to Bill Colby for his temporary use. In late September, the three men of Jedburgh team Bruce returned to London for their debriefing. Both Favel and Giry later returned to the French Army, Favel becoming a liaison officer with an American unit.

Roger Bardet, the man who had betrayed so many in the resistance and had been an unknown threat to Jedburgh team Bruce, successfully kept a low profile for many months. Once he saw that Allied victory was imminent he essentially became a bench-sitter, doing nothing to aggravate either side or to draw attention to himself. In the end, though, he was found out and was arrested, tried, and convicted of treason after the war.

Meanwhile, as Third Army was making its dash across central France in August 1944, the First U.S. Army was doing the same, though with much less fanfare, just to the north. And Jedburgh teams, dropped much later than they should have been, struggled to work in an area increasingly crowded with retreating Germans.

9

A RAINY NIGHT IN PICARDY

UNDER the terms of the 1940 armistice with conquered France, Germany had allowed the collaborationist Vichy regime to retain a small army. Permitted to carry only small arms, this Armistice Army had been limited in size to one hundred thousand in metropolitan France and an army in North Africa which eventually numbered more than twice that.[1] Among the officers assigned to that Armée d'Afrique was a former sergeant by the name of Jean Delviche and, like most Frenchmen, he had seen his world turned upside down when France capitulated to the German invaders. The handsome native of the Picardy region of northern France had gone through officer training and earned a commission in the artillery. When the German invasion came that summer, he fought with distinction, commanding a battery of guns. But then France fell.

The young lieutenant had remained in uniform as part of the Armistice Army and been sent to a small garrison in Morocco. He had gotten married and he and his new wife had been able to obtain military family housing at the garrison. There was great camaraderie among the soldiers and their families at the small post and they had many friends, and Lieutenant Delviche had grown content with the military life in sunny French North Africa.

All that changed when U.S. and British forces stormed ashore in

Morocco and Algeria in November 1942. The Vichy French forces at first offered token resistance but were quickly persuaded to lay down their arms and throw in with the Allies as Free French. Germany had responded by occupying what had been the unoccupied southern portion of France. For the French military community in North Africa, all ties with France had been severed and they soon found it impossible to get many items from their homeland, including badly needed medical supplies.

Lieutenant Delviche's wife had been carrying their first child and there were difficulties with the birth. Because the medical care was not what it should have been, both mother and baby died. Grief-stricken, Delviche sought any opportunity to leave the land where he had once been so happy. He applied to his commander to be sent anywhere, as long as it would get him away from that place. When recruiters came looking for French volunteers for a secret mission involving parachuting behind enemy lines, Jean Delviche was one of the first to step forward.[2]

Delviche was a little older than most of the French Jeds, and while most of the men at Milton Hall had taken advantage of every opportunity to visit a pub in the evening or to get a pass to London, Delviche had seldom joined them. He was a captain by the time the Jedburgh trainees had begun forming teams in the spring of 1944, and he had hooked up with a likable American, Major John Bonsall.

Like Delviche, Bonsall was an artillery officer. He hailed from Morristown, New Jersey, where he had been raised by his mother and her parents. He had been named for a father he never knew. John Bonsall's mother had been carrying him when his father left for France in the First World War. A lawyer in civilian life, his father had died in France, a victim of the great influenza epidemic which swept through Europe in 1918, killing more American soldiers than German guns did. News of his death had hit John's mother hard, and it was then that his grandparents moved in to help raise John and his older sister, Katherine.[3]

John had attended The Haverford School, a prominent school for boys in Pennsylvania, had been a top student there, and graduated with honors. In other ways, as well, he had shown himself to be an unusually bright and talented young man. He learned French at an early age, and proved himself to be mechanically clever. As a teenager, he would find old cars, have them towed home, tear them apart, and rebuild them to running condition. And he demonstrated that he had inherited his family's love of music by learning to play the piano—and play it well.

From Haverford Bonsall had gone on to Princeton. Outgoing and sociable, he had joined the University Cottage Club—which had been whimsically characterized by F. Scott Fitzgerald in *This Side of Paradise* as "an impressive mélange of brilliant adventurers and well-dressed philanderers." John Bonsall at least qualified as the brilliant adventurer. He stood around six feet tall with an athletic build; he made friends easily and was known to have a mischievous sense of humor. He had talked of a future in law following the war, but law school would have to wait. For among his many activities at Princeton, Bonsall had been in the ROTC program, and when graduation came in 1941 he received an army commission in the artillery. His call to active duty came in August of that year. Two years later he volunteered for the Jedburghs, made it through the selection and training process, and was standing by with all the others at Milton Hall, awaiting his call to London. His twenty-fifth birthday came just five days after the Allied landings in Normandy.

Joining Major Bonsall and Captain Delviche as the team's radio operator was a twenty-one-year-old sergeant from Manchester, New Hampshire, named Roger Côté.

Finally, two weeks into August, Bonsall's team was summoned to London for its mission briefing. There the men learned that they were bound for the department of the Aisne in the northern region of Picardy, where Captain Delviche had his roots. It was an area surrounded by battlefields of the last war: Soissons, Arras, Cambrai, the Somme, Verdun, and Château-Thierry. When the briefing concluded, the three men were driven to an airfield. It was not a particularly good night for jumping; the weather was nice, but there was no moon at all. The next full moon would not come until the beginning of September, but London had many teams to get into the field soon if they were to be of any use. The plane carrying team Augustus took off late on Tuesday night, August 15, just twenty-four hours after Bill Colby's team had left for the Yonne.

*   *   *

First thing Thursday morning, Sergeant Côté broke out his radio gear and got his first message off to London. The message simply read, "AUGUSTUS ALL WELL. RECEPTION PERFECT."[4] It was succinct, but it told those at SFHQ all they needed to know at that time. Team Augustus's jump had gone well; the men landed in flat farmland about a hundred miles northeast of Paris. Once all of their gear had been collected from the drop zone, the Jeds had been driven to the departmental FFI headquarters for a brief rest and then on to a farm in a more remote area. There, the men were briefed by FFI leaders on the status of maquis groups throughout the area.

Roger Côté was well-suited for the job of Jedburgh radio operator. His father, Elzear Côté, had been a radio operator in World War I and had shared some of his knowledge of radios with Roger, even teaching him some Morse code. Like Major Bonsall, Roger Côté was a French speaker, but to Côté the language came naturally, a result of his family's French Canadian roots. He had been born in Manchester in southern New Hampshire, where his parents had been married, and had grown up in the area.

Elzear Côté had, for a time, sold Singer sewing machines door to door. Then he had worked in a bakery, but the flour-saturated air caused some health problem and, on a doctor's advice, the family moved to a farm. Because of his poor health, Roger's father had often been out of work, and the family never had much money. Roger had a younger brother, Roland, an older sister, Zita, and two younger sisters, Violette and Jeannine, and they were a close and devout Catholic family.

Roger was of slight build and no more than about five feet, two inches tall, with hazel eyes; people around Manchester sometimes commented that he looked like a little Frenchman. He had been a good student at St. Anthony's High School in Manchester and had harbored a desire to go to college, but it was out of the question because there was no money. Halfway through his senior year, he quit high school and, in early November 1942, joined the army along with two of his friends. Roger's family had thrown a farewell party for the three young men, complete with a large American flag and a cake decorated with many smaller flags. Elzear Côté wore his World War I uniform—which still fit him perfectly—for the occasion.

Roger had asked for a Signal Corps assignment at the time of his enlistment because of his early interest in radio. The army had sent him to the radio school at Fort Monmouth, New Jersey, and it was there that he had heard the Jedburgh recruiter's briefing and volunteered.

Because of the secret nature of his assignment, the Côté family knew nothing of what Roger's role in the war would be when he shipped out in December 1943. But, with his son off to do his part, Elzear Côté decided that the whole family should get involved in the war effort. And so they had packed up and moved to Newton, Massachusetts, where Violette, Zita, and Elzear took jobs with the Raytheon Company in Waltham, making radio tubes for the army.

The family missed Roger, and was always glad to get his letters and hear how he was doing—even if he couldn't say what he was doing. Roger always wrote to his family in French, and in his last letter home he had asked the family to pray for him.[5]

At the farm in northern France, Major Bonsall, Captain Delviche, and Sergeant Côté were enjoying true château living, with good French cooking and plenty of wine. But there was work to be done, and the Jeds soon got started. Resistance leaders from throughout the area gathered to meet with the Jeds on Saturday, August 19. The group decided that the Jeds should begin their work in the southern part of the Aisne department, in the area around Soissons. The Germans had built some fairly extensive fortifications in that area which might be of interest to the Allies. Besides, there were many Germans in the Soissons area and a move southward would allow the Jeds to quickly arrange the delivery of weapons so badly needed by the resistance there.[6]

In a message to London on the twentieth, the Jeds told of their conference with the resistance leaders. They reported that there were some eleven hundred men armed and trained throughout the Aisne department and nearly five thousand more in need of arms. The message conveyed the Jeds' confidence in the FFI leaders and the team's readiness to get to work. But because the area was saturated with Germans, and perhaps at the suggestion of the FFI leaders, the Jeds had decided that the only way they could move about the area would be in civilian clothes. Already the FFI was at work preparing false papers for the men to carry during their journey southward.[7]

About an hour before noon on Monday, a man called Seigneur arrived in a gasogene-powered truck to pick up the Jeds and take them south. Driving the truck was a man named Gaston Costeaux; and another FFI man named Fontaine, who was the operations officer for the department, was with them. Seigneur and Fontaine went into the house while Costeaux prepared a hiding place in the back of the truck for the team's radios and rucksacks. When everything had been loaded aboard the truck, the Jeds thanked their hosts and said their good-byes and climbed aboard for the sixty-mile journey to Soissons. Captain Delviche and Sergeant Côté climbed into the cab of the truck with Costeaux, while Major Bonsall got into the back and found a place to sit on a pile of rabbit skins. Seigneur and Fontaine joined the American in the back and by eleven-thirty they were on the road.

The resistance people had produced false identity papers for the Jedburghs and the team had received them that morning. As the truck rolled along the men studied the papers. Every detail about their new identities had to be quickly committed to memory in case the truck was stopped along the way and they were questioned. In the cabin, Sergeant Côté learned from his papers that he was a student named René Chabaud. He had been born in 1928 at a place called Motteville in the Seine-Inférieure department, and he was currently living in St-Quentin. When he had studied this for awhile, Captain Delviche tested him.

"What's your name?"

"René Chabaud," said the sergeant. Gaston Costeaux noticed that the American rolled his R's slightly.

"Where were you born?"

"In the USA," responded Côté.

"No! If you fall into the hands of the Gestapo you'll be a goner. Come on. Again, where were you born?"

"In Motteville, in the Basse-Seine."

"Not *Basse*-Seine, it's Seine-*Inférieure*. You're a student in St-Quentin, but you are on vacation and staying with us. I am your uncle."[8]

Delviche's assumed identity was that of a thirty-three-year-old wood merchant from Coucy-le-Château named Jean Derval. "As for you," he said to Costeaux, "you picked us up hitchhiking on the road."⁹

In the back of the truck, with Seigneur, Major Bonsall studied his own identity. His papers described him as Joseph Porteval, a forester from Anizy-le-Château.

As the old truck plugged along southward, the men saw many convoys of German army vehicles. For many weeks, Hitler had refused to listen to all proposals from his commanders in France for a withdrawal in the event of an Allied breakthrough. He had refused, that is, until it was too late for any sort of organized withdrawal.

Although a considerable number of Germans, including some panzer units, had succeeded in escaping encirclement by withdrawing through the narrow Falaise-Argentan gap before the Allies could close it, they had paid a heavy price. Of an estimated one hundred thousand German troops caught in the pocket, only half had been able to escape. Some forty thousand troops from fifteen German divisions had been captured and another ten thousand killed.¹⁰ Those lucky enough to have escaped were making a mass exodus eastward to man the defense works on the Siegfried Line.

Passing through one village, the FFI truck suddenly met an oncoming German truck convoy. The German driver in the lead truck was taking too much of the road as they met on a curve, and the truck carrying the Jeds, which had built up a respectable speed for a gasogene, was forced off the street and onto the sidewalk. But Costeaux was familiar with the road, and he remained calm and kept the truck under control.

Just outside a village on the Oise-Aisne canal north of Soissons, Costeaux stopped the truck when he recognized a man standing with his bicycle as a friend named Jean Nöel. Nöel told Costeaux that a German tank had broken down about a half-mile from the village and was blocking the road. He added that Costeaux should be able to get around it with the truck, so Costeaux drove on toward the village.

As the truck came around a curve in the road Costeaux saw the tank, a model known as the Panther, and he slowed as they approached it. The gray forty-four-ton behemoth was eleven feet wide, nearly ten feet tall, and almost thirty feet long—and it was indeed blocking the road. Then, just when the Jeds feared the worst, a German soldier walked out and calmly guided the truck around the tank and they were once again on their way. The Panther was obviously flotsam from one of the many columns of retreating Germans.

At last, at two-thirty in the afternoon the truck pulled into Braine, a town about eleven miles east of Soissons, and drove directly to the Costeaux home, where Madame Costeaux was waiting for the men with lunch prepared. The men climbed out of the truck and went into the house; and when they entered the dining room, they were surprised to find it all done up in red, white, and blue—the colors of the Allies. Jean Delviche also noticed that the dishes were decorated with the Cross of Lorraine. They sat down and enjoyed the fine lunch and good wine and topped it off with champagne.

At eight that evening, the men climbed back into the truck to go to the farm where they were to stay. Seigneur, Costeaux, and another FFI man named Jean Plantier got into the truck with the Jeds and they got underway. When they'd left Braine they found their route blocked by a train, which was stopped at a road crossing, obstructing traffic. After waiting for about ten minutes, the men decided to try a different route. They drove around the train station and made what they considered a long enough detour before heading back to the main road. But then a column of German army trucks cluttered the road and, as if that weren't enough, it began to rain.

Eventually, the road cleared and the men drove on to the farm, near the hamlet of Rugny, where the Jeds would be staying with a family named Mathieu. The team was cautioned to remain as inconspicuous as possible, for there were an estimated three thousand Germans in the immediate area.

In the week that followed, the Jeds of team Augustus helped the FFI get organized for guerrilla operations and sent messages urging Special Force Headquarters to drop weapons. German convoys continuously passed through the area and would have made lucrative targets, but the FFI lacked enough weapons and explosives to carry out anything more than harassing attacks. If only the Jeds had arrived back in June.

While they waited for London to come through with the parachute drops, the men gathered information about enemy activity in the area and radioed it back to SFHQ. During their first three days at Rugny, they reported on German train and convoy movements and on the general disorganized state of the enemy units withdrawing through the area to the northeast. They also informed London that they had gotten their hands on German demolition plans for the channel port of Le Havre. The port was a hundred and forty miles west of the Jeds' location, and the plans apparently had been smuggled out to an area where the resistance could hand them off to the Allies. Of more immediate interest to team Augustus, though, were details they were given on some extensive fortifications located just north of Soissons.

Four and a half miles northeast of Soissons, the Margival fortification had been constructed early in the war to serve as Hitler's headquarters during the planned invasion of England. It was an expansive steel-reinforced concrete bunker system, complete with shelters and pillboxes, underground and above-ground command posts, and a network of connecting trenches. Ingeniously well-camouflaged in a sheltered and heavily wooded valley, the complex was difficult to see at ground level, and had been built away from cities to protect it from Allied bombing. Anti-aircraft batteries had been placed in surrounding villages. Comfortable accommodations lay inside the thick concrete walls and the bunkers had armored roofing. There were well furnished and decorated quarters for the theater commander and his staff, conference rooms, and an operations room complete with map cases. Outside the buildings, concrete streets and winding, paved walkways were lined with lampposts and large camouflage netting covered the entire works.[11] There was even a swimming pool.

But the Margival complex had gone largely unused since its construction, although Hitler had met there with Field Marshals Gerd von Rundstedt and Erwin Rommel on June 17 to discuss operations in Normandy.[12] Major Bonsall, probably unaware that the complex might be unoccupied, was determined to get details of the Margival fortifications, as well as the Le Havre demolition plans, to London.

Bonsall and Côté didn't leave the Mathieu farm very often, but occasionally would walk to Seigneur's command post located in a village about a mile up the road. Otherwise, contact between team Augustus and the command post was maintained twice each day through a young female courier. Captain Delviche often accompanied Seigneur to meetings with FFI leaders in the surrounding area. On Wednesday, August 23, all three Jeds met with the departmental FFI chief and the chief of the Soissons FFI at Rugny to discuss planned guerrilla operations. Still, though, little could be done without the delivery of arms and other supplies from London.

Every night, remnants of the German armies from Normandy continued to shuffle through the area to the northeast. Most didn't remain in the Soissons area for long. The Panzer Lehr Division, for example, had been ordered to an assembly area just north of Soissons on August 17 but, by the twenty-fourth, most of the division had moved on to the east.[13] The Panther tank which the Jeds had seen stalled on the road as they neared Soissons from the north on the twenty-first might have belonged to the Panzer Lehr.

Special Force Headquarters in London heard from team Augustus again on the twenty-fifth, and the message was one of frustration. "IMPOSSIBLE TO FORM MAQUIS NOW DUE TO ONE, TOO MANY BOCHE; TWO, LACK OF GOOD HIDING AREAS; THREE, VERY FEW ARMS."[14] The remainder of the message reiterated the Jeds' assessment of the quality and potential of the guerrilla forces in the Aisne. Many small maquis groups had been trained and they all had good leaders, but they were ineffective because of the shortage of arms. The Jed team repeated its urgent need for an immediate arms drop and asked for a second load to be dropped two days after the first.

The Allies had gotten most of their lead divisions across the Seine by August 26, and were pushing eastward on the heels of the retreating Germans. At the northern extent of the Allied lines, General Montgomery's army group drove northeastward toward Belgium and Holland, following the coastline. To his right was General Bradley's army group, whose First Army was attacking to the northeast, along Montgomery's right flank, while Patton's Third Army attacked due east toward Metz.

Brigadier General Maurice Rose's 3rd Armored Division—spearheading First Army's attack—set out on a northeasterly track from its starting point near Paris, a course which would take it straight through Soissons and Laon and on into Belgium. Following close on its heels were two infantry divisions, one on each flank.

After pushing off from the Seine, the 3rd Armored Division fought through a German infantry division which had been deployed as a covering force for the withdrawing enemy. Rose's division initially followed a broad corps reconnaissance screen but, as the division picked up speed, the cavalry group split to the north and south to provide flank security and Rose's tanks rolled forward in the lead.

The pursuit by Bradley's armies quickly became a rout, a war of attrition, the Allies intent on destroying as much of the German army in France as possible before it reached the frontier. For once the Germans reached the Rhine and the Siegfried Line—their string of fortifications along the border—they surely would throw up a stiff defense. Breaking through such a fortified line could be costly for the Allies; the more Germans that could be knocked out of the war—before they reached the Rhine—the better.

The 3rd Armored Division approached Soissons from the west and southwest, and its first objective—much more important than capturing the city—was the seizure of crossings over the Aisne River, which runs on an east-west course through Soissons. From there, plans called for the division to continue moving toward Laon, capital of the Aisne department, which lay about nineteen miles to the northeast.

Eager to contribute to the Allied advance, just as it had done in Brittany and the Loire Valley, Special Force Headquarters proceeded to drop Jedburgh teams ahead of the divisions driving eastward. Divisions of the First and Third Armies began advancing much more rapidly than expected, however, overpowering everything in their path, and they overran some of these Jed teams shortly after the teams jumped in.

Jeds operating ahead of General Bradley's army group found life behind enemy lines to be even more hazardous than usual as areas became congested with retreating German formations. Movement by Jeds became so risky that some teams, like Augustus, found it necessary to operate in civilian clothes, forfeiting whatever protection of combatant status the uniform might have provided in the event of capture. The provisions of the Geneva Conventions offered no protection to soldiers operating in civilian clothes and carrying false identification papers.

News soon reached team Augustus that U.S. ground troops were approaching Soissons, and the Jeds decided to attempt to get through to them. They discussed how to go about it with Seigneur and Costeaux and made plans to leave on Monday morning, August 28.

German forces withdrawing through French towns and villages often grabbed everything they could carry—and it wasn't just a matter of soldiers filling their pockets. In one case, an Allied unit captured a thirty-four-car train headed for Germany, loaded to the hilt with wine and cognac, liver paste and sardines, canned foods and margarine.[15] On Sunday morning, Seigneur and Costeaux went out to get tobacco, but a German convoy had pulled out at five that morning and enemy troops had beaten them to it—there was none to be had. Some SS troops broke the lock to the courtyard where Costeaux kept the truck and looked it over, seeming tempted to take it. Costeaux and the others felt very lucky, for they had just removed some munitions from the vehicle and hidden them nearby. The truck didn't prove enough of a temptation, though, and the Germans left it alone. Luckily, it would still be available to haul the Jeds the next day.

The Jeds planned to head out to the west of Soissons on Monday, because that was where they expected to find U.S. troops approaching the town. But the Americans weren't the only ones heading for the Soissons area. Germans, too, would soon be approaching, from the northwest.

By late August, Germany's Fifth Panzer Army was an army in name only. On the twenty-eighth, the army reported that it had only twenty-four tanks, thirteen hundred men, and sixty artillery pieces remaining. In all, only about one hundred and twenty German tanks had made it back across the Seine to join in the withdrawal toward Germany.[16] The Allies estimated that, since D-Day, the enemy had lost the equivalent of about thirty divisions.[17] What remained of the enemy marched eastward, occasionally making a stand to fight for time to create a more orderly withdrawal. Rear guard formations tried to slow the advancing Allies, tried to provide some protection for the dusty columns of tired tanks and half-tracks, trucks and staff cars, horse-drawn artillery, and even troops on bicycle. The rear guards were often overrun or cut off by Allied units, however, or were simply brushed aside to be mopped up by follow-on units or by the FFI.

Overwhelmed by the speed of the Allied advance, German troops often were taken completely by surprise. On one occasion, the 3rd Armored Division caught a group of Germans resting under a stand of trees, drinking wine. The Wehrmacht was fleeing France like a street gang being run out of a rival's turf. It was as if the great blitzkrieg machine had been thrown into reverse.

Hauptmann (Captain) Helmut Ritgen, a tank battalion commander in the Panzer Lehr Division, later wrote that, for stragglers and small groups of Germans, the retreat was "like running the gauntlet through a hate-filled enemy country in an uprising." Which, of course, is exactly what it was. Going on to assess the effectiveness of the Jedburghs and the FFI, Ritgen (who would retire from Germany's NATO contingent as a colonel in 1976) wrote, "As time went by and they gained experience, they developed into a real threat for the German withdrawal."[18]

Seigneur and Jean Plantier were in the Soissons area on Monday morning, and they needed to return to Rugny to pick up the Jeds. But Germans were on the roads in such numbers that the men could not risk making the trip with their weapons, so they hid the guns in Vaux, a hamlet just west of Soissons. Then they drove back to Seigneur's command post, arriving at noon, and began preparations for driving the Jeds toward the American lines. More Germans had arrived in the village and, when it came time for the men to leave, they had to be careful.

The Jeds had heard that American forces were only seven or eight miles away, and they had heard right. The 3rd Armored Division had crossed the Marne on Sunday and was approaching Soissons and Braine, fighting through elements of two German divisions to get there.

At one o'clock the truck arrived at the Mathieu farm. The FFI men helped the Jeds load their equipment in the back and hide it under a pile of rags. An FFI man named Émile Fortier joined them as they all climbed aboard and got under way. They headed for a town on the Oise River about nineteen miles west of Laon, where they thought they could make contact with an American unit, but they first intended to stop at Vaux and retrieve the weapons Seigneur and Plantier had hidden there that morning. Suddenly, about a half mile before reaching Vaux, the men saw a column of tanks on the horizon.

"What's that?" asked Fortier.

"They're American tanks," answered Major Bonsall.

"Hell, they're shooting. Maybe they'll shoot at us."

"Maybe," Bonsall said, "and they aim well."[19]

The men in the truck had made it this far without incident, so they took a chance and drove straight for the lead tank. Bonsall and Delviche were determined to get the information they had gathered on German defenses north of the Aisne to the American commander. After delivering the information, the Jed officers hoped to be able to make their way back behind German lines again to continue their work. Perhaps, they thought, they would be able to break back through the lines tomorrow with the help of a patrol of three or four Sherman tanks.

When the truck reached the tank column, the Jeds got out and approached the lead tank. The men identified themselves and Major Bonsall asked to see the commander of the column. When they met the commander, Bonsall said he needed to be taken to the commanding general of the division, and arrangements were quickly made. Captain Delviche then told the FFI men to take the truck and return to Rugny and wait for the Jeds there.

The tanks were from the 3rd Armored Division, and by day's end they would seize two crossings over the Aisne, one at Soissons and another nearby. But they quickly ran into increased resistance from

ABOVE: Jedburgh team Frederick, one of the few teams with three nations represented, (left to right): Lt. Paul Bloch-Auroch (alias Aguirec) of France, 1st Sgt. Robert Kehoe of the U.S., and Maj. Adrian Wise of Britain. (*Robert R. Kehoe*)

RIGHT: Capt. Paul Cyr, American officer of Jedburgh team George. (*Donna J. Cyr*)

TOP: Troopship HMT (RM as a peacetime ocean liner *Queen Mary*, shown here arriving at New York in June 1945. The *Queen Mary* carried American Jedburgh radio operators from New York to Englan in December 1943, while her sister ship, HMT *Queen Elizabeth*, carried the officers. (*National Archives*)

LEFT: Main wing and front entrance of Milton Hall near Peterborough, Cambridgeshire, England. The Elizabethan country estate served as home for the Jedburghs from early February through mid-September 1944. (*National Archives*)

LEFT BOTTOM: Jeds firing .45-caliber pistols on the small arms range at Milto Hall. (*National Archives*)

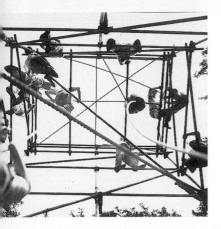

TOP LEFT: Jeds scaling a brick wall on the obstacle course at Milton Hall. (*National Archives*)

LEFT: Jeds on the confidence course at Milton Hall. (*National Archives*)

ABOVE: Jedburgh radio operators practice wireless Morse telegraphy communications at Milton Hall. (*National Archives*)

BELOW: Demolitions lecture in a gilded classroom at Milton Hall. (*National Archives*)

ABOVE: Lt. Jack Singlaub, Jedburgh and future major general in the U.S. Army, models full Jedburgh rigging for parachute jumping. The British parachutist helmet and jump smock were discarded, buried or otherwise hidden, upon landing. (*National Archives*)

RIGHT TOP: U.S. Army soldiers of the Office of Strategic Services at Area H near Holme, England, packing canisters to be parachuted to the French Resistance. (*National Archives*)

RIGHT MIDDLE: Ground crew personnel refuel a special operations B–24 Liberator at Harrington airfield in England. The specially modified bombers and their crews at Harrington belonged to the U.S. 801st Bombardment Group (Heavy), whose nickname was the Carpetbaggers. Similarly modified British bombers flew from secret bases such as Tempsford. (*National Archives*)

RIGHT BOTTOM: A maquis reception committee clearing a field serving as a drop zone after a parachute drop. Horse-drawn hay wagons owned by French farmers were often used to haul away the heavy metal containers which were filled with weapons and other supplies. (*Her Majesty's Stationery Office*)

TOP: An FFI group in Brittany flying the French tricolor in August 1944. Once provided with the tools of war, the Bretons proved themselves aggressive and effective in combat. (*National Archives*)

MIDDLE: The members of Jedburgh team Bruce in photos taken at Milton Hall for identification papers. (Left to right): Capt. William E. Colby (U.S.), French Lt. Camille M. Lelong (alias Jacques Favel), and French Lt. Roger Villebois (alias Louis Giry), the team's radio operator.

RIGHT: Lt. Col. Robert Powell (center) and members of his Special Forces Detachment 11, attached to the operations staff of General Patton's Third Army headquarters. (*National Archives*)

TOP LEFT: Maj. John H. Bonsall, U.S. Army, leader of Jedburgh team Augustus, was captured and killed on the night of August 30, 1944, in the hamlet of Barenton-sur-Serre in the Aisne department of France. (*Katherine Bonsall Strong*)

TOP MIDDLE: 1st Sgt. Roger E. Côté, U.S. Army, radio operator on Jedburgh team Augustus. Côté was captured and killed at Barenton-sur-Serre, France, on August 30, 1944, along with the team's two officers. (*Violette Côté Desmarais*)

TOP RIGHT: Three commanders who relied heavily on the FFI and Jedburghs in support of Operation Dragoon, the invasion of southern France. (Left to right) Lt. Gen. Lucian K. Truscott, VI Corps, Lt. Gen. Alexander M. Patch, Seventh Army, and Lt. Gen. Jacob L. Devers, Sixth Army Group. When Jedburgh Capt. Doug Bazata (U.S.) and British SOE Capt. George Millar sped on motorcycle across a bridge guarded by Germans to deliver information to advancing American forces, Gen. Truscott invited them to dine with him in his tent. Gen. Devers recommended approval of the Jedburgh concept as commander of American troops in the European Theater in 1943. (*National Archives*)

ABOVE: Jedburgh team Chloroform, accompanied by men of the local maquis, enter the mountain town of Gap in southeastern France on the day of its liberation, August 20, 1944. Lt. Henry D. McIntosh (U.S.) is the tall figure, fourth from right. (*Henry D. McIntosh*)

TOP: Lt. Gen. Alexander M. Patch, Seventh Army commander, reviews FFI troops in St-Tropez, France, in August 1944. (*National Archives*)

BOTTOM: Teenage FFI members in southern France bring in a wounded German prisoner. All three maquisards are armed with British Sten submachine guns, while the center man also carries the German soldier's rifle. (*National Archives*)

TOP: The town of Besançon, on the Doubs River, near the area where Jedburgh team Cedric operated with SOE circuit organizer Capt. George Millar. (*U.S. Army photo*)

LEFT: 1st Sgt. Richard C. Floyd, American radio operator on Jedburgh team Cedric. (*Richard C. Floyd*)

Germans dug in north of the river. The Americans were probably unaware that they were running Hitler's senior commander in the west out of his headquarters. Field Marshal Walther Model, commander of Army Group B and acting commander in chief of Germany's Western Front, had temporarily occupied the Margival complex north of Soissons. After less than two weeks in the place, however, he was now forced to scurry sixty miles to the north to relocate his headquarters west of Cambrai.[20]

It was a thin defense which the Germans had thrown up along the Aisne; and by the morning of the twenty-ninth, in bleak weather, Americans were pouring across the river. Near Soissons and Braine tanks and anti-aircraft guns of the 3rd Armored Division shot up three German trains.

Late that day, Jedburgh team Augustus briefed officers of the 3rd Armored Division's tactical command post, which was setting up in a village about six miles east of Soissons. The division staff was very interested in any information the Jeds had on the Margival fortifications. Division units were already crossing the Aisne and earlier FFI reports had indicated the existence of expansive concrete fortifications in the area.[21] The Jeds gave them everything they had.

That evening, team Augustus was driven by jeep back to the village where Seigneur had his command post. The village was by then in American hands, and Gaston Costeaux decided to drive the three Jeds to Soissons, where they took a room at the Hotel de la Croix d'Or and remained there until five the next afternoon.

Sherman tanks and self-propelled artillery, tank destroyers and anti-aircraft guns, trucks and half-tracks continued to pour across the Aisne throughout Tuesday and Wednesday as the 3rd Armored Division expanded its bridgehead, seizing the high ground north of the river and then pushing out to the northeast. Troops soon found the extensive concrete fortifications at Margival and, to their great relief, they found the complex vacant. The enemy had fallen back to the north. And the Allied troops had no idea of the prize they had just missed—Field Marshal Model, senior German commander in the west.

A dozen miles ahead, atop a long narrow ridge, with its thirteenth-century Gothic cathedral rising above all else like an over-sized cake decoration, lay the town of Laon, capital of the Aisne department. A thousand years earlier it had been a royal city and capital of all of France. From its ridge-top perch, Laon looked out over the broad flat plains of the Aisne more than three hundred feet below, a panorama of pasturelands and rivers and gray villages huddled around church steeples.

Wednesday, August 30, began as another day of dreary weather with an overcast sky. Troops of the 1st Infantry Division, on the 3rd Armored's left flank, had been marching through the same wheat fields south of Soissons, up the same chalky-white farm roads, through the same homely villages, that the division's dough-boys had known twenty-six years earlier during the great Aisne-Marne counteroffensive of World War I. Now they entered Soissons and took over security of the crossing sites while the 3rd Armored Division pushed on, moving into Laon in force, catching up with lead elements which had entered the town the night before. There the division shot up three more German troop trains, and reconnaissance elements moved out about three miles to the north and east of the town. That afternoon the Germans began forming another thin defense, this time north of Laon.

Fifth Panzer Army had ordered its 116th Panzer Division, after crossing the Seine, to pull back to an area east of Laon, where it was to be refurbished. By the twenty-ninth, the division was still about seventy miles west of Laon, but another German tank division was much closer.

With the British pushing them from the west, officers of the Fifth Panzer Army began to see a new threat from the U.S. forces advancing along their right flank. Swift action was needed to avoid encirclement by the American First Army's drive to the northeast across the Germans' path of retreat. The 9th SS Panzer Division had been ordered to pull back eastward to the Somme, and while the division's rear guard was still engaged by British armor west of Amiens, its lead units were sent southward to establish blocking positions in the area between Laon and Soissons. In fact, the regimental-size combat group, or kampfgruppe, which attacked toward Soissons to establish the blocking positions constituted virtually all the division's remaining effective combat power. The group probably had no more than five to ten tanks left, however, and it was stopped cold when it ran into the 3rd Armored Division at the Oise-Aisne Canal north of Soissons.[22]

That same day, lead elements of the 116th Panzer Division began arriving in the area northwest of Laon. At around noon on Wednesday, Generalleutnant (Major General) Gerhard Graf von Schwerin, commander of the 116th, learned that the Americans had already taken Laon. He immediately decided to establish an east-west defense line along the Serre River, about nine miles north of Laon. Units of the 116th began moving into position along the north bank of the Serre immediately and continued to do so throughout the night.[23]

By late in the day of August 30, units of the 9th SS Panzer Division were falling back from their fight with 3rd Armored Division on the canal north of Soissons. Moving northward, they skirted around to the west of American-occupied Laon. Then they turned back to the northeast and pulled into the area north of Laon and south of the Serre River.

By nightfall, American forces of the 3rd Armored Division had begun probing to the north of Laon.

Stormy weather had moved into the Aisne, and it had been cloudy and rainy all day on the thirtieth, although the sun briefly peeked through the clouds in the evening. Major Bonsall's team did not consider its mission complete, even though it no longer was needed in the southern Aisne because the area was in American hands. So the Jeds were determined to get back behind German lines and continue their work farther north. And they were certain that this was the time to cross back over the lines, while the stormy weather could help conceal their movement.

Because the Jeds had been operating in civilian clothes and had obtained false French identity papers, they decided that their best means of getting through would be to travel in one of the horse-drawn peasant carts so common to the area. Among the maquisards that team Augustus had been training was a somewhat older local farmer by the name of Magniez. The Jeds decided to go to his farm and seek help.

At about five in the afternoon the men left the hotel in Soissons. They had arranged for a 3rd Armored Division jeep to take them to Laon, and from there got a lift on a tank to their starting point, Magniez's farm, a few miles northwest of Laon. Captain Delviche was familiar with the area, and the team soon arrived at the home of Monsieur Magniez, whose farm was scarcely more than a mile from the village where Delviche had been born. The Jeds dined at the Magniez home and then prepared for their journey.

The three men still all wore civilian clothing: Bonsall in gray pants with a white shirt with black stripes; Delviche in black pants, a white shirt and a black tie with white polka dots, a gray hat, and a black leather jacket; and Côté in a gray woolen sweater over a blue shirt, and a Basque beret on his head.

Magniez arranged for the men to use a horse-drawn cart that the Germans had abandoned earlier that day. He hitched one of his horses to it and the Jeds loaded their gear on the cart and hid it as best they could. By about nine-thirty they were ready to leave.

According to the latest information the Jeds had, they judged that the German lines should be just south of Froidmont, a town about nine miles, by the main road, north of Laon. Magniez gave the men directions to the home of his brother-in-law in Froidmont and told them to go straight there. Captain Delviche was anxious to avoid any main roads, such as Route Nationale 2, which ran north from Laon to Froidmont. They would be less likely to run into German convoys, strongpoints, or roadblocks if they stuck to back roads.

Magniez explained that there was another route, a road which passed through a few villages before reaching Froidmont. It was a longer way—about fourteen or fifteen miles long—but it should be safer. The farmer then decided to ride with the Jeds part of the way, until he was sure they were on the right road. As the Jeds and Magniez set out in the cart, others from the local maquis, mostly armed farmers, waited in the barn next to the old man's farmhouse.

At around ten o'clock, confident that the Jeds knew the way, Magniez left them and returned to his farm. The road took the Jeds past one village, then along a stretch of about five miles before they reached the next. A mile or two after that, the road curved to the right, crossed a railroad track, then curved back to the left and through another village. The men still were about five miles from Froidmont and had one more village, Barenton-sur-Serre, which was a couple of miles short of their destination, to pass through.

Barenton-sur-Serre was a quiet commune of about a hundred people. The roar of guns and the bedlam of battle had been almost continuous in this area during the First World War, and the village had been partly destroyed by shelling. The place had been mostly spared devastation during this war, although it had been in this very area, back when the Germans invaded in May 1940, that a young brigadier named Charles de Gaulle had led his tank division in a briefly successful counterattack. All told, in two world wars the good people of Barenton had lived through eight years of German occupation.

By the evening of August 30, the Germans were attempting to stabilize their retreat somewhat by establishing, as much as their reduced capabilities allowed, a line of defense north of Laon, running east-to-west generally along the Serre River. Any delay of the Americans along this line would aid in the retreat of the German armies to the northeast. Barenton-sur-Serre lies just south of the Serre, in an area where there now were scattered elements of the 9th SS Panzer Division. The 116th Panzer Division occupied positions along the river's north bank. Small strongpoints or roadblocks—often consisting of a few tanks and some infantry—were hastily thrown up at key road intersections throughout the area.[24] And it was into this area that Jed team Augustus now drove the horse-drawn cart.

A light rain had begun falling earlier that night and at about 10:15 it became a downpour. Lightning and thunder added to the miserable wetness of the driving rain, making visibility and hearing hopeless for the Jeds in the horse cart.

Two and a half miles short of Froidmont the cart approached Barenton-sur-Serre from the southwest. They crossed over a railway bridge and came to an intersection just inside the village, near the station, and the men possibly did not even see the three German tanks which were posted at the crossroads.

Although no one in the village witnessed what happened next, the Jeds were apparently stopped by German troops who then searched the cart and found the team's American weapons, British radios, and other gear hidden in the back. At ten forty-five that night, the people of Barenton heard seven shots. First there were two, followed a short while later by five more in rapid succession. About thirty minutes later the German tanks pulled out and left Barenton-sur-Serre.

Sixteen-year-old Armand Rot was at his home—about a hundred and fifty yards from the intersection—when he heard the shots. Just as he looked outside he saw a frightened horse pass by pulling an empty cart.

Back at the Magniez farm, the small group of farmers gathered in the barn wondered if the Jedburghs had been successful in crossing the lines. Outside, the storm continued to rage. Suddenly, the barn door blew open and the men saw a huge shape silhouetted against the night. They watched as the huge figure slowly entered and approached Magniez. Then the men recognized the outline of the horse, which had come home.

When morning came, young Armand Rot and others from the village discovered three bodies lying in the mud near the intersection. None of the villagers recognized the dead men. But among the items found on the bodies were military identification cards. The bodies of John Bonsall and Jean Delviche were found side by side. That of Roger Côté was about a dozen yards away, on the other side of the road. He lay face down, his arms twisted, looking as if he had tried to make a run for it. Around his neck the villagers found a silver chain with a tiny cross and a medal inscribed: "I am a Catholic; please call a priest."

All three men had large head wounds. Nearby lay a seat from the cart and it looked as if it had been ripped out during a search. The cart would later be found in a village just north of Barenton.

The mayor and people of Barenton-sur-Serre buried the three men in unmarked graves in the cemetery next to the village's small St. Martin church. Armand Rot went home and made a French flag from pieces of cloth he found in his mother's chiffonier, then lay the tricolor on the graves. Members of a nearby maquis arrived and, despite the fact that Germans were still in the area, formed a guard of honor and performed a military funeral ceremony.

Later, Armand Rot recovered the flag he had made and gave it to some American soldiers who mounted it on their jeep.

The meager defense line which the Germans had established along the Serre quickly dissipated when the 3rd Armored Division began its attack northeast from Laon later that morning. From Laon, the division pushed on to the northeast for about twenty miles and then straight north toward Mons, Belgium, crossing the border on September 2, just eighteen days after crossing the Seine.

In a final attempt to reach Jedburgh team Augustus, which had gone silent, Special Force Headquarters transmitted a message on September 16, informing the team that its mission was ended and that the men should return to London at once.

Jedburgh team Augustus was one of many teams dropped into eastern France in late August and September that found it nearly impossible to do its job. Major Bonsall's team had been able to provide some information to the 3rd Armored Division, but even that was of no great importance by then. The team simply had not had enough time to properly organize, arm, and train the maquis of the Aisne to take advantage of the lucrative targets provided by the German convoys withdrawing through the area. And it might have been this which caused the men to believe that their mission was not accomplished, and compelled them to attempt to re-cross to enemy territory and continue on, when they could just as easily have considered their work finished once they had briefed the staff of 3rd Armored Division.

In the end, more than anything else, the Jeds of team Augustus fell victim to simple bad luck. They had really not done anything unsound, and they had been correct in reasoning that the storm would help to conceal their movement. Of the many times Jedburgh teams would pass through German checkpoints, they were the one team unlucky enough to be caught.

Only one other complete Jedburgh team was lost in France. Team Jacob, dropped into the Vosges Mountains of eastern France on the night of August 12–13, lost its French officer when he was killed in action and lost both British members when they were captured. The radio operator spent the rest of the war in a prison camp and was liberated at war's end, but the British officer was executed.

*   *   *

Just one month after Patton's Third Army had broken out at Avranches and swept into Brittany, the Allies were on the frontiers of Belgium and Luxembourg and were about to enter the regions of Alsace and Lorraine in eastern France. But they were soon to be joined by another American army and a Free French army, which were driving northward from the Mediterranean coast. For, on August 15, the same day that Jedburgh team Augustus had departed England for the Aisne, Allied forces had made amphibious and airborne landings on the south coast of France. And roughly two dozen Jedburgh teams would be dropped into southern France to organize FFI support for those ground forces.

10

WAR COMES TO THE RIVIERA

ONE danger that the Jedburghs, and the circuit organizers before
them, always warned resistance groups about was that of
attempting a full-scale uprising before the time was right.
Guerrillas were most effective against modern mechanized armies
when those armies were simultaneously fighting conventional
forces, or were at least under the threat of imminent engagement
by such forces. Any attempt by guerrillas to engage large conventional combat forces in a toe-to-toe fight could be disastrous for the
guerrillas. But the Allies were not always successful in persuading
the FFI to wait for a signal that the time was right to begin full-
scale guerrilla attacks against the Germans.

The fact that Grenoble, in the Alps of southeastern France, is
known today as a former site of the Winter Olympics says much
about the terrain of the region. Southwest of Grenoble lies a high
mountain plateau, twenty-five miles long and ten miles wide,
called the Vercors Massif. It is a natural citadel, a spectacular
mountaintop wilderness of dense pine and beech forests with intermittent rolling grasslands, and in 1944 it could be reached only by
discreet trails up steep, craggy mountain walls. There were deep
gorges and mountain outcroppings, with one peak reaching nearly
seven thousand feet.

Shortly after the Allied landings in Normandy, a large resistance force, which had been gathering on the Vercors Massif for the past year, had prematurely risen so boldly and in such numbers that the Germans could not ignore it. By the middle of June, some four thousand guerrilla fighters had rallied on the plateau and a German division based in Grenoble had begun probing the Vercors defenses. American bombers dropped more than four hundred containers of arms on June 25 and on Bastille Day, July 14, seventy-two B-17 Flying Fortresses from England dropped another 862 containers.

These drops were made in daylight, however, and as the maquis tried to gather up the containers from the open fields, German planes arrived and strafed them. Then, on July 19, German forces numbering nearly fourteen thousand, with tanks, armored cars, and artillery, attacked the resistance stronghold. After fighting for two days, and losing more than six hundred men, the overmatched maquis were forced to disperse. And then the Germans began taking their revenge, pillaging and burning villages on the plateau and killing innocent civilians.[1]

The FFI had learned a tough lesson, but the survivors of the Vercors debacle would be ready to work with Jedburgh teams and other special forces to rebuild, rearm, and re-engage the Germans. An American OSS Operational Group had fought on the Vercors plateau and a few Jedburgh teams had been in southern France at the time, but soon the region would receive many more.

When Henry McIntosh left his West Palm Beach, Florida, home in the fall of 1939 his goal was to become a physician. He entered the pre-med program at Davidson College in North Carolina just about the time Hitler's armies were pulverizing Poland to begin the European war. By the end of 1942, McIntosh had completed all requirements for his BS degree and had been accepted to the medical schools of the University of Pennsylvania, Johns Hopkins, and Thomas Jefferson University in Philadelphia. He was to begin medical school in January.

But that winter McIntosh enlisted in the army and because he had been in the ROTC program at Davidson (though he hadn't completed it) he was inducted as a corporal at Camp Blanding, Florida, in February 1943. Almost immediately, the army sent him to Officer Candidate School at Fort Benning, and he graduated with a commission in the infantry in late May. He stayed on at Benning for further training, completing the parachute jump course and the parachute demolition course, and then he was assigned to the post's 542nd Parachute Infantry, an airborne replacement training unit, in July.

That fall, the Jedburgh recruiter came to Fort Benning, and when he reviewed the qualification records of the regiment's officers he noticed that Second Lieutenant Henry McIntosh had taken two years of French in college. The twenty-two-year-old platoon leader was summoned to a large gym to hear the recruiter's pitch along with a few dozen other officers. McIntosh volunteered and reported to Washington in early November.

By the spring of 1944, McIntosh was going through the Jedburgh training program at Milton Hall. But in late April his team and fourteen others were told to pack up their gear; they were being shipped out to North Africa. Earlier that month, British and American special operations planners had proposed sending fifteen Jedburgh teams to North Africa to prepare for insertion from there into the south of France. Eisenhower's operations officer approved the transfer and, on May 2, the fifteen teams boarded a ship called the *Capetown Castle* bound for Oran. They would be joined by another ten teams in June.

To administer the insertion and resupply of special forces teams into southern France, and to maintain radio communications with them, an organization similar to Special Force Headquarters was created in North Africa. The British had established an SOE mission near Algiers in 1942. Code-named Massingham, it was located at a former seaside beach resort called the Club de Pins, at Cap Matifou, fifteen miles west of Algiers. OSS had set up its own office in Algiers the following year, and in May 1944 the two were combined to form the Special Project Operations Center, or SPOC.[2] Although SPOC was administratively subordinate to Allied Force Headquarters (AFHQ), the Mediterranean Theater command, it was to be under the operational direction of SHAEF headquarters in London. It was to be, in effect, a satellite office of Special Force

Headquarters. All operational orders and guidance would pass directly from SFHQ in London to SPOC, although close coordination was maintained with the operations section at AFHQ. A compound of tents and Quonset huts was built to house the Jedburghs as well as OSS Operational Groups. Most missions would be flown from an airfield near the town of Blida, about thirty miles southwest of Algiers.[3]

Lieutenant Henry McIntosh, the lanky six-foot-two future physician, liked the medical significance of the code name given his Jed team during their mission briefing.[4] The team of McIntosh and two Frenchmen would be known as Jed team Chloroform. Leading it was Captain Jacques Martino, a personable man in his early twenties—about the same age as McIntosh—athletically thin, and dark-haired. Martino had been recruited in North Africa, and he knew that his parents' home in France had been taken over by the Germans. Corporal Jean Nicole would be team Chloroform's radio operator.* The team had first been alerted soon after the Allied landings in Normandy, but bad weather had postponed its deployment until the end of June. This team would be the sixth Jedburgh team to deploy to southern France from North Africa.

Team Chloroform's mission would take the men to the beautiful Rhône Alps of southeastern France, between the valley of the mighty south-flowing Rhône River and the mountainous Italian border. There, they were to organize guerrilla operations in the departments of the Drôme and the Hautes-Alpes (High Alps), a land of breathtaking mountain scenery.

A few days after Jedburgh team Chloroform's jump to a drop zone in the Drôme on the night of June 29, the men were taken to a meeting of resistance leaders and special forces men. They were to meet some of the officers with whom they would be working.

One of the men they met was a handsome British officer who went by the field name Roger. A six-footer in his late twenties with

---

* Jacques Martino's real name was Jacques Martin; that of Jean Nicole was Jean Sassi.

a manicured mustache, he was actually Lieutenant Colonel Francis Cammaerts, and he had been the head of one of SOE's most successful circuits since March of the previous year.

Cammaerts' Jockey circuit was one of the largest and one of the longest-surviving because of his strict security practices. He never spent more than two or three nights in the same place and almost no one in the circuit knew exactly where he was at any given moment.[5] In fact, Cammaerts seemingly had something of a sixth sense when it came to security. When SOE sent him to the field in the spring of 1943, they had intended for him to become Henri Frager's lieutenant, before Frager had gone north to set up the Donkeyman circuit. But Cammaerts had backed out of that relationship largely because he mistrusted Frager's sidekick Roger Bardet.[6]

Cammaerts was a former schoolmaster, and he might have seemed an unusual choice for a circuit organizer. He had come from a distinguished family, his father a well-known Belgian poet, his mother a Shakespearean actress, and his grandmother a former Bayreuth opera singer. Early in the war, he had registered as a conscientious objector, but the death of a brother in the RAF had helped to change his outlook on the war.

By the summer of 1944, Cammaerts controlled a circuit with some ten thousand maquisards, about half of them armed, spread over an area that essentially included all of France south of Lyon and east of the Rhône River. He had so much territory to cover that he often used a motorcycle to travel about.

One man who was at the gathering of resistance leaders needed no introduction to the Jeds of team Chloroform. He was Major Neil Marten, the British officer and only surviving member of Jedburgh team Veganin, which had been dropped into the Drôme on the second night after D-Day. Marten's team had run into trouble that very first night when his radio operator was killed on the jump because his static line had not been hooked up securely. He and the French officer on his team had just received reinforcements, though, in the form of a two-man Jed team—an American officer and a French-Canadian radio operator—sent in four days ago to join them. (Six weeks later, the American officer was captured and spent the remainder of the war in a prison camp in Germany.)

The Jeds also met an FFI leader who was introduced as General

Joseph. He was actually General Henri Zeller, FFI commander for the entire southeastern part of France.[7] Zeller was a career army officer who, after the fall of France, had served as a colonel on the general staff of the Armistice Army at Vichy until it was disbanded in late 1942. As with many of the army's officers, he had then joined the resistance, and worked hard to maintain a military command structure within the FFI of the southeast.

The men of team Chloroform also met a subordinate of Zeller's, an FFI major called Hermine, who was military chief for the Drôme department. Hermine was a former sergeant who had been mobilized in 1939 and later had entered the French air academy. He, too, served in the Vichy government's Armistice Army after the French defeat in 1940, then later joined the resistance and made a name for himself as a flamboyant leader in the Lyon area. Hermine was the type of person who is often described as "colorful"; his fulsome personality made him popular with some but antagonized others.

In early 1944, the Drôme was estimated to hold slightly fewer than five hundred active maquisards, backed up by as many as fifteen hundred sédentaires, as the sedentary reserve—those ready to leave home and join the active maquis as soon as more arms were available—were called.[8] About 70 percent of the Drôme maquisards belonged to the communist FTP, however, and they had grown tired of Hermine's pompousness. The group was demanding his removal from command of the department, and General Zeller had finally agreed to move him. But Zeller thought highly of Hermine and he decided to move the young officer by promoting him to lieutenant colonel and giving him command of the entire "Central Alps" region. Jedburgh team Chloroform had arrived just as Hermine was moving his command post to an area north of Gap, the principal town of the Hautes-Alpes department farther to the east.[9]

One of the sabotage tasks which had been assigned to team Chloroform during its mission briefing was the destruction of a railway line between Gap and Valence. But the men learned from Zeller and Hermine that the FFI had already blown the line three times since D-Day, removing the rails from the scene each time to make repair by the Germans more difficult. In fact, the men were told, the line had not been put back into full operation since the Normandy invasion had begun. The Jeds were taken to inspect some of the maquis troops in the area and to verify the destruction of the Valence-Gap rail line.

Then Hermine and General Zeller asked the Jeds to go with Hermine and to work with him in the Hautes-Alpes, where there were an estimated three thousand Germans. To the Jeds, Hermine appeared to be a strong leader, and they seemed to get on well with him. They also thought that they would be more useful in the Hautes-Alpes, where there weren't as many Allied special forces already operating as there were in the Drôme, and so they agreed to move east into the mountains.

The Jeds set out with a small group of maquisards in a car and a truck on the fourth of July and soon found themselves in the beautiful terrain of the High Alps. They crossed rugged mountain ridges and passed through green meadows, where intermittent scrublands and wheat fields surrounded quaint gray villages with tile roofs the color of old pennies. Towering abruptly in the background were impressive, sometimes snow-capped mountains, with sparse stands of fir and pine clinging to the lower slopes.

After a journey which included a three-day gun battle with Germans in a mountain pass, team Chloroform arrived at a village in a valley northeast of Gap on the night of July 9. But the men soon realized that the villagers here were unaccustomed to resistance activity. Mistaking the Jeds for the hated Milice, the civilians ran for their homes. Then, as Henry McIntosh later reported, "One youngster rushed at us with a Sten and demanded our surrender." The Jeds, however, soon convinced the boy that they were friends, and he ran off to inform the rest of the town.

The Jeds set up a command post nearby and immediately radioed Algiers for a supply drop. They were now about twenty miles northeast of Gap. In addition to arming maquis groups throughout the area, the team needed replenishment of their own supplies, having left theirs cached back in the Drôme.

Then the men met a priest from a nearby village who told them of a drop which had been made in the area about a year earlier. The priest had helped to hide the weapons at the time, and he led the Jeds to the storage site. Luckily, they were also able to find some old French rifles and, at last, the team got down to the business of training guerrilla fighters.

For the next month Martino, McIntosh, and Nicole armed and trained maquis groups throughout the wild, roller-coaster alpine country around Gap, from the rugged Dévoluy Massif in the west to Barcelonnette and the rugged Queyras region in the east, and from Sisteron in the south to Briançon in the north.[10] The men joined the maquis in skirmishes with Germans along Route Nationale 85, the major north-south highway through the mountains which was lined with terraced villages. The highway entered Gap from the south and continued on northward from there to Grenoble. Since 1932, the road had been known as the Route Napoléon because it was up this road that Napoleon Bonaparte and his supporters had journeyed in March 1815 after his escape from exile on the island of Elba.

Team Chloroform also tried to bring in more arms and supplies for the survivors of the Vercors maquis. They began receiving air drops on July 24 on a plateau in the mountains northwest of Gap. Weasel was the code name given to the drop zone atop the plateau—some fifteen hundred to eighteen hundred meters above sea level—and by month's end the Jeds had received more than sixty tons of weapons and ammunition there. They tried in vain to get some of the material to the Vercors. But in the end they distributed all of it among their own maquis.[11]

By early August the Jeds estimated that they had armed and trained approximately fifteen hundred men in the area around Gap, and Hermine thought that his FFI was strong enough to force the town's German garrison to surrender.

The southern Alpine town of Gap sat in a glacier-carved valley where agriculture benefited from a richly fertile soil. It had been a staging post on the north-south route since Roman times and was still a key town on the Route Napoléon. And it would be an important route northward to Grenoble for Allied armies when the invasion of southern France came. From Gap, roads led eastward up to the mountain passes into Italy—roads which could be an avenue of approach if the Germans chose to send armored units across the border and into France.

But before he tried to gain the surrender of the German garrison in Gap, Hermine first wanted to further isolate the garrison by closing off the escape route to the east, a route which might also be used to reinforce the enemy in Gap. To cut this route, a key bridge over the Durance River in the mountains east of Gap, at a village called Savines, would have to be blown. On the afternoon of the fourteenth, the Jeds took forty men and the necessary explosives and set out. The steep approach to Savines was murderous to anyone unaccustomed to walking over such mountainous terrain. The maquis of the region had grown up hiking these mountains, but Lieutenant McIntosh—although in peak condition from months of Jed training—strained to keep up. Leg muscles screamed for relief as lungs labored in the thin mountain air. Eventually the men reached the long bridge and placed their charges. Then, on the afternoon of the fifteenth, a tremendous blast dropped the bridge into the Durance. Every escape route out of Gap had been cut with the exception of the road heading south toward the coast.[12]

An invasion of southern France had been envisioned by the Allies since the fall of 1943. Early plans for Operation Anvil, as it was called, envisioned landings on the beaches of the French Riviera at about the same time as the Overlord landings in Normandy. Such an assault in the south, it was hoped, would hold German forces in southern France that might otherwise be sent to Normandy. The British had argued instead for an operation in the Balkans, with Allied forces striking northward toward Austria. But in the end, and despite British objections, the coast of southern France was chosen as the landing site as much for logistical as for operational reasons; the capture of Marseilles would provide the Allies another badly needed port.

The timing of the invasion, however, came to be driven not by strategy but by landing craft production. To ensure availability of the required number of landing craft for Overlord, the Anvil operation had to be postponed for more than two months.

Commanding the invasion force was a veteran of the fighting on Guadalcanal, Lieutenant General Alexander M. Patch. Troops of his Seventh U.S. Army began coming ashore in the St-Tropez area on the morning of Tuesday, August 15. Patch's invasion force included an American corps of three infantry divisions pulled fresh from the fighting in Italy, Free French forces eventually amounting to an army of two corps, a division-size provisional airborne unit which included both British and American paratroopers, and an independent American-Canadian special forces unit. Air support was provided by a tactical air command operating from Corsica. Because it was feared that the operation's code name, Anvil, had been compromised, the name was changed to Dragoon two weeks before the landings.

German forces defending the Mediterranean coast of France belonged to the Nineteenth Army, and in the middle of August it consisted of five infantry divisions and two reserve divisions. Then, virtually on the eve of the invasion, the Germans had sent the 11th Panzer Division, then at nearly full strength, from the Atlantic coast to the southeast to reinforce the Nineteenth Army.

Seventh Army commanders were relying on strong support from the French resistance, and planners estimated that there were as many as fifteen thousand to twenty thousand trained and armed maquis fighters in southeastern France. Another thirty thousand to forty thousand were estimated to be standing by, waiting for additional arms to be dropped. In fact, the expectation of strong support from the resistance had been a factor in the Allies' decision to launch the invasion.[13] General Eisenhower had reported on how FFI support for the Overlord operation had "exceeded his most optimistic anticipations," and the Allies hoped to build an FFI force as large as eighty-four thousand in southern France.[14] General Wilson, the theater commander in the Mediterranean, planned to drop as many supplies as he could, but he had a limited number of aircraft in North Africa for such missions. Eisenhower offered to help from his end by arming fifty-three thousand guerrillas through air drops from England-based American bombers, two hundred to three hundred sorties in all.[15]

Wilson's staff had coordinated with the Special Project Operations Center to provide the FFI with a list of targets to be attacked in support of the invasion. The staff had been kept abreast of German movements and activity throughout the planning period by reports from the maquis. And, as with the Overlord operation, execution orders signaling the FFI to hit their designated targets had been broadcast by the BBC on August 14 in the form of pre-arranged messages.[16]

At General Patch's Seventh Army headquarters, special operations planning and coordination was the responsibility of a sixty-four-man British-American attachment called No. 4 Special Forces Unit.

By this time, it had become obvious to the German high command, and even to Hitler, that France was all but lost, and that Germany's only hope lay in saving the greatest number of tanks, artillery pieces, and troops as possible to defend the homeland at its western border. On August 17, two days after the Dragoon landings, Hitler sent a message to his army group commander in southern France ordering him to begin withdrawing all of his forces back toward the Rhine. The only exception was to be a small force remaining at the ports of Marseilles and Toulon, and they were to be ordered to fight to the last man to keep these ports out of the hands of the Allies. Because the message went out by radio on an Enigma cipher machine, however, its contents were quickly provided to General Patch in the top secret Ultra message traffic. So Patch was reading the withdrawal order at about the same time as the German commander.[17]

Major General Lucien Truscott, the American corps commander under Patch, had planned, once his force was firmly ashore, to create a small, rapidly mobile strike force. While the main thrust of Seventh Army would be up the valley of the Rhône River, this force would strike northward farther to the east, up the historic highway known as the Route Napoléon, with the objective of reaching Grenoble as quickly as possible. Information about the planned withdrawal of the German Nineteenth Army added the opportunity of an envelopment by such a rapidly moving Allied force, hoping to drive northward fast enough to cut off the retreating Germans.

On August 18, the provisional unit was quickly formed—a battalion of motorized infantry, two companies of Sherman tanks, a company of tank destroyers, a battalion of self-propelled artillery, a cavalry reconnaissance squadron, and engineers and other support units. Command of the unit went to the deputy corps commander, Brigadier General Frederick B. Butler, and the unit became known as Task Force Butler.

Throughout the planning for Operation Anvil (Dragoon), and during the two-week period immediately following the landings, Seventh Army had some concern about the possibility of German reinforcements arriving from northern Italy. Along the mountainous border with France, there were five Alpine passes through which such a threat could emerge. On August 18, the Jeds of team Chloroform received word that a Panzer division was approaching Gap from Italy and would be coming south and west on the hairpin mountain road from Guillestre. It had to be stopped. The Jeds saw three possible routes which might be used by the tanks to cross the wide Durance River. They could use a bridge on the main route or they could take either of two secondary routes. Knowing that the Allies might need to use the bridges later, the Jeds decided to block all three routes without destroying them.

In the early morning hours of the nineteenth, trucks were put in place to block the main bridge. But when the Jeds went to the two smaller bridges they found that an FFI group from another district had already blown both of them.

If the Route Napoléon was to be used by the Americans as a speedy road to Grenoble to outflank the Germans, some key towns along the route had to be secured as soon as possible. One of these key towns, Gap, was in Jedburgh team Chloroform's area. Hermine had sent a message to the thousand-man German garrison in Gap on August 17 demanding its surrender, and two days later the Germans gave their answer. They understood the hopelessness of their situation but preferred to wait and surrender to an American unit, which they understood was already in Sisteron, thirty miles to the south.

So on the morning of Saturday, August 19, Captain Martino, Lieutenant McIntosh, and two FFI officers headed south to make contact with the American unit. They soon met vehicles of the 117th Cavalry Reconnaissance Squadron, the vanguard of Task Force Butler. It was the highly mobile recon squadron's job to probe ahead of the main part of the advancing task force with its half-tracks, light tanks, jeeps, and command cars, and locate the enemy. The main body of Task Force Butler had advanced roughly ninety miles inland, a third of the way to Grenoble, and was at Sisteron.[18]

The Jeds and the FFI officers proceeded to General Butler's command post, descending from the limestone mountains around Gap into the valley of the broad Durance River. They headed southward until the valley closed in at the confluence of the Durance and another river and where the Durance then cut between two mountains. At that spot lay the town of Sisteron, stretched out along the west bank of the Durance. It was an ochre town—pale yellow buildings with old rust-colored tile roofs—and it had a Mediterranean look and feel about it, unlike the more alpine character of Gap and the country to the north. At the point where the mountains on either side of the Durance pinched right up to the river's banks, the town was squeezed tight and narrow between the river along one side and the base of a nearly vertical wall of rock on the other.

Perched on a mountaintop high above were the remains of an impressive eleventh-century stone citadel, indicating that the strategic importance of the town's location, sitting as it does at a natural choke point, had been recognized for a very long time. Sadly, American bombers had largely destroyed the medieval citadel only four days earlier, at the time of the landings on the Riviera coast, because it had been occupied by German troops. Only the fortress's keep and sentry walk remained undamaged.

The Jeds found General Butler's command post just south of town. Martino and McIntosh met the white-haired Butler and explained the situation in Gap, and told of the German desire to surrender only to American forces. Could the general send an element of his task force ahead with the Jeds to accept it?

Butler agreed and sent a platoon of tanks and a reconnaissance element back with the Jeds at five that afternoon. The Jeds arranged for maquis groups to approach Gap from the direction of the three blocked roads while the tank platoon approached the town from the south. But it soon became clear that the Germans had changed their minds about surrendering, and a fierce battle raged for two hours. When the fighting was over, some twelve hundred Germans surrendered to the maquis and were turned over to the American recon force. According to General Truscott, the American corps commander, similar action occurred not far away five days later, when some four thousand Germans surrendered to the U.S. 36th Infantry Division rather than to the maquisards who had them surrounded.[19]

Intelligence reports indicating that the German Nineteenth Army had been ordered to withdraw northward up the eastern bank of the Rhône had now reached General Truscott, commander of the American VI Corps. Late on the night of the twentieth, he sent a message to General Butler ordering him to move his task force west to Montelimar, on the Rhône River, to block the enemy's withdrawal. The 36th Infantry Division, which had been following Butler, would continue north on the Route Napoléon, through Gap and on toward Grenoble.

Seventh Army, in what came to be called the Champagne Campaign, pushed northward at a pace the troops had never known during the months of fighting in Italy. Division command posts moved many times a day, and signalmen laid as much as a hundred and sixty miles of wire every twenty-four hours.[20] Quartermaster drivers stayed at the wheel twenty to twenty-four hours a day to keep up, as supply lines from the beaches grew steadily longer. One driver, returning to the beaches with a truckload of German prisoners, reported to those in the rear that the maquis was "going wild" and that the Germans were "surrendering by the thousands."[21]

All along the Rhône Valley the maquis were taking a terrible toll on the enemy. Sergeant Audie Murphy of the 3rd Infantry Division—later to earn the Congressional Medal of Honor, a battlefield commission, and the distinction by war's end of being America's most decorated soldier—later recalled how the infantry would sometimes "find whole towns liberated by the FFI and waiting our entrance."[22] When a *Stars and Stripes* correspondent asked a staff sergeant in the 45th Infantry Division about the maquis, the noncom remarked, "They've been terrific. Boy have they saved us trouble."[23]

With help from the FFI, the 36th Infantry Division took the

mountain resort city of Grenoble on August 23, and the bells of the city's university echoed throughout the valley. Back on the coast, Marseilles and Toulon, with their valuable ports, were in Allied hands by the twenty-eighth.

Tough battles were fought by American and Free French forces at blocking positions north of Montélimar, on the Rhône, through the end of August. But, in the end, the better part of five German divisions broke through and continued up the valley toward Lyon, France's second city, eighty miles to the north.

On August 30, just as the Americans were approaching Lyon, General Truscott learned that the FFI wanted to take the city, which had been a hotbed of resistance since early in the war. And, for political reasons, the Allied high command preferred that French forces enter the city first. So when an American division reached Lyon in the first days of September, it was ordered to stay to the east of the city. The maquis, aided by two Jedburgh teams and four OSS Operational Groups, were already fighting within the city. When the commander of the 36th Infantry Division finally sent a patrol of officers into Lyon on September 2, the men found that the maquis had cleared the city of Germans. The next day a Free French infantry division entered Lyon from the west.

Team Chloroform continued to work with the maquis of the Hautes-Alpes on into September, providing protection to Seventh Army's right flank and blocking German forces on the roads leading from the mountain passes along the Italian border. By September 20, however, its work was finished. Nearly three months after jumping into the Drôme, team Chloroform went to Grenoble, then on to Paris, and on the twenty-fifth they flew to London.

Seventh Army continued the chase, advancing twenty-five to forty miles a day in an attempt to keep up with the Germans as the enemy raced toward the Belfort Gap. The Germans would next try to delay them at Besançon, a fortified city of about eighty thousand on the Doubs River southwest of Belfort.

11

UKRAINIANS IN THE FFI

BY late August, General Bradley's and General Montgomery's army groups were pursuing the Germans eastward from Normandy while American and French forces were driving northward after landing on the Mediterranean coast. The east-bound and north-bound Allied armies were on a course to converge near the town of Dijon in eastern France.

What remained of Germany's army in southern France was racing to reach an area in the mountainous eastern part of France near the borders of Germany and Switzerland. Known throughout history as the Gate of Burgundy, the Belfort Gap is a natural fifteen-mile-wide pass between the Jura Mountains, girdling the Swiss Alps to the south, and the much older and heavily forested Vosges Mountains to the north, in Alsace, just across the Rhine from Germany's Black Forest. It had been a strategic corridor since Roman times, and in August 1944 it provided the surest route for German forces trying to withdraw into southern Germany to establish a defense along the Rhine. And the primary route for the Germans to use through this picturesque region called the Franche-Comté was the road leading up the valley of the Doubs River, running northeastward from Besançon to Belfort.

Special Force Headquarters hoped to make the most of the guerrilla warfare opportunities provided by such a concentration of enemy movement through such a narrow corridor. On Friday, August 11, SFHQ called three more Jedburgh teams down to London from Milton Hall to be briefed for deployment to the region. One of those teams was assigned the code name Cedric, and it was led by probably the most flamboyant of the American Jedburgh officers.

Captain Douglas DeWitt Bazata was a modern-day swashbuckler. In a unit full of colorful personalities, he was in a class by himself, unabashedly contemptuous of military rank and never fully submissive to uniformed authority. Fellow Jedburgh Captain Bernard Knox would later write that Bazata "was famous among us for a brazen audacity, both physical and verbal, that took people's breath away and enabled him to get away with actions and remarks that were, in a military milieu, outrageous. He used to address full colonels, for example, as 'Sugar.'"[1] The rusty-haired thirty-three-year-old former Marine from Pennsylvania had proved himself as a boxer and as a marksman by the time he accepted an army commission in 1942, and he had joined OSS a year later.

Bazata's French counterpart on team Cedric was Captain Chapel,* a dark-haired man of medium height with a quick, handsome face. Like most of the French Jeds, he had been a soldier in the regular army before the war. The two officers had settled on a tall, quiet young American as their radio operator. He was Technical Sergeant Dick Floyd, a handsome nineteen year old from Brooklyn who had entered the army in April 1943 after having graduated from high school in January of that year.[2]

Bazata's team was to jump into the department of the Haute-Saône, in the upland region of eastern France known as the Franche-Comté, bordering the northwest corner of Switzerland. The quiet Franche-Comté, with its heavily forested hills laced with winding roads, had been largely overlooked by pre-war tourists, and had slumbered through much of the war. Captain Chapel had originally come from the area but had not been there since his youth, though he retained the distinct Franc-Comtois accent.

* Chapel's real name was Louis Lesne.

This had been an active, but perilous, territory for SOE's F Section circuits since April 1943. Jed team Cedric's mission, the briefer explained, would be to work in support of one of those circuits known as Treasurer. Specifically, the team would be working for a British agent whose code name was Émile.

When the briefer had finished providing the Jeds with details of their mission, he introduced a British army captain named Harry Rée, who was to provide the team with some additional background on the area they were going to, and it was information based on first-hand experience. It had been Harry Rée who had steered Francis Cammaerts, organizer of the Jockey circuit in southeastern France and an old friend, to SOE. Like Cammaerts, Rée had been a schoolmaster before the war and had been a conscientious objector for a time after the war began. And, like Cammaerts, he eventually saw reason to change his views and to volunteer to fight the Germans. What made Harry Rée of interest to Jedburgh team Cedric was that he had worked with the resistance in the very area to which the team was headed.

After joining Special Operations Executive and completing training, Rée and another lieutenant had been dropped into France in April 1943. Not long afterward, he had been sent to help an SOE captain establish a circuit known as Acrobat in the area of the Doubs encompassing Besançon and Belfort, and he eventually broke off and created a sub-circuit of his own called Stockbroker.

Rée soon showed an aptitude for sabotage work, and he pulled off one of the more innovative industrial sabotage schemes of the war. A Peugeot factory in the town of Sochaux was making gun carriers and tank turrets for the German army. Factory owner Rudolphe Peugeot carried on such work in compliance with the orders of the German occupation authorities, but he was no collaborator. In fact, Peugeot was secretly a patron of the resistance.

Rée met the industrialist and got him to agree to allow saboteurs to make a surgical strike in his factory, one which would not greatly damage the plant but would halt production of the war material for the Germans for some time. The Royal Air Force had already tried bombing the factory and had only caused minor damage. If the saboteurs were unsuccessful, Rée convinced Peugeot, the air force bombers would return, and his factory could face total destruction and innocent townspeople could be killed. Peugeot not only agreed to cooperate, he also provided plans of the factory and arranged for the help of workers inside the plant. The operation was a complete success, not only halting production but also destroying a large stock of finished tank components.[3]

Then, over the span of a few months in the latter half of 1943, the F Section organizer and many other members of the Acrobat circuit were arrested by the Gestapo. When, at last, a Gestapo man came for Lieutenant Rée, he fought with the German and was able to get away, although he was shot twice during the struggle. Friends were able to get him across the border into Switzerland, where he recovered in a hospital. Rée then made his way across France and over the Pyrénées to Spain, and by early July 1944 he was back in London. Since his return to England he'd made himself useful by talking to Jedburgh teams bound for the Jura and the Doubs, telling them of the country and its people, and warning them of the dangers.[4]

And the area did indeed remain treacherous. An American civilian sent there in April 1944 to rebuild Captain Rée's Stockbroker circuit had been killed just two days after his arrival. When two American OSS lieutenants had then jumped in to establish a new circuit to replace Stockbroker they, too, met with trouble and had to escape.

But one portion of the Stockbroker circuit had survived, the sub-circuit called Treasurer, and since D-Day it had been very active in attacking telecommunications and railway targets. Then, in the middle of July, the circuit's organizer had sent his lieutenant, Émile, to take control of some small maquis groups near Besançon. This was the man that Jedburgh team Cedric was being sent to support.

Based on reports from the field, it was known that Émile was working in the area north of the road that connected Besançon and Belfort and that he had two maquis groups—one outside a village called Vieilley and another one nearby. Both camps were fairly well hidden deep in the forested hills. Small as these groups were, Émile had been successful in training the men in the use of weapons and explosives, and in carrying out some sixty-four attacks on local road and railway targets—bringing traffic to a virtual standstill on three major routes.

Émile was actually Captain George Millar, a British army officer in the SOE whose war had already included enough excitement for most men. He was the thirty-four-year-old son of a prosperous Glasgow architect, and had studied architecture while at Cambridge. After leaving the university, he had learned to fly, had worked for a time as an ordinary seaman on a freighter, and then, in 1936, had taken a job with the *Daily Telegraph*. Millar later moved to the *Daily Express* and soon was working out of its Paris office, having proved himself a talented journalist. When war came, he had returned to Britain and enlisted in the army.

Millar had received his commission through an officer cadet training unit, becoming a second lieutenant at the age of thirty-one. He soon was off to fight Rommel's Afrika Korps in North Africa but was captured by the Germans while leading a scout platoon on reconnaissance. Millar escaped from a prisoner of war camp in Italy, made his way through southern France, across the Pyrénées, and returned to England in January 1944.

By April, he was interviewed by Special Operations Executive and, largely because of his fluent and almost accent-free French, was accepted. The organization's French Section had then rushed Millar through training so that he could be dropped during the upcoming June moon period. And just a few days before D-Day, he had jumped from a Liberator in civilian clothes into eastern France to serve as assistant to the organizer of the Treasurer circuit. He had been promoted to captain just before leaving England.[5]

The maquis leader whom Captain Millar had been sent to assist near Besançon was an FFI chief named Joseph Bartholet. An intelligent man in his thirties, he was tall and thin and carelessly dressed, and the men of the maquis called him Boulaya. He and his family had lived for a time in England, but he was a native of Besançon and he knew the area well. Boulaya had brought his family back to France in 1938 and opened a business school for women in Metz. Early in the war he served as a captain in the army, was captured, and escaped. He made his way to Besançon and when his family got word of his whereabouts, they joined him. There was no question of returning to Metz, for the Germans had occupied their house and carted off all their furniture and other belongings.

In Besançon, Boulaya had again opened a school, but his hatred for the German occupiers continued to grow, and he had soon begun working with the resistance, eventually becoming chief of all the FFI in the Besançon area.

Millar had also come to rely on another exceptional resistance man in the area by the name of Georges Molle. Boulaya and Molle and Millar liked each other, and they worked well together. The Briton learned much from the Frenchmen about the region, about the people, and about the meager maquis forces and their needs. As they bicycled throughout the area Boulaya showed Millar hideouts, told him whom he could trust in each town and village, and explained where Millar could get a meal or seek medical care.

As the weeks passed, Millar saw the maquis force in his area grow, and new young leaders took their places in key positions. But he also saw the desperate shortages that existed—in arms and explosives, in clothing and blankets, in boots and bicycle tires, in food and money and all the other things necessary for a guerrilla force to survive and be effective when called on to perform. He looked forward to the day when these things would begin to arrive from London.[6]

Team Cedric's destination, the Franche-Comté, had, like Brittany, always existed on the periphery of France proper. It had always been considered somewhat remote, even when Caesar's legions settled in the area. Politically, it had more recently been an appendage of Germany, only permanently becoming part of the French nation in the eighteenth century. But, unlike the predominantly Catholic Brittany, the Franche-Comté was strongly Protestant. And while Bretons lived off the sea and the soil, the Franc-Comtois were more likely to build clocks, watches, and music boxes; to tan hides; or to work in foundries or cotton mills. There was some agriculture, of course—dairy cows, fields of corn and hay, vineyards, and rolling meadows and pastureland in the lower lying valleys. In general, the people of the region were well-educated, healthy, courteous, and amiable.

The Jeds were to be dropped near the border between the departments of the Haute-Saône to the north and the Doubs to the south, an area characterized by long forested ridges running from southwest to northeast. Along the valleys between these ridges ran southwesterly flowing rivers such as the wide, swiftly flowing Doubs and the smaller and somewhat slower Ognon. Along their banks lay rich flatlands with fields of wheat and corn.

George Millar had learned soon after his arrival in the Franche-Comté that arranging for parachute drops in this part of France would be a challenge. His area of operations lay in the farthest eastern part of the country, midway between London and Algiers. This meant, first of all, that he was the farthest of all organizers from the front lines and, therefore, that many circuits which were closer to the fighting would have priority for arms and supplies. Secondly, he knew that he was located at the farthest extent of the range of the aircraft flying such missions from either England or North Africa. As the war drew closer in the last half of August 1944, however, with the British and American armies approaching from the west and American and French forces approaching from the south, the majority of supply drops began to focus on Eastern France.

Millar had done everything he could to prepare for the day when London would turn its attention to his remote corner of France. He had selected and trained people for the reception committees, found a safe house for operators who jumped in and places where arms and supplies could be taken and stored, and arranged for the use of draft horses and wagons to haul containers from the dropping grounds. He also had gotten the maquis in the habit of listening to the BBC twice each day for the personal messages —impatiently awaiting the one which would signal the impending arrival of the group's first air drop. And then it came.

A girl in the village of Vieilley had been tasked with listening for the message, "La langoureuse Asie et la brûlante Afrique" ("The languishing Asia and the burning Africa"). She jumped with excitement when she finally heard it on August 27. She ran off at once to find George Millar and Georges Molle, for this was the signal that they were to receive a parachute drop that night from two planes on the drop zone code-named Onion, a field not far from the village, next to the brown Ognon River.[7]

Millar and Molle made the final arrangements on the drop zone, which was about eight miles north of Besançon. Unlike the FFI in Brittany, though, they ran a textbook reception operation with a minimal number of people involved.

Captain Chapel was the first to arrive at the assembly point on drop zone Onion, led by a maquisard carrying his parachute. Captain Millar greeted him and introduced himself as Émile. Chapel asked for some wine and was given some in a tin cup. Next, Millar's driver came in leading a tall American, and Millar noticed a procession of maquisards following closely as the American officer laughed and cheerfully handed out chewing gum and chocolate. Millar met Captain Bazata and wondered what sort of rascal was joining him. Again introductions were made and Bazata explained that they had been trying for three weeks to get to France. As soon as the plane dropping the parachutists had passed overhead, Georges Molle had yelled to the maquisards to put the bonfires out, and they had all been extinguished by the time the third jumper arrived. Millar watched as a thin, six-footer with dark hair was brought in. Without the glow from the fires, Millar had to use his flashlight to get a look at the young man who was introduced as Sergeant Floyd, the radio operator.

Soon the men heard the drone of aircraft engines again, and Millar and Molle ordered the maquisards to re-light the fires for the second Liberator.

Bazata was impressed with the efficiency of the reception committee; it was clear that the resistance here had been well trained. Millar, the "Émile" whom Bazata's team had been sent to assist, turned the three Jeds over to his driver and returned to his spot in the center of the drop area to prepare for the arrival of the second plane.

The driver was René Berger, the tall, strong-looking man who had led Captain Bazata in from the drop zone. Berger had a swarthy complexion and wore an absurd-looking leather helmet when carrying out his driving duties. He had been a house painter before the war.

Twelve more canisters and some packages fell from the second plane. But unseen—because they were dropped wide of the drop zone—were two more parachutists, and they walked up just as Millar and Berger were guiding the Jeds to their car hidden in a wooded area. The two unexpected arrivals introduced themselves as Colonel Relativite and Captain Masure. Captain Millar greeted the two men and led all five jumpers to his car. The vehicle was a large and fairly new black Citroën "familiale" with red wheels and, being the family model, a roomy interior. It had been given to Millar by a small man named Jacques Painchaux, a garage owner and leader of a nearby maquis band.

Millar grew restless as the parachutists all began asking for the containers that carried their equipment. The circuit leader wanted to get the new men clear of the area as quickly as possible in case a German patrol arrived. He assured them that their luggage would be brought to them later. With some coaxing, he got four of the jumpers to crowd into the back seat of the Citroën. Then Sergeant Floyd crawled into the front seat next to Berger, who was behind the wheel and had fired up the engine. Millar took the window seat next to Floyd and they were off, down rough back roads along the south bank of the river.

"Shall I use lights, mon capitaine?" asked Berger.

"Only dipped," replied Captain Millar. "Full speed through Venise, Moncey, Rigney. No lights after the hairpin two kilometers before la Barre, and then avoid making tracks." Glancing at their five passengers, he asked, "Are you armed, gentlemen? The roads in this part are still unsafe for people like us, I regret to say."[8] Millar carried a .45-caliber pistol in the pocket of his denim jacket and kept a Sten on his lap pointed out the window.

Soon they turned off the road, pulled into an orchard, and got out. The men followed the British officer as he walked through the orchard and across a garden to a house called the Château de la Barre. They were taken inside the old house, where a woman and her daughter lived, and the parachutists stripped off their jump smocks and all their gear and piled it on the floor of the living room. In their haste to leave the drop zone, they now realized, not all of the leg bags and other gear which had been strapped to the jumpers had been picked up, and the team's radio was among the missing items. But the men were assured that the equipment would be recovered and brought to them. Captain Bazata then asked the woman if they might have some coffee.

Millar and Berger left to check that the drop zone had been thoroughly cleared and to look for the missing items. The Jeds and the other two jumpers remained in the care of the very capable woman of the house, who was a war widow and mayor of the hamlet of La Barre. She saw that they were given a place to sleep.

Back at the drop zone, Millar found the work of clearing the field to be capably overseen by Georges Molle, and almost finished. All the canisters had been loaded aboard horse-drawn hay wagons and driven off to the designated arms storage location. The priceless cargo of weapons, ammunition, and explosives would be hidden in a place unlikely to attract German interest—the Vieilley garbage dump—there to be neatly stacked and covered with rubbish.

Millar and Berger helped the others as they swept through the entire area, up to a mile from the drop zone, to make sure that nothing was left for the Germans to find. Millar eventually found the package containing the Jed radio as well as a leg bag containing twenty-four million francs in cash. He thought that the Jeds had been careless in not maintaining more control over these items, but he was even more disturbed by his discovery of a parachute left in the field by one of the two men who had jumped from the second plane. (The other man's chute would be found and hidden by an alert farm boy the next day.)

Millar was furious at such blatant disregard for security. German planes overflew the area every day and the discovery of parachutes would have resulted in widespread searches and reprisals. He and Berger gathered up the remaining Jed gear, including the radio, and drove back to the château and dropped it off. Then, after one more trip back to Vieilley to check on the storage of the supplies, the two tired men drove back to the château at La Barre and fell asleep in the garden.

Early the next morning, Millar and Berger entered the house for breakfast. The two men who had jumped from the second Liberator, Colonel Relativite and Captain Masure, came into the room dressed in civilian clothes. They told Millar that they had orders to report to a man called Ligne, who was General de Gaulle's appointed military delegate for the region, so Millar had them load their gear aboard the Citroën and Berger drove them to Boulaya's command post at Vieilley.

Then, to Millar's dismay, the three Jedburghs of team Cedric appeared for breakfast in full uniform. Millar explained to the newcomers that the Germans were very active in the area and that the Jeds would certainly not survive long in uniform. They would have to operate in civilian clothes, and he asked that they change as soon as they had finished their breakfast. While they ate, the Jeds had their first relaxed conversation with the man they knew as Émile. They saw that he was in his mid-thirties, with boyish good looks, reddish fair hair, and blue eyes.

Captain Millar was interested to know more about the Jeds. What sort of team was this? Why had the men come here? What was their mission? Who were they supposed to work for?

Captain Bazata spoke up and explained the Jedburgh concept, and made it clear that the team was there to serve Millar (Émile).

As Millar listened, he quickly came to realize that his private guerrilla war, small and fairly easily controlled, would never be the same. These Jeds, and especially the man named Bazata—clearly the dominant personality of the trio—seemed eager to make a much more active war of it. But Millar didn't think the time had yet come for that. He was clearly uneasy about doing anything to further agitate the enemy in this region and possibly bring vicious reprisals down on the villagers. Millar brought the Jeds up to date on the local situation. Many Germans, he explained, were moving through the area to the northeast, seizing all available means of transportation and severely punishing the people for any interference.

Most of the work Millar had done with his maquis thus far had been in the area around Besançon, the old clock- and watch-making city and departmental capital of the Doubs. He told the Jeds that he had been organizing a small maquis band in an area along Route Nationale 83, the highway running northeast from Besançon to Belfort. The department of the Haute-Saône, lying north of the

Ognon River, Millar explained, was largely devoid of any organized maquis.

To Bazata, the Besançon-Belfort road appeared to be the main German artery for withdrawal through the area, and he agreed that the valley of the Doubs should be the focus of their work. Millar added, though, that he still hoped to eventually expand northward into the Haute-Saône.

Geographically, the Doubs is an area of transition, where the great river valleys and gently rolling plateaus of eastern France and the Saône River basin give way to forested ridges, where the foothills of the Doubs rise to the Jura mountain range which, in turn, hugs the Swiss Alps to the east. As the hills of the Doubs push closer to the Swiss border, they grow steadily steeper, rising like stadium seating, wrinkling into deep, narrow gorges lined by craggy ridges. Forests of oak and beech give way to pine and fir— many of which reach heights of more than a hundred feet. Some of the ridges slope to lush mountain valleys, with winding roads and turbulent streams alive with pike and trout, and placid lakes nestled among the hills.

Such terrain as that of the eastern Doubs might be picturesque, but it was hardly conducive to the speedy movement of large columns of vehicles. The German Nineteenth Army's shortest and fastest route back to the Rhine clearly followed the gentle valley of the Doubs River in the western part of the department. Up Route Nationale 83, through the orchards and vineyards and poplar groves that skirted the north bank of the river. The valley was also a busy air corridor, and every day lumbering German Junkers 53 transport planes passed overhead toward Belfort and on to Germany. Millar thought they probably carried German soldiers wounded in the fighting in southern France.[9]

The men decided that they first needed to arm some two thousand guerrillas, and they planned to prepare four fields to receive air drops.[10] Sergeant Floyd set up his radio in his bedroom at the Château and, with Captain Chapel turning the hand-cranked generator, he got a message off to London reporting the team's safe arrival and requesting another delivery of arms and supplies. Captain Millar couldn't help noticing how Floyd tapped out his message while lying on the floor, unlike his own radio operator, who preferred sitting at a desk or table while working. Floyd had grown accustomed to his method after lengthy training in the transmission of messages from remote outdoor locations. But Millar also noted that the thick walls of the old house were unable to completely muffle the piercing whine of the set's generator, and he worried for the safety of the old woman and her daughter. He would have to find another place for these Jeds to stay.

Jacques Painchaux, the little garage owner who doubled as a maquis leader, suggested moving the Jeds to a convent outside a village not far away. He knew the Mother Superior there and was sure that she would be glad to help. Millar found the thought of housing Bazata in a nunnery appealing, and he agreed at once to meet with the Mother Superior. She turned out to be as charming and hospitable as Painchaux had described her, and the men were shown five rooms which the three-man Jedburgh team, plus Millar and Berger, could occupy. Millar happily accepted.[11]

When Millar returned to the château at la Barre, he and the Jeds dined together with the old woman and her daughter, and he revealed the new billeting arrangements. Bazata again dominated the conversation, speculating on the value of various items of antique furniture in the château.

Next morning, Millar and the Jeds were just about to leave in the Citroën for the convent when a messenger from Jacques Painchaux arrived on motorcycle and stopped them. Painchaux himself soon arrived on a moped and explained that the nunnery was out—they would have to find another safe house. The old gardener at the convent, it seems, had gone into a café in town and announced that the supreme Allied command was coming to set up a radio station in the convent. If the Germans had not already heard the news they soon would, and would be keeping an eye on the place. So Millar again began looking for a new hideout.

In the meantime, Millar and Painchaux decided to put the Jeds up for one night in a mill near the village where Painchaux lived. When they arrived at the mill, sentries, arranged for by Painchaux, were posted on the approaching roads and Berger hid the car nearby. Inside, the miller made the men comfortable and provided a supper of roast duckling.

By evening a terrific storm rolled into the area, with wind and driving rain. While the men were eating and enjoying the miller's champagne, a maquis leader by the name of Menigoz arrived with news of a revolt by Ukrainian troops from one of the East European units which had been integrated into the German army. According to Menigoz, an entire six-hundred-man battalion had overthrown their German officers and wanted to fight on the side of the Allies. They came armed with German weapons, including mortars and anti-tank guns, and they had horse-drawn transport. Menigoz had taken charge of them and had put them in the Cherlieu Forest, about thirty miles north of Besançon.

There were actually two battalions of Ukrainian mutineers, double the number that Menigoz was aware of at the time. The bizarre revolt was all a result of Germany's ill-conceived practice of putting East Europeans into uniform to fight for the Third Reich.

Desperate for manpower on the Western Front, in early August the German high command had formed a Waffen SS grenadier division in East Prussia from battalions of anti-Soviet Russians, Belorussians, Ukrainians, and Cossacks. The Waffen SS was the armed branch of the SS. It was composed of army-like regiments and divisions, such as the 9th SS Panzer Division which Jedburgh team Augustus had run into farther north, but they were not part of the army. In addition to the pure German Waffen SS units, the German high command organized such divisions from volunteers from occupied countries.

In the middle of August, the SS grenadier division composed of East European troops had been shipped to the German Nineteenth Army in eastern France to fight the maquis of the Franche-Comté. German officers held all key leadership positions within the division, and German military police units were added to help enforce their commands. Some units within the division, however, clearly were not inclined to fight anything other than Soviets for the Fuhrer.

On the night of August 26—just twenty-four hours before team Cedric jumped into France—a battalion of Ukrainians billeted at a camp twenty miles southeast of Besançon attacked the barracks of their German officers and noncommissioned officers and killed them all. The following morning, another Ukrainian battalion from the same division, deployed to an area north of Besançon, likewise killed their German leaders—all twenty-five officers and seventy noncoms. The two battalions then openly defected to the FFI.

In addition to nearly thirteen hundred trained combat troops, the two Ukrainian battalions brought anti-tank guns, dozens of mortars and machine guns, and hundreds of small arms. They also came with a considerable stock of ammunition, thousands of grenades, a cavalry unit complete with ninety mounts, and a transportation unit which included more than two hundred wagons and five hundred draft horses.[12]

Menigoz asked Captains Bazata and Chapel if a message could be sent to London explaining the situation and requesting an arms drop for the Ukrainians. The maquis leader was concerned that the defectors' supply of ammunition for their German weapons would not last long. A switch to Allied weapons would make it easier to keep them resupplied. Millar was glad to let the restless Bazata and his team handle the situation. Bazata, who hoped that such an act would encourage other groups of Russians nearby to turn against the Germans as well, drafted the message and Sergeant Floyd sent it. Captain Chapel agreed to accompany Menigoz on a visit to the Ukrainians first thing in the morning.

The Ukrainians, in the woods north of Besançon, were shelled by German artillery on the third and fourth of September, but they were able to hold out. Special Force Headquarters received team Cedric's request for an arms drop for the two battalions, but decided instead to send a small OSS team on the night of the seventh to make an assessment of the situation.

Meanwhile, accommodations had finally been found for Millar, Berger, and the Jedburghs.

12

ON THE REICH'S DOORSTEP

A WELL-TO-DO citizen by the name of Landel, who was mayor of a town called Loulans and a member of the local maquis, offered to provide room in his home for Jedburgh team Cedric and Captain Millar. Monsieur Landel was a small, nice-looking man with white hair, and he smoked continuously. He owned and managed a cheese factory and was the richest man around.

Landel lived in a roomy chalet on the outskirts of town with his wife, their ten children, a few grandchildren, and some children of friends. It was common during the war for large households in rural areas to keep the children of friends or relatives living in urban areas. It protected the children from bombings and usually meant better access to dairy products, which were all but unavailable in the cities. In Landel's case, because of the cheese factory the family had a steady supply of milk and butter and cheese—one of the reasons that there were so many children staying with them.

By sending eight of the younger children off to stay with Madame Landel's sister in the next village, the family could make room for the men. Of course, the entire family understood the risk inherent in housing a team which would be transmitting radio signals, but they accepted the risk without complaint.[1]

The arrangement worked out well. While staying at the Landel house, Sergeant Floyd would often go out into the woods nearby to transmit his messages. Landel's eldest son, Bernard, about twenty years old and also a maquisard, helped Floyd by turning the hand-cranked generator during radio transmissions. At times, one of the older daughters also performed this chore.

The house was spacious and warm and dry, and the men enjoyed generous meals with the family around a large table. Captain Millar contributed by providing the Landels with food which his maquisards had stolen from German stocks.

With a base of operations established, Jed team Cedric and Captain Millar began a campaign of sabotage on the road and railway running between Besançon and Belfort. Until they were able to bring in more air drops from London, the men would be limited to the small number of arms and the meager amount of explosives which Millar's maquis groups had been able to acquire and store. To this, of course, would be added the material which had been dropped with team Cedric.

With so many German units passing through the area, the Jeds wanted to keep the telephone lines constantly cut to make communications more difficult for the enemy. They found this particularly easy to do. They soon became adept at hitting larger targets as well—targets with a much higher payoff. On Sunday, September 3, the men blew a section of the Besançon-Belfort railroad, cutting the track and derailing a German troop train. On the same day, they also ambushed an artillery convoy north of Besançon.

But the village of Loulans lay north of the Ognon River in the Haute-Saône department. Working from their command post at the Landel house in Loulans, the men gradually began shifting their operations more to the north, away from the department of the Doubs south of the Ognon. Bazata soon found that what George Millar had said about the maquis north of the river, in the Haute-Saône, was true. Maquis bands were scattered about and poorly organized. They lacked arms, were largely untrained, and their security was weak.

Because of the danger involved in moving about with so many Germans in the area, Bazata decided to have Sergeant Floyd remain with the radio either at the Landel house or with the maquis of Loulans. Captain Chapel was spending most of his time with a maquis group north of Besançon, and Bazata decided that he would be most useful sticking by Millar's side. So he began accompanying the British officer everywhere he went—an arrangement which, at times, must have tried the patience of both men.

Doug Bazata and George Millar were clearly a contrast in personalities. Politically, militarily, and in seemingly every other way, they each saw the world through different eyes. Once, while the two were bathing on the south bank of the Ognon, Millar spoke of his admiration for President Roosevelt and his policies and programs. But Bazata, he quickly learned, was an ardent Republican. The two men also could not have been more divergent in their approaches to irregular warfare. Millar, whom Dick Floyd would later describe as quiet and aloof, was content to continue the small-scale sabotage that had worked so well for him in the past, waiting to be eventually overrun by Allied ground forces. He had seen many months of war, had been a prisoner of war, and had little stomach for killing. But Bazata was new to the war, had come in full of piss and vinegar, and clearly preferred a more aggressive approach. Millar later would write that, whenever he found a chance to rest, Bazata would spoil the moment by demanding, "For Pete's sake, Émile, let's get down to that road and bag us a couple of Krauts."[2]

Jedburgh team Cedric had yet to receive an air drop from London and, as supplies of ammunition and explosives dwindled, sabotage and guerrilla warfare opportunities were missed. It was the same old problem that had plagued Jed teams George and Augustus. For whatever reason, team Cedric was having trouble getting Special Force Headquarters to respond to its needs, and the team was quickly running out of time.

Americans of the Seventh Army were rapidly approaching from the southwest, with some forces only about fifty miles from Besançon, and more and more German convoys were moving through team Cedric's area. Captain Chapel had been organizing road blocks with the maquis on the major routes north of Besançon and, with the successful attacks on the Besançon-Belfort route by team Cedric and the maquis groups in the Doubs Valley, vehicle convoys of the German Nineteenth Army were being forced onto secondary roads. Some of these convoys chose to take the D15 route, a secondary road which would allow them to cut farther to the east in search of an open northbound road. And route D15 passed right through the village of Loulans.

On Monday, September 4, Millar and Bazata, trying to appear as just two more curious villagers, ambled to the center of town to watch the enemy retreat. A lengthy convoy of camouflaged cars, poking along at about thirty-five miles per hour, took an entire day to pass through town. Some of the soldiers even rode on bicycles.

Bazata was irritated that London had not come through with the air drops. The roads were rich with targets, if only the Jeds had the means of attacking them and had had more time to organize and train the maquis of the Haute-Saône. He noticed that most of the cars in the convoy were on the verge of breaking down—and he was certain that, had the maquis been sufficiently trained and armed, they could have inflicted a good deal of damage on the enemy. As it was, all they could do was radio messages to London asking for air strikes. At least the Jeds and the maquis, by forcing the Germans to use the slower secondary roads, were making such air strikes more effective.

Back at the Landel house, however, while Bazata and Millar were watching the German convoy and ruing their lack of means to attack it, Sergeant Floyd received a message from London which offered hope. The Jeds were to expect a drop the following night on field Onion, the same drop zone where team Cedric had arrived a week earlier. On Tuesday morning, excited at the prospect of receiving the air drop, Bazata and Millar departed to check out the field. But what they saw when they approached the field next to the river gave them a jolt. An estimated eight hundred Germans were camped on the drop zone known as Onion.

George Millar and Doug Bazata had to decide whether to radio London and warn headquarters of the danger—and risk losing the arms and equipment they so badly needed—or to let the mission continue in the hope that the Germans would pull out before nightfall.

Before heading back to Loulans, the two men decided to stop in Vieilley for a bite of lunch at the home of a family that Millar knew. While the men ate in a room at the back of the house, a few villagers came by to share the news that American forces were near. Rumor had it that they were just south of the Doubs, and indeed they were. Lead elements of the 3rd Infantry Division were just southwest of Besançon and were beginning their attack on the city.

But there was also bad news. German troops had begun arriving in nearby villages, one just a mile and a half to the west, and American shells were pounding another village about six miles away.

Suddenly, the woman of the house broke in with news that Germans had arrived in Vieilley, and she urged the men to leave at once. Millar and Bazata scrambled out the back and hurried to their car, which they had left behind the house, and sped out of town to the north and back to Loulans. Finding that village also full of Germans, they snuck to the Landel house by a back route and hid the car in the garage.

Later that day, Berger came to Millar and reported that he had seen two German soldiers in the garage eyeing their car. Millar feared that the soldiers might have gone to report the vehicle to their commander, and he was anxious to keep it out of enemy hands. The car had been essential in helping the men move among the scattered maquis elements. Berger had worked hard to keep the large black Citroën washed and shined. Such a car, rolling through the countryside and passing quickly through towns and villages, appeared to the casual observer to be a Gestapo vehicle, and it had allowed the men to enjoy a certain lack of scrutiny by German soldiers.

The German army, particularly during the hectic weeks of the withdrawal from France, often seized whatever means of transportation they needed, and especially such attractive vehicles as the big black Citroën. Millar knew that he had to get the car out of there before the Germans could return and commandeer it. So he, Berger, and the Jeds hastily gathered up their gear, loaded it in the car, and sped off down a back road.

Five miles southeast of Loulans they approached a village on the north bank of the Ognon. Suddenly, just outside the village, they drove upon a German roadblock. Berger braked the big car to a stop and quickly began to wheel it around for a hasty departure. But just as he had gotten the car turned halfway around it stalled, sitting crosswise in the middle of the road.

While Berger struggled to bring the Citroën back to life, the Germans sensed that this was not a Gestapo car, but rather one full of "terrorists." They opened fire with rifles and submachine guns. While dozens of rounds ripped the air around the car, Millar and Bazata fired back as best they could with pistols and somehow avoided being hit. Finally, the car came to life and Berger, who had been nicked in the ear by a bullet, sped back down the road, around a bend, and off into an adjacent woods. Amazingly, they had driven at least a hundred yards under fire and had gotten away, and Millar and Bazata laughed heartily, as if they had just pulled off a high school prank.

When Berger had driven up a rise and into the woods as far as he could, the men jumped out, hid the car in a thicket, and continued on foot until they thought it was safe to stop. They hid in the woods for the remainder of the night, high up on a hill and hidden by thick brush. Late in the night, a German cavalry unit left the road below and came up into the woods to rest before moving on. Soon Millar, Bazata, and Berger could hear German voices all around them, and they wondered what the morning would bring. Then it began to rain.

As they lay in the woods, sometime after midnight, the men could hear four-engine planes circling overhead. They were sure the planes were their bombers, looking for the lights marking drop zone Onion, and they agonized at the thought of losing the badly needed arms.

The German cavalry unit left at four in the morning. At first light, about two hours later, the men crawled out of the woods and made their way to the home of a man Berger knew. There they were fed breakfast. Then Millar gave his weapons to the others and set off on foot alone to learn what, if anything, had happened at drop zone Onion. Bazata and Berger headed in the opposite direction, toward Loulans, so that Bazata could check for any radio messages from London.

When George Millar neared the drop zone he discovered that Georges Molle had come through again. The imperturbable Frenchman had arrived at the field the night before just in time to hear the approaching planes and flash the recognition signal on his flashlight. Even though the area was still saturated with Germans, Molle and his maquisards were able to recover all forty-eight containers from the drop, including three which had landed in the river. That day, Millar saw that the weapons were distributed, including a number that were given to local villagers who needed them to protect their homes and families. The Germans had begun burning some villages in retaliation for maquis roadblocks.

General Wiese, commander of the German Nineteenth Army, had chosen the Doubs River as a place where he could fight a brief delaying action against the pursuing Allied Forces by blowing all bridges across the river and forming a hasty defense line along the valley. Wiese also sent an infantry division into Besançon with orders to hold the town at all cost for ten days to protect German units withdrawing through the area.

Much of the heart of Besançon is encircled by a large loop in the Doubs River, and the town is surrounded by hills and encircled by seven massive stone forts. The greatest fort among them had been designed by Vauban, Louis XIV's brilliant military engineer. German troops now occupied the forts, intent on stopping the Americans. But after just three days of fighting, the town fell to American infantry, and by September 8 it was cleared of all German troops.

Word soon reached Jedburgh team Cedric that American troops were in Besançon. Bazata convinced Millar that they should make their way through the German lines and link up with the nearest division. The Jeds had much information on German troop locations and activities that would be useful to the Americans.

Before sunup on Thursday, September 7, Millar and Bazata set out on foot, proceeding in a southwesterly direction along the river. They walked through two villages and had just reached a third when it began to rain. The two men ducked into a barn to take shelter from the downpour, but a villager soon came by and told them that German soldiers had surrounded the village and were rounding up all males aged sixteen to sixty. Millar and Bazata feared that the Germans might be organizing a mass slaughter in retribution for maquis attacks, and they chose not to wait around.

Slowly, the two men made their way to the edge of the village, where they stopped at a house and borrowed two blankets from the woman who lived there. Then, stooped over with the blankets draped over their backs and heads, hoping to appear as elderly peasants, they puttered across a neighboring field, picking the mushrooms which were abundant in the area as they proceeded. Once they had wandered far enough from the village and were certain that they had made it through the German cordon, they took off and made it back to an unoccupied village. There, Bazata insisted on having a mushroom stew prepared. It had been a very close call.

That afternoon, the men tried once again to cross the German lines and link up with the Americans. This time they would be accompanied by Georges Molle, whom they met outside Vieilley. Molle was reputed to be the best poacher in the region, and he knew the local hills as well as anyone. With him as their guide, Millar and Bazata set out across the hills to the south and up into the Chailluz Forest. They found the woods thick with Germans— thousands in Bazata's estimation. The men took careful note of the German defensive positions along the road and even talked to some of the German soldiers, hoping to gain information which they could pass on to the American forces. They had to be careful, however, for the slightest mistake would invite closer scrutiny by the Germans—and the men had some close calls.

Soon they could go no farther without arousing suspicion, and so the three men spent a wretched night in the forest. All night they suffered the cold and the rain—and Georges Molle quickly tired of hearing Bazata say, "If only it would *rain.*"[3] It had become a favorite expression of Bazata's in such circumstances but, to Molle, on this night it was not funny, and he asked Millar to keep the American quiet. Doug Bazata was determined to get through to American units with the information they had gathered, but another way would have to be found.

The next day the men walked back to Vieilley and got a ride from there to Loulans, which by then was overrun with Germans. Captain Bazata checked with Sergeant Floyd for an update on message traffic from London, and learned that a message from Special Force Headquarters told of a thousand-man force of paratroopers which could be dropped to team Cedric's area if needed. The ever-cautious Millar was against it, sure that it would result in greater danger for the local people. Bazata, though, saw this as just one more piece of information requiring delivery to the approaching American forces. So he and Millar began planning another attempt at passing through the German lines.

General Wiese's weak defense along the Doubs had hardly caused the three infantry divisions belonging to Major General Lucien Truscott's VI Corps to break stride. They had jumped that river and were on the banks of the Ognon.

Late on the afternoon of the eighth, Bernard Landel arrived home on a bicycle with startling news. American forces had advanced beyond Besançon and were in Rigney, on the south bank of the Ognon, not far from the Château de la Barre where the Jeds had spent their first night. That put them just a few miles south of the Landel house. Millar and Bazata decided to head south to the village of Cenans, where they could cross the Ognon and go into Rigney. But Bernard then told them that German soldiers were preparing to blow all bridges across the Ognon. He had just seen ten Germans and two trucks on the Cenans bridge.

Millar and Bazata decided on a highly risky method of getting across the bridge before the Germans blew it. Some time earlier, Millar had gotten his hands on huge Terrot motorcycle—a popular pre-war French model. He had kept it well hidden among some thick shrubbery near the Landel house. With the motorcycle, Millar thought, they might be able to shoot across the bridge before the Germans could blow it, but they had to move at once. Millar instructed Bernard to go immediately and get his maquis to attack the Germans on the bridge. "But hold your fire when you see me coming on the Terrot. I'll have Captain Bazata up behind, if he's managed to stay on that far."[4]

With help from some of the Landel boys Captain Millar pushed the Terrot out and got it started. Bazata climbed on back, held Millar around the waist, and they tore off down the road toward

Cenans, armed only with pistols. It was only a mile to Cenans, and Millar raced down the road at nearly seventy miles per hour, almost losing Bazata, at times, when he couldn't avoid hitting potholes. When they reached the village, Millar slowed the big bike and cruised through the place at a steady pace. Then, upon hitting the downhill slope to the bridge southeast of town, he opened it up. They hit the bridge at full speed and a bump at the entry sent them briefly airborne. Bazata held on and they roared straight across—right through the startled Germans.

In his post-war memoir, George Millar would describe how, through tearing eyes, he only saw the German trucks and soldiers on the bridge as grey blurs. But the grey blurs quickly recovered from their initial shock and opened fire at the motorcycle as it disappeared up the rise on the opposite bank and around the bend. Once again, Millar and Bazata had made it through a tight spot. The Terrot roared down the road to Rigney and pulled up to a group of American soldiers in front of the Hôtel de la Gare. The stunt had worked.

Once the Americans (who turned out to be from the 3rd Infantry Division) saw Captain Bazata's papers, the two men were put in a jeep and driven back to the division command post in Besançon. There they met with the division commander, Major General John W. O'Daniel, a stout man with a hard face, who listened to Bazata's report and decided that the two men should be taken on back to VI Corps headquarters at Tarcenay, south of Besançon.

A jeep deposited the men at the VI Corps command post, and Major General Truscott, the corps commander, invited Bazata and Millar to dine with him in his tent. Staff officers served Bazata and Millar dry martinis while they visited with the general.

Captain Bazata briefed the general on German locations and activities ahead of the corps. Interestingly, in the mission report which Bazata filed upon his return to London, he indicates that Truscott, when told of SFHQ's proposed dropping of paratroopers, asked Bazata to radio a request that they be dropped to a spot in the Vosges Mountains. In his book *Road to Resistance*, however, George Millar wrote that Truscott rejected the proposal outright, and he quotes Bazata's later description of the general's opinion of the idea: "He pissed on it from a great height."[5] The general then asked Millar how long he had been in the area and expressed admiration for the work of Special Operations Executive.

When their audience with General Truscott had ended, Bazata and Millar were taken by jeep back to Rigney, arriving there at about three in the morning. Millar had been very much impressed with what he saw of the American soldiers and their leaders. He knew that they must be as exhausted as the Germans were, but they showed no signs of it.

Bazata was eager to return to the Landel house to get a message off to London. When the American lieutenant in Rigney saw that the two men planned to re-cross the German lines on the motorcycle, he told them they were crazy. But, against the lieutenant's advice, the men tore off on the big bike for the return trip to Loulans. The motorcycle's headlight did not work, but there was sufficient moonlight for them to find their way. They were stopped by an American patrol at one point, but were eventually allowed to proceed. The men learned from the American troops that the Germans had blown the bridge they had crossed earlier at Cenans, so they had to make a detour to another village which still had a bridge up. There they were able to cross and they sped back to Loulans, killing the engine as they neared the Landel house and then coasting into the driveway. Bazata ran into the house to get a message off while Millar hid the Terrot under a weeping willow.

Loulans was full of Germans, many of them searching for food or temporary billeting; it was inevitable that some would find their way to the large Landel house. One day two German officers, one of them a colonel, came to the house and knocked on the front door. When Monsieur Landel answered, the colonel politely asked if he could use the house for his headquarters. But Landel explained to the Germans that he had a large family and that many of his daughters and grandchildren were living with them. The house was full. Millar, Bazata, Chapel, and Floyd listened to the conversation from the other side of the wall in the next room. Fortunately, the German said that he understood and then left—although the Germans did take the liberty of billeting some troops in the Landels' farm buildings.[6]

Millar grew increasingly concerned about the high concentration of Germans in Loulans. Loud singing by German soldiers, seemingly inspired by alcohol, drifted to the Landel house from nearby buildings. Apparently fearing the possibility of a search, Millar saw that all of Sergeant Floyd's radio gear was gathered up and stored in a cupboard in an upstairs bedroom. He then persuaded the Landels to place their baby's bed closely against the cupboard to discourage any inspection.

In the second week of September, acting on a request from Special Force Headquarters, Millar, Berger, and Bazata attempted to get through to the OSS mission which had jumped in to join the Ukrainians in the forest north of Besançon. London had asked Bazata to provide the OSS team whatever assistance he could. But the 3rd Infantry Division was attacking the nearby town of Vesoul that day, and the three men were unable to get through to the Ukrainians' position. Suddenly the men found themselves caught in the middle of an artillery duel. The Americans were attacking Vesoul from the south and, for a time, the men were on the receiving end of both German and American artillery fire. But they came through all right, except for a small shrapnel wound which Bazata received on one hand. Then, after the men made it back to the Landel house, the Germans began shelling Loulans.

At this same time, farther to the west, Allied forces from the Dragoon landings in southern France were linking up with the Overlord forces driving eastward from the Normandy breakout. On September 11, Third Army patrols made contact with a French element of Seventh Army west of Dijon. The two converging armies linked up in force shortly thereafter. In doing so, the Allies effectively cut off the escape route of the remaining German forces in southwest France. Most of the German First Army had long since been pulled from southwest France to reinforce the armies in the north. What remained of Germany's Atlantic defenses, not much more than a corps, had been repeatedly and mercilessly harassed and ambushed by maquis and Allied special forces. For a month the Germans had been struggling to get back to the Rhine while at the same time trying to avoid being slaughtered by the maquis.

The maquis had been urging General Elster, senior commander of the remaining German forces in the southwest, to surrender. But

Elster demurred. With his personal honor—as well as that of his army—at stake, the general said that he would only discuss surrender with American ground forces. The maquis relayed this message to the U.S. 83rd Infantry Division north of the Loire. And at three-thirty on the afternoon of September 17, Major General Robert C. Macon, commander of the 83rd, accepted the surrender of the German general and nearly twenty thousand troops at a bridge southwest of Orléans.[7]

According to the Overlord invasion plan, Field Marshal Montgomery was to be in overall control of the ground campaign in northern France until the Allies had broken out of the lodgment area and advanced far enough for General Eisenhower to fully relocate his headquarters to the Continent. At that time, the supreme commander would assume control of all ground forces. This Eisenhower did on the first day of September. Two weeks later he also assumed command of the Dragoon invasion forces from southern France as they linked up with the Allied armies in northern France to form one continuous front from the channel coast to the Swiss border. Furthermore, the Seventh U.S. Army and French Army B (to be renamed the French First Army) now would be controlled by a newly activated headquarters, Sixth Army Group, commanded by General Devers. Soon after the fall of Vesoul, the new army group changed direction, attacking directly eastward toward the Vosges mountains and the Rhine River beyond.

One afternoon, not long after Doug Bazata, George Millar, and René Berger had escaped the artillery duel, the three men were in the woods just outside Loulans. Artillery rounds exploded not far from the Landel house. The men were trying to determine whether the shells were coming from German guns or American guns when suddenly they saw American army vehicles coming down the road from the west. An armored car was in the lead, and right behind it were three Sherman tanks with infantrymen riding on top. They were from the 3rd Infantry Division, and they drove on into the center of Loulans, where the armored car shot a German engineer truck loaded with explosives, causing a tremendous explosion.

When Dick Floyd heard that American troops had arrived, he ran out to the road and stopped the first jeep full of GIs he saw. Floyd approached them and said, "You guys aren't going to believe this, but I'm a first sergeant in the United States Army. If you could direct me to your S–2 [intelligence] section, I'd appreciate it."[8]

The Landel property became host to the 3rd Infantry Division's vehicle maintenance facility. In thirty days the division had come four hundred miles. Tracks were falling off tanks and other vehicles were likewise in need of work, so the maintenance shop was a busy place.

George Millar and the Jedburghs of team Cedric would never get over the way the Landels had taken them in—risking arrest or worse by the Germans—and made them feel at home. One morning, near the end of their stay, Millar counted seventeen at the breakfast table, children included.

Bazata, Chapel, and Floyd spent their remaining days in France serving the 3rd Infantry Division as liaison to the maquis, helping units clear out bypassed pockets of Germans and sending maquisards through the lines to gather intelligence. One day, a message came from General de Gaulle's military deputy for the region—ordering Captain Millar back to London. Millar was puzzled and sent a message through Sergeant Floyd to F Section asking for confirmation of the order. London confirmed the order and informed Millar that a plane would be sent to pick him up. As Millar would later learn, General de Gaulle, in one of his smallest acts, had ordered all British agents of SOE out of France that day. The general had always been at odds with F Section's work, and now that he was firmly in power he declared F Section's circuit organizers to be nothing more than British mercenaries.[9]

That night, Captain Millar went into Besançon to attend a dinner party, found an old friend in town—CBS war correspondent Eric Sevareid, one of (Edward R.) "Murrow's Boys"—and took him along. Sevareid had been with the Dragoon forces since they came ashore and would stay with them all the way to Germany.

The next day, Bazata and Berger went to the airfield to see George Millar off to London; Boulaya was going with him. The four of them, and Georges Molle, who was absent, had been through a lot together. Now that peace had returned to the valley of the Ognon, however, Molle was on the river with his skiff, relaxing and getting reacquainted with the fish. So Bazata and Berger and Millar said their good-byes. "If only it would *rain*," added Bazata.[10]

In the end, some of the German Nineteenth Army succeeded in making it all the way back to Germany, but there were at least as many Germans who were stopped along the way—never making it to the Belfort Pass or the Rhine. Roughly half of the two hundred and fifty thousand troops of Hitler's army group in southern France had been lost. Allied losses had been a fraction of that. Dozens of Jedburgh teams throughout the south and the eastern portion of France had participated in the campaign and had contributed to the victory.

In the south and in the east, however, just as had happened in the north of France as the Allied forces grew nearer to the German frontier, many Jedburgh teams—like Cedric—were sent in too late and were poorly supported from London once they were in. It is hard to imagine how much more they could have contributed had they been given the time and the support to organize, arm, and train a resistance force to the level that should have been possible.

But team Cedric, and the Jeds of many other teams who ended up in that situation, had managed to find ways to help the Allied cause. In team Cedric's case, the men were successful enough in their sabotage of the highway and railway in the Doubs valley to force the Germans to use the secondary road network, further slowing and complicating their withdrawal and making them more vulnerable to air attack. Captain Bazata's team also provided much valuable information to the Americans as they prepared to advance northward toward Vesoul, and continued to assist them as guides afterward.

Team Cedric also had alerted London to the status of the turn-coat Ukrainian battalions. No sober-minded military man would ever consider such units dependable as a fighting force. The Ukrainians had betrayed their own Soviet government and army and then had betrayed the Germans. They certainly gave little reason for anyone to trust them. By sending in an OSS team to stay with the Ukrainians for the short time until they were overrun by Allied forces, however, those in London were at least able to keep tabs on them. And, at the very least, it removed two combat battalions and much equipment from the German order of battle.

Other Allied successes came farther to the north, with Montgomery's forces capturing Brussels on September 3, and Bradley's armies taking Luxembourg on the tenth and Nancy on the fifteenth.

By October 1944, nearly all of France had been liberated. But as Eisenhower's armies approached the threshold of Hitler's Germany, the enemy which they had chased across France from Brittany in the west and from the shores of the Mediterranean in the south began to fight with a new fierceness. More Jedburgh teams were dropped into eastern France and took part in the fighting in the Vosges Mountains and Alsace and Lorraine, areas which would not be completely liberated until early February 1945.

The sons of the Reich, determined to protect home and family, would give the western Allies some of the war's bloodiest fighting along Germany's western border, in places such as Arnhem in Holland, and Aachen and the Hürtgen Forest in Germany. "By this time," a member of an American division later noted, "we had lost a colorful and gallant team that had been fighting with us." He was referring to the men the division's chief of staff called the "dashing soldiers" of the FFI.[11]

Punishing German offensives in the Ardennes Forest of Belgium and in the Colmar area of France still lay ahead. Once those battles were won, though, the armies of the Third Reich were beaten. Allied forces swept through Germany without the support of active resistance elements. In Germany such irregulars—and the special forces to fit them and train them and guide them—were not needed. For the Reich had been scraping the bottom of the manpower barrel for a year, and the barrel was dry.

EPILOGUE

Most provisional military enterprises, like summer help, sooner or later reach the point where their missions have been accomplished, their purposes fulfilled. That time came for the Jedburgh project—indeed for virtually all of the special operations work shepherded by Special Force Headquarters—in the late fall of 1944. Nowhere in the German homeland were there resistance movements—indigenous or otherwise—strong enough to be worthy of exploitation. The work of the Jedburghs and other special forces in France was finished.

A half dozen Dutch Jedburgh teams deployed in September during Operation Market-Garden, the bold and ambitious plan conceived by British Field Marshal Bernard L. Montgomery to seize three bridges in Holland and the road corridor connecting them, as a means of gaining a bridgehead across the Lower Rhine. Unfortunately, the operation fell short of its objective and cost many casualties.

By October, much of the FFI had been incorporated into the French Army by General de Gaulle and would march into Germany alongside the Anglo-American armies.

On October 13, Special Force Headquarters ordered all American and British Jedburghs still in France to return to England. Upon completion of their Jedburgh missions in France, team members were asked to volunteer for missions in other countries or other theaters. Most Jeds did so, with a considerable number going on to fight the Japanese in the China-Burma-India (CBI) Theater. For the most part, the British who went this route were reassigned to Special Operations Executive's Force 136, operating out of India and Ceylon (now known as Sri Lanka). Americans mostly went to an Office of Strategic Services detachment in China. The French Jeds who went to the Far East usually ended up in French Indochina (the area today known as Vietnam, Laos, and Cambodia), which had been a French colony before the war.

Some Jeds found other work in Europe, such as those who volunteered for a provisional unit called the Special Allied Airborne Reconnaissance Force, which prepared teams to parachute into areas by German POW camps. Near war's end, these soldiers were to make contact with German camp administrators and coordinate the medical treatment and evacuation of Allied prisoners.

Major Bill Colby led a Norwegian special operations team on a sabotage and guerrilla warfare mission in Norway. Captain Aaron Bank prepared for a mission, in German uniform and leading a makeshift unit of German POW volunteers, which was to have dropped into the Austrian Alps where it was believed the Nazi leaders were establishing a redoubt. The team's mission was to capture as many of the top leaders as possible. For a number of reasons, however, the mission was aborted.

Special Force Headquarters was, quite simply, going out of business.

The swiftness with which the end came can be seen in the personnel strength figures of the American contingent of SFHQ. As of the end of September 1944, the OSS Special Operations Branch had 1,114 personnel in the European Theater of Operations. More than seven hundred Americans had received special operations training in SOE schools between July 1943 and November 1944. By the end of November, all American personnel had returned from France, and by December 30 the roster numbered only 437.[1]

SFHQ's Mediterranean alter ego, the Special Project Operations Center in Algiers, was shut down on September 12, 1944. On the day after Christmas, General Gubbins, the head of Britain's Special

Operations Executive, recommended to General Donovan, director of the U.S. Office of Strategic Services, that Special Force Headquarters be officially dissolved.

On May 7, 1945, Eisenhower's headquarters announced the surrender of all German air, sea, and land forces.

Bernie Knox, the U.S. Army captain on Jedburgh team Giles, whose jump into France is described in the prologue to this book, completed a very successful mission with his team in western Brittany, including leading maquis attacks on elements of the hard-core German 2nd Parachute Division. OSS later sent him to Italy, where he led Italian partisans in the mountains until the Germans surrendered. He was back in the States on leave, en route to the Pacific to fight the Japanese, when the war ended. Discharged in September 1945, Knox began graduate work in the classics at Yale, under the GI Bill, in the spring of 1946. Two years later, he received his doctorate and a teaching position in the Yale classics department. He later served as director emeritus of the Harvard Center for Hellenic Studies in Washington, D.C. He was awarded the Croix de Guerre from France for his service with the Jedburghs. Dr. Knox has written a number of books, and the introduction to his *Essays Ancient and Modern* (Johns Hopkins, 1989) includes an account of his wartime Jedburgh experiences. He lives with his wife, Bianca, in a Maryland suburb of Washington, D.C.

Adrian Wise, the British major and team leader of Jedburgh team Frederick, went on to serve as a career officer in the British Army. He retired as a brigadier in the early 1970s and died in 1980.

Paul Bloch-Auroch, who, under the pseudonym Paul Aguirec, served as the French officer on team Frederick, played a big part in the effort to prepare leaders of the FFI and the FTP to serve in the regular French army. Once France had been liberated, the French established a number of schools for this purpose and Bloch-Auroch headed one in the Aisne department, where he had six former Jeds on his staff of instructors.

In late 1944, several of the French Jeds volunteered to go to Southeast Asia to carry on Jedburgh-like missions against the Japanese. But in fighting to regain their pre-war colony of French Indochina they also found themselves battling anti-French Vietminh insurgents. This conflict would continue beyond the end of World War II. Paul Bloch-Auroch (Aguirec) was among those who volunteered, and in late August 1945 he parachuted into Indochina with four other French Jeds on a mission to make contact with Bao Dai, the former figurehead emperor of Vietnam, in Hue. The team was headed by Captain Paul Grall, who had been the French officer on Bernie Knox's Jedburgh team Giles in France. Bloch-Auroch was second in command. The team was captured by Vietminh guerrillas, however, shortly after its arrival. The men were able to escape at the end of October, but were re-captured almost immediately. They escaped again on March 8, 1946. Late in March, as the Jeds were being pursued through the jungle, Bloch-Auroch became separated from the others and was never seen again.[2]

Bob Kehoe, team Frederick's radioman, received the Distinguished Service Cross, the French Croix de Guerre, and a Mention in Despatches from Britain for his service in Brittany. Kehoe had completed two years of college before entering the army. After the war, he went to Rutgers for two years to finish his undergraduate degree, then on to Columbia where he earned a master's degree in international relations. In 1970, he was granted a Ph.D. in Far Eastern studies from American University. Dr. Kehoe began work as an analyst for the Central Intelligence Agency in 1949 and spent thirty-five years with the agency, including work in the training division and in management. He has kept in touch with many of the men and women of the resistance who worked with Jed team Frederick in 1944, and he has visited many of them in France over the years since the war. Dr. Kehoe now lives in retirement with his wife, Ann, in Boulder, Colorado. They have a daughter, two sons, and four grandchildren.

* * *

Marceau, the resistance leader who had worked so closely with Jedburgh team Frederick in the Côtes-du-Nord, abandoned his career as an educator, as well as his political ambitions, to serve as a regular officer in the post-war French Army.

Jedburgh team George returned to France on a second mission in early September 1944. Working in support of a special inter-Allied mission called Shinoile, the team, reinforced by four additional Jedburgh teams, organized the FFI investment of the German fortresses at La Rochelle and St-Nazaire. The mission concluded in November of that year.

Philippe Ragueneau, the French captain who led Jedburgh team George under the assumed name of Erard, began a lengthy and distinguished career in journalism and broadcasting following the war. Beginning in 1947, he took a leading role in Charles de Gaulle's new political party, becoming a member of the party's executive commission in 1951. He later served de Gaulle—upon his return to power in 1958—as a member of his private cabinet, charged with handling press relations. In 1959 he began a career as an administrator in French television and went on to become a successful television writer and producer, as well as the author of more than twenty books.

Mr. Ragueneau was made a commander of the Legion of Honor and a companion of the Order of Liberation. Among the military decorations he received for his service in the war were three awards of the Croix de Guerre and the Medal of French Resistance. From Great Britain he received the 1939–45 War Medal with the emblem signifying a Mention in Despatches, and from the United States he received the Silver Star. He was married to Catherine Anglade, who died in 1994. Mr. Ragueneau died at Gordes, in the Vaucluse, on October 22, 2003, at the age of eighty-five.

Paul Cyr, the American captain on Jedburgh team George, received the Distinguished Service Cross for actions during his first Jedburgh mission in France. After his second mission in France, he was transferred to the OSS detachment in China. There, he led team Jackal—made up of OSS men and Chinese guerrillas—on a demolition job to destroy a mile-long railway bridge over the Yellow River in August 1945. The bridge was blown just as a Japanese troop train was crossing it, dropping the train and its cargo of two thousand Japanese soldiers into the Yellow River. Cyr's account of the mission was published in *The Saturday Evening Post* ("We Blew the Yellow River Bridge," March 23, 1946).

Mr. Cyr made an unsuccessful bid for a congressional seat from Indiana in 1950, and later went to Washington as aide to Indiana Republican Senator Homer E. Capehart. He subsequently served as a government civilian employee of the Army Materiel Command and with the Federal Energy Administration. He lived in retirement with his wife, Donna, in Mt. Pleasant, South Carolina, until his death on September 5, 1994.

Pierre Gay (pseudonym Christien Lejeune), the French lieutenant and radio operator on Jedburgh team George, joined Bloch-Auroch and the others who volunteered to go to Southeast Asia to fight the Japanese and the Vietminh. He parachuted into Indochina with Bloch-Auroch's team in late August 1945, and escaped with the others in early March 1946 after they had been captured and imprisoned by the Vietminh. Lieutenant Gay, like Bloch-Auroch, became separated from the others while being pursued through the jungle in late March and was never seen again.[3]

Today, the Museum of Breton Resistance is located in a wooded park on the outskirts of St-Marcel, not far from a monument to the resistance which stands on the grounds of the farm called La Nouée, where Jedburgh team George fought in the battle to defend the Dingson SAS base. The farmhouse at La Nouée, destroyed during the battle, has been restored.

* * *

Bill Colby, the American major on Jedburgh team Bruce, followed his Jedburgh mission by leading a Norwegian special operations (Norso) group on a daring mission to occupied Norway in the spring of 1945. He received the Bronze Star Medal and the French Croix de Guerre for his service in France, and the Silver Star and Norway's St. Olaf's Medal for the Norso operation.

Colby returned to New York at the end of the war, left the army, and entered Columbia Law School. He married Barbara Heinzen in September 1945, and the couple had five children—three boys and two girls. Upon his graduation from Columbia in 1947, Colby joined the law firm of Donovan, Leisure, Newton, Lumbard and Irvine.

He began work for the National Labor Relations Board in Washington in 1949, and joined the Central Intelligence Agency in November 1950. Mr. Colby served in various CIA positions in Stockholm, Rome, Saigon, and Washington. President Richard Nixon appointed him director of central intelligence in September 1973 and he served in that capacity until January 1976. At his departure, President Gerald Ford awarded Colby the National Security Medal. Mr. Colby then returned to the practice of law and later worked as a consultant in Washington. He and Barbara were divorced in 1984, and he later married Sally Shelton, a former ambassador and a top official at the U.S. Agency for International Development. Mr. Colby authored two books, *Honorable Men: My Life in the CIA* (Simon and Schuster, 1978) and *Lost Victory* (Contemporary Books, 1989), the latter covering his service in Vietnam. He died in a canoeing accident, at the age of seventy-six, on April 27, 1996, and was buried at Arlington National Cemetery.

Roger Bardet, the Frenchman—and traitor—who was Bill Colby's contact in the Yonne resistance, survived the war. He was arrested at war's end, tried for treason in a French court, and sentenced to death in December 1949. The sentence, however, soon was commuted to a term of imprisonment and, in 1955, he received a reprieve and was released from prison. Mr. Colby told me in 1989 that Bardet subsequently disappeared and had not been seen nor heard from since that time. According to one source, Bardet changed his name and became a prosperous businessman.

Upon completion of team Bruce's mission, Lieutenant Camille Lelong (pseudonym Jacques Favel) served as French Army liaison officer to an American unit. After the war, he returned to Louisiana to look after his family's eight-thousand-acre plantation there, raising cotton, corn, and cattle. He now lives in retirement with his wife in the town of Coushatta, Louisiana. They have three daughters and a son, and several grandchildren and great-grandchildren.

Roger Villebois, the French lieutenant who, under the name Louis Giry, served as radio operator on Jedburgh team Bruce, joined those French Jeds who transferred to the Far East. He and two other French Jeds parachuted into the Tonkin area of northern Vietnam on the first day of March 1945. Shortly thereafter, they joined a French unit which was garrisoned in the imperial city of Hue, near the coast of central Vietnam. Lieutenant Villebois was killed in action during a Japanese assault on the garrison on March 9, 1945.[4]

The three members of Jedburgh team Augustus who were killed on that rainy night of August 30, 1944—Major John Bonsall, Captain Jean Delviche, and First Sergeant Roger Côté—have not been forgotten. Every year since 1944, in late August or early September, a small ceremony is held in Barenton-sur-Serre at the spot where the men were killed. On September 9, 1984, in commemoration of the fortieth anniversary of their liberation, the people of Barenton-sur-Serre named the village's main street after Captain Jean Delviche, the French member of the team. A bronze plaque bearing the names of all three men was mounted on a stone wall at the cemetery to mark the site where they had initially been buried by the villagers. Jean Delviche remains interred there.

The remains of John Bonsall and Roger Côté were later moved to the Épinal American Military Cemetery located in the Vosges foothills. Both men were posthumously awarded the Distinguished

Service Cross and the Purple Heart. John Bonsall's sister, Mrs. Katharine B. Strong, established a music scholarship in his memory at Princeton University in 1950. The John Halsey Bonsall Fellowship in Music is still awarded each year to an outstanding graduate student in the university's music department.

Jacques Martin (pseudonym Martino), the French captain who led Jedburgh team Chloroform, served as one of the instructors at the school in the Aisne run by Paul Bloch-Auroch to retrain resistance fighters for service in the French army. After the war, he went on to a distinguished career in the diplomatic service. He was France's ambassador to Yugoslavia during the 1970s and was serving as deputy head of the Direction Politique in the French Foreign Ministry at the time of the Jedburgh reunion in Paris in 1984.

Henry McIntosh, the American lieutenant on Jedburgh team Chloroform, returned to the United States for a month-long leave before shipping out to the China-Burma-India Theater. There, he served with OSS behind the lines in China, much as he had in occupied France. At war's end, he returned home and married Harriet Lee Owens—the sister of a close friend and fraternity brother—on November 6, 1945. He was discharged from the army as a captain the following month. McIntosh's war decorations include the Silver Star, the French Croix de Guerre with Silver Star, and a Mention in Despatches from Britain.

He resumed the study of medicine which had been interrupted by the war, and graduated from the University of Pennsylvania Medical School in 1950. Dr. McIntosh taught medicine at Duke University, Baylor University, the University of Florida, and the University of South Florida, and joined the Watson Clinic in Lakeland, Florida, as a cardiologist in 1975. He served as president of the American College of Cardiology (1974–75) and chairman of the Council of Clinical Cardiology of the American Heart Association (1975–76). In 1984, Dr. McIntosh founded and served as Chairman of the Board of Heartbeat International, an organization committed to making cardiac-related medical devices (cardiac pacemakers) available to needy patients worldwide. President Ronald Reagan recognized his work by presenting him The Presidential Citation in the Rose Garden of the White House in June 1986. Dr. McIntosh is retired and lives with his wife, Harriet, in Lakeland, Florida.

Lieutenant Jean Sassi, who served as radio operator on team Chloroform under the name of Jean Nicole, was another who made the journey to the Far East to fight the Japanese. He jumped with two other Jeds as team Vega into northern Laos in June 1945 to gather intelligence and organize guerrilla strikes against Japanese lines of communication. Sassi survived the war and was among a number of French Jeds who were instrumental in creating the French special forces in the immediate post-war years. He later became an executive with the Citroën automobile manufacturing company.[5]

Doug Bazata, the American captain on Jedburgh team Cedric, earned the Distinguished Service Cross, four Purple Hearts, and the French Croix de Guerre with two palms during the war. After leaving the army as a major in 1947, he studied wine making in Paris and spent a number of years working in the wine industry in Europe. In the fifties he became an artist, painting in the abstract expressionist style so popular at the time, and held one-man shows in France, England, Germany, and the United States. In Maryland, in the early 1970s, he ran a pheasant preserve and hunting club. Government work followed with service in the Veterans Administration and at the Navy Department, where, in the 1980s, he served as a special assistant to Navy Secretary John Lehman. Mr. Bazata lived with his wife, Marie-Pierre, in Chevy Chase, Maryland, until his death at the age of eighty-eight on July 14, 1999. He is buried in Arlington National Cemetery.

Doug Bazata had a well-earned reputation among the Jeds as a great storyteller, and I never tired of listening to him during the few opportunities I had to spend time with him. My last visit with him, in 1988, resulted in an unforgettable incident. I was in a roomful of Jeds and their families at the French Embassy in Washington for an award ceremony. There were perhaps three hundred people in the crowd. I was standing next to Mr. Bazata, with whom I had been chatting before the ceremony began, about three-fourths of the way back in the crowd. The French ambassador began speaking and a hush fell over the crowd. Suddenly, Bazata leaned over to me and asked, "Hey Will, did I ever tell you about the time I slept with Bill Colby's daughter?" And he said it loud enough for everyone within a radius of about six feet to hear him. What's more, Bill Colby was standing immediately in front of me!

I responded negatively and hoped that he would drop it at that, but Bazata went on to say that it was true, even though she always denied it. Just then, Mr. Colby turned around with a grin on his face and said, "I think I need to tell you the rest of that story." As it turned out, Colby had been a major when the war ended in 1945 and had received orders to Fort Leavenworth to attend the Army's Command and General Staff College. But he had decided to get out of the army and resume his studies at Columbia Law School. So he and Barbara had taken a small apartment on Manhattan's upper west side. One day, a year or two later, Bazata showed up at their door, having just returned from Europe and needing a place to stay for the night. So the Colbys let him sleep on the floor in the nursery, where their baby girl, only weeks old, was asleep in her crib. When Colby finished explaining this, everyone within earshot began laughing and the French ambassador had to stop the ceremony and ask us to keep quiet.

Bazata was just an unforgettable character, plain and simple. Eric Pace of *The New York Times*, in his August 16, 1999, obituary of Mr. Bazata, wrote that Salvador Dali, whom Bazata had known, once painted a likeness of Doug "done up as Don Quixote," and called the painting "Homage to Bazata."

Louis Lesne (pseudonym Chapel), the French captain on team Cedric, is deceased.

Dick Floyd, team Cedric's radio operator, was discharged from the army in October 1945 and started school under the GI Bill at St. John's University in February 1946. He finished his degree and then stayed at St. John's to complete law school. He married Sheila Charles—whom he met on a blind date shortly after leaving the army—on March 26, 1951. Following graduation from law school three months later, Mr. Floyd went to Europe as an employee of the Central Intelligence Agency. He crossed the Atlantic traveling First Class on the *Queen Elizabeth*, and found it to be a decidedly better voyage than his crossing on the *Queen Mary* in December 1944. He remained with the CIA from 1951 to 1953, then began a career in sales and marketing in the paper business, working for Owens-Illinois, Inc. The Floyds now live in Berkeley Heights, New Jersey. They have five sons (a sixth died shortly after birth) and twenty-two grandchildren—fourteen girls and eight boys.

George Millar, the British captain who, as a Special Operations Executive agent in the Doubs, worked so closely with Jedburgh team Cedric, returned to England immediately upon the completion of his mission. He received the Distinguished Service Order and the Military Cross for his service in France.

In the years following the war, he authored nine books and edited a tenth. Among his books are three in which he relates his war experiences: *Maquis* (William Heinemann Ltd., 1945; published in the United States by Doubleday & Company, Inc., in 1946, as *Waiting in the Night*), *The Horned Pigeon* (Doubleday & Company, Inc., 1946), and *Road to Resistance* (Little, Brown and Company, 1979). Despite being ordered out of France by General de Gaulle, along with all the other SOE circuit leaders, in September 1944, Millar was later invited to visit President de Gaulle in his office in Paris, and de Gaulle told Millar that he had read his book *Maquis* and had enjoyed it immensely. He told Millar that, on a recent trip to eastern France, he had even gone out of his way to visit the village of Vieilley.

Sir Peter Wilkinson, KCMG, DSO, OBE, who, as a Special Operations Executive staff officer in 1942 was the principal author of the Jedburgh concept, commanded No. 6 Special Force (SOE) from 1943 to 1945. He entered the Diplomatic Service in 1947 and subsequently served in the British Embassies in Vienna, Washington, and Bonn. In 1955, he served as secretary general of the Geneva Summit. He was later under secretary at the Cabinet Office and a senior civilian instructor at the Imperial Defence College. He served as British ambassador in Saigon and Vienna, retired from the Diplomatic Service in 1972, and became coordinator of intelligence at the Cabinet Office that same year. Mr. Wilkinson published his war memoir in 1997 under the title *Foreign Fields: The Story of an SOE Operative* (I. B. Tauris Publishers, 1997).

The Jedburghs held their first reunion, a four-day affair, in Paris in late May 1984, marking the passage of forty years since their wartime exploits. An American Jedburgh reunion was held at Fayetteville and nearby Fort Bragg, North Carolina, in 1985. In May 1988, the second international Jedburgh reunion took place in Washington, D.C., drawing fifty-one American, eighteen British, and twenty-six French Jedburgh veterans, as well as their families.[6] The next such gathering was held in England in May 1991. At the earliest of these reunions, Jeds often found themselves greeting old friends whom they had not seen since Milton Hall, before departing for missions in France or Holland. Some first learned the real names of their French colleagues, whom they had only known until then by their noms-de-guerre. Most recently, twenty-two surviving Jedburgh veterans were among the attendees at a reunion held in Peterborough, England, near Milton Hall, in June 2004.

The Jedburgh project was a bold experiment. We should remember that as late as 1943 the outcome of the Second World War was, at the very least, uncertain. Allied success in the invasion of France was by no means guaranteed and, because of that, military leaders were reluctant to turn their backs on any option which might contribute to final victory.

How successful was the project? The value of any special operation, particularly within the context of total war, is difficult to assess, and people often minimize the contributions made because there is a tendency to overestimate the expected results of such operations. Maurice Buckmaster, who headed Special Operations Executive's French section, later wrote of early unfriendly attitudes of the high command toward SOE. "They demanded miracles and when we failed to work them they became disillusioned and sarcastic."[7] The Jedburghs and other special forces did not win the war in Western Europe—far from it. Nor were they designed to or expected to. Like the signal corps or the artillery or the air force, they simply did their part to *help* win the war.

The answer to the question of how successful the Jedburgh project was, I think, is in the effectiveness of resistance activities in support of the Allied campaign in France. Resistance folklore aside, operations carried out by the FFI in the summer of 1944 would have been far less effective if they had not been tied to the Allied ground campaign. And they would have been of little consequence at all without the tons of material and the training and advice provided them by the British and Americans. Special forces such as the Jedburghs played such a key role in making all of that happen, and in effecting such close coordination between the conventional and the unconventional war efforts, that no other measurement of their success seems appropriate. What is certain is that the activities of these special forces and the resistance groups they worked with helped to shorten the Allied campaign in France.

The most important task assigned to the resistance was that of disrupting the movement of German reinforcements to the Normandy beachhead or to oppose the Allied landings in southern France. And this they did remarkably well, delaying many divisions and completely stopping others. According to British historian M. R. D. Foot, the resistance kept eight German divisions from ever reaching the Overlord and Dragoon battlefields.[8]

An often unrecognized contribution of the Jedburghs was their ability to keep maquis groups of wide-ranging political and ideological backgrounds focused on working together to defeat the common enemy—the Germans. More than a few Jedburgh veterans have told me that they expended as much effort in preventing clashes between rival maquis groups as they did in fighting the Germans.

General Bradley referred to the maquis as a valuable ally in the Brittany campaign, and he often paid tribute to their work in his messages to SHAEF. Ralph Ingersoll, a planning officer on Bradley's staff, shortly after the war wrote about how he and others, while still in England, had not been impressed with the romantic tales they had heard of the resistance. After entering France, though, they were able to witness firsthand the FFI's "solid efficiency and hard accomplishments." Ingersoll went on to explain that, "what cut ice with us was the fact that when we came to France the resistance was so effective that it took half a dozen real live German divisions to contend with it, divisions which might otherwise have been on our backs in the Bocage."[9]

Colonel Robert S. Allen, a staff officer at General Patton's Third Army headquarters, also wrote of the FFI's contribution. During Third Army's sweep through Brittany, Allen later wrote, "over 30,000 armed FFI rendered invaluable fighting and intelligence aid to the spearheads. These unknown and humble resistance combatants, fighting heroically and effectively, deserve undying tribute for their great contribution to this crucial victory."[10] Allen's praise continued when writing of how the resistance later helped protect Third Army's right flank during its race across France, including the capture of an entire German corps approaching from southwest France. "To these unknown resistance fighters and the XIX [Tactical Air Command] pilots," wrote Allen, "belongs the real credit for the capture of [German Major General Eric] Elster's command."[11]

General Patton received laudatory comments about the work of special forces in a letter from one of his corps commanders, who wrote: "SF operations, including the employment of FFI personnel in support of this corps, have been particularly effective. . . . It is believed that a very definite role has been created for SF personnel in support of this corps and that continuing support will definitely be gained from their activities."[12]

Patton himself was so pleased with the work of Special Force Detachment 11, which was attached to his army staff, that in September, when operations in France were all but over, he requested to keep the detachment when Third Army moved on into Germany.[13]

Praise also came from the officers and men of the Seventh Army who came ashore in southern France, where the FFI was credited with the capture of an estimated forty-two thousand German prisoners. Brigadier General Frederick B. Butler, the commander of Task Force Butler, acknowledged that "without the Maquis our mission would have been far more difficult."[14]

Butler is also supposed to have judged that the FFI who supported Operation Dragoon were equivalent to four or five divisions.[15] Echoing that sentiment, the 3rd Infantry Division's official history of the campaign states: "A major factor aiding the speed and success of our movement was the activity of the French resistance groups." All along their northward march, the division's history records,

> whole towns were seized and held to await our coming. In addition to this sabotage activities were coordinated with our movements. If the Air Force failed to destroy a bridge, that bridge might be demolished anyway—from the ground and with hand-laid demolitions. Speeding convoys of enemy reserves ran into mysteriously laid roadblocks, and ambush.[16]

In the war report of the U.S. 180th Infantry Regiment we read of how the "continual harassing by the Maquis cost the Germans heavily and rendered them unable to put up an organized resistance."[17] The regiment's history, however, also recognizes how the maquis helped in so many other ways. When, for example, a regimental reconnaissance element was surrounded by Germans northeast of Lyon, the maquis rescued all but two of the Americans and saw them safely back to friendly lines.

The 179th Infantry Regiment's official history explains how the FFI initially helped by ambushing German columns and blowing up enemy munitions dumps, and how they would then seize towns and bridges and await the arrival of the tanks and infantry. "Then, when the doughboys did arrive, the local FFI served as informants and guides. After four years of spying, these men knew everything there was to know about the enemy. And they knew the terrain."[18]

Knowledge of the terrain was particularly valuable to American armored and motorized units that were moving too fast for map supplies to keep up with them. Tactical elements typically operated from Michelin road maps rather than from detailed military topographical maps. Seventh Army's official war report elaborates on the importance of this information, explaining how "the FFI had made careful note of German gun positions and their fields of fire, the location of pillboxes, minefields, and antitank obstacles, they were of invaluable service in guiding patrols to objectives with least loss of time and lives."[19]

Lieutenant General Lucien K. Truscott, Jr., the U.S. corps commander in southern France, later expressed his admiration for the work of the resistance and the Jedburghs when he wrote,

> So effective were the Maquis that the Germans moved only in large numbers. The Maquis were well provided with arms and explosives by the Allies, and Allied officers with communications had parachuted in to assist them in coordinating their operations. We had expected a good deal of assistance from them, and we were not disappointed. Their knowledge of the country, of enemy dispositions and movements, was invaluable, and their fighting ability was extraordinary.[20]

British General Sir Henry Maitland Wilson, supreme Allied commander in the Mediterranean Theater and responsible for the launching of Operation Dragoon in southern France, was equally generous with his praise when he estimated that the FFI "reduced the fighting efficiency of the Wehrmacht in southern France to forty per cent at the moment of the Dragoon landing operations."[21]

Not all Allied units shared these views of the FFI, though. Sadly, a few units saw only those "eleventh-hour" resistance fighters— bands of men who appeared only after the fighting was over and then boasted of their role in capturing a town. Others witnessed small groups, often claiming to be of the leftist FTP, whose members were little better than gangsters and seemed only interested in exacting revenge on alleged collaborators. Such groups as these were small in number, however, and were equally despised by the true resistance fighters.

Much was learned about the effectiveness of the resistance from captured German officers. "And it made the most cynical sit up and take notice," observed Ralph Ingersoll, "when we learned from German field officers that the Germans in central France were truly terrified, had to live under arms, could not move freely, had lost all control in sizable sectors even before we came."

Attempts by the Germans to deal with the threat had only made the guerrillas more effective. "Caught between the devil and the resistance, the German High Command had finally to draw on its police divisions in central France to reinforce its army in Normandy." But as they thinned out such police forces in the interior, "the effectiveness of the maquis increased in geometrical proportion."

Ingersoll's final assessment of the contribution made by the resistance was that:

> [i]t would be an empty history of the campaign in France and Belgium that tried to credit the success of the Allied arms in those countries to the Allied weight of guns and aircraft alone. It was a military fact that the French were worth at least a score of divisions to us, maybe more.[22]

He concluded by comparing the way the Allies sliced through France to the bloody fighting at the German border, when they no longer had "any friends beyond our own lines."[23]

One German officer referred to the Jedburghs in a post-war memoir when he wrote of how they helped in increasing the effectiveness of the FFI by August 1944. "As time went by," he wrote, "and they gained experience, they developed into a real threat for the German withdrawal."[24]

Field Marshal von Rundstedt, German commander on the Western Front, had recognized as early as 1943 that "a serious turning point in the interior situation of France" had been reached when the "organized supply of arms from England to France became greater every month." By the end of that year, he observed, "It was already impossible to dispatch single members of the Wehrmacht, ambulances, couriers or supply columns without armed protection to the First or Nineteenth Army in the south of France."[25]

By 1944, according to von Rundstedt, the situation in southern France had become

> so dangerous that all commanders reported a general revolt.
> . . . Cases became numerous where whole formations of

troops, and escorting troops of the military commanders were surrounded by bands for many days and, in isolated locations, simply killed off. . . . The life of the German troops in southern France was seriously menaced and became a doubtful proposition.[26]

In a telephone conversation with a general on Hitler's staff, just five days after the Normandy landings, the German commander-in-chief in the west explained how the morale of his troops was suffering as the FFI, "feeling the end approaching, grow steadily bolder."[27]

But probably no one was in a better position to offer an informed opinion on how well those resistance activities directly supported the Allied ground campaign—which was the whole purpose of the Jedburghs—than the supreme commander himself. And General Eisenhower never hesitated to express his admiration and appreciation for the work of the irregular warriors. He did so to his superiors in Washington and to others on many occasions during the war. In his 1948 war memoir, *Crusade in Europe*, Eisenhower judged that, "[w]ithout their great assistance the liberation of France and the defeat of the enemy in western Europe would have consumed a much longer time and meant greater losses to ourselves."[28]

At the close of the war in Europe, General Eisenhower wrote to Major General Colin Gubbins, SOE director, and Colonel David Bruce, head of OSS in the European Theater, to express his thanks and admiration for the work of SFHQ and the many special forces missions it directed.

"In no previous war," wrote Eisenhower,

and in no other theater during this war, have resistance forces been so closely harnessed to the main military effort. While no final assessment of the operational value of resistance action has yet been completed, I consider that the disruption of enemy rail communications, the harassing of German road moves and the continual and increasing strain placed on the

German war economy and internal security services throughout occupied Europe by the organized forces of resistance, played a very considerable part in our complete and final victory.[29]

It also was recognized at the highest levels that the French resistance would have been much less effective without the assistance of Allied special forces. In a secret assessment of resistance and special forces contributions provided to the Combined Chiefs of Staff in July 1945, U.S. Lieutenant General Walter Bedell Smith and British Lieutenant General Sir Frederick E. Morgan, Eisenhower's chief of staff and deputy chief of staff, respectively, wrote that "without the organization, communications, material, training and leadership which SOE supplied, . . . 'resistance' would have been of no military value."[30]

Lastly, author Blake Ehrlich quotes former United States Army chief of staff, General of the Army George C. Marshall, as stating in 1946 that, "[t]he resistance surpassed all our expectations, and it was they who, in delaying the arrival of German reinforcements and in preventing the regrouping of enemy divisions in the interior, assured the success of our landings."[31] As this book hopefully has shown, the Jedburghs contributed to that success.

As successful as they were, however, the Jedburghs perhaps could have made even greater contributions, as the teams were not always used as effectively as they might have been. The complaint most often heard from the Jeds themselves is that they were sent in too late. Sir James R. H. Hutchison, a Jedburgh officer who would later serve as Britain's under-secretary of state for war, probably best articulated this sentiment and hinted at lost opportunities in his mission's after-action report.

Jedburgh teams were more than justified. The pity is that more were not sent sooner as requested. The maquis wanted them and asked for them. Their help in carrying out a common training and a coordinated tactical policy was invaluable; their example in action and their acceptance of a military discipline and hierarchy would have borne unconscious fruit in the minds of maquisards now relapsing into unrestrained and violent action reminiscent of the middle ages. The arrival of Allied officers in uniform was, not only to the men of the maquis but also to the civil population, an earnest that the Allies took resistance seriously; a pledge that the people's gallant and tragic resistance throughout the years had not gone unnoticed or uncounted. Allied officers were recognized immediately as having and offering views unbiased by French internal questions; they could have no axe to grind. The Jedburgh conception was truly founded. It was, alas, not used to the full.[32]

The work of the Jedburghs, it should be added, would never have been possible without the facilities, the expertise, and the indoctrination so magnanimously provided by Britain's Special Operations Executive. And it certainly could not have been done without the support of the British and American air force special operations squadrons responsible for delivering the teams to the field and responding to their requests for air resupply drops. A generation before FedEx and UPS, these British Special Duty Squadrons and American "Carpetbaggers" were providing next-day (actually next-night) delivery from England and Algiers to points throughout Western Europe and the Balkans. Approximately four thousand supply drop sorties, delivering more than six thousand tons of arms and other supplies, were flown to the French resistance from July through September, when the Jedburghs were most active.[33] The Jeds in Brittany alone armed more than twenty thousand men of the maquis with weapons from such drops.[34]

For the men who served in the Jedburghs, it was the defining experience of their young lives; it changed these men, forever bonding them and setting them apart from all others. In some ways, the Jeds were a reflection of their time—a time of segregated armies and of limited opportunities for women. As with most front-line units of the Allied armies in Western Europe during the war, there were no blacks in the Jedburghs. Nor were there any women, even though many brave women had performed superbly in the field as members of SOE circuits and were decorated for their actions. The men who served with the Jeds, however, laid the foundation for the special forces of the future—special forces which grew even stronger and more capable by becoming more ethnically diverse in their makeup.

In 1989, William E. Colby sent me a photocopy of a memorandum he had written in May 1945. Colby had carried out guerrilla warfare with the French resistance as a member of a Jedburgh team and had led a special forces team into German-occupied Norway on a railway sabotage mission. In the memorandum, addressed to the chief of the Special Operations Branch of the Office of Strategic Services in Washington, Colby offered suggestions on how special forces teams should be organized and how they should function in the future. The team he proposed would be organized similarly to the American Operational Groups employed in France, Italy, and Norway, but its methods would be closer to those used by the Jedburghs. It was a concept, in fact, not far from that of the Green Beret "A-detachments" of the future.

America's special operations capability was lost when President Harry S. Truman ordered the Office of Strategic Services disbanded at the end of WWII. Five years later war erupted in Korea, however, and the need for an unconventional warfare force once again became apparent. So, in 1952, the United States Army Special Forces officially was established, and the first group activated was commanded by Colonel Aaron Bank—a former Jedburgh.

Many French Jedburgh veterans carried their experiences with them in the development of that country's modern special force, the 1er (Premier) Regiment Parachutiste d'Infanterie de Marine (1st Marine Parachute Infantry Regiment)—not a naval marine force, as the name implies, but more a descendent of the French SAS of World War II. And in the United Kingdom, the legendary Special Air Service remains the premier special force.

Today, these units carry on the Jedburgh tradition, and the same high-caliber young people continue to come forward to aid those living under the yoke of oppression—especially those who decide to stand up and fight for the freedoms which we, ourselves, too often take for granted.

APPENDIX
THE FRENCH JEDBURGH TEAMS

The following is as accurate a roster of Jedburgh teams and person-nel deployed to France as I could put together from the sources at hand. I have relied most heavily on the information provided in the OSS Special Operations (London) Branch *War Diary*, as well as sim-ilar documentation prepared by the Special Project Operations Center in Algiers. While these sources contain most Jedburgh team after-action reports, they do not contain them all. I have been able to locate other reports as separate documents in the National Archives. Jedburgh veterans have helped with corrections to some name spellings which are incorrect in *War Diary* or other docu-ments. Especially helpful in this respect were Arthur Brown, Général Paul Aussaresses, Joe de Francesco, Lou Lajeunesse, and Camille Lelong.

In the interest of standardization, I have chosen to cite the rank of personnel—as accurately as official documents and other sources allowed me to—as the rank held when the team deployed to the field—even though many of the men subsequently were promoted. Ranks that may be unfamiliar to some readers are explained in the notes following the roster. The initials "W/T" following a name identify the wireless telegraph, or radio, operator.

Lastly, casualties shown in the remarks column refer only to those casualties suffered on that specific mission or as a direct result of that mission. Some of these men later were killed or wounded elsewhere during World War II or in later conflicts. Gaston Vuchot, for example, was killed in action while fighting in a conventional French army regiment during the battle for Colmar in February 1945.

French Jeds killed in action in Indochina in 1945 and 1946 include: Paul Bloch-Auroch, Pierre Gay, Jean-Pierre Herenguel, Alexandre Martelli, Lucien Paris, Pierre Rousset, Maurice Stasse, and Roger Villebois. Pierre Bloch, Roger Crétin, and Paul Scherrer were killed in action in Algeria during the 1950s insurgency there. British Jeds Godfrey Marchant, Peter Vickery, and Peter Colvin were killed in 1945 in India, when they were leaving for a mission in Burma and their plane crashed during takeoff.

Mission
Rank,* Name & (*Nom-de-guerre*)

ALAN
Deployed from Tempsford, England, to the Sôane-et-Loire
department of Central France on the night of 12–13 August 1944.
Capt. Robert Toussaint (*André Gairaud*)
Capt. Stanley M. Cannicott
S/Lt. Robert Clause, W/T (*François de Heysen*)

ALASTAIR
Deployed from Harrington, England, to the Vosges department of
Northeast France on the night of 24–25 August 1944.
Maj. Oliver H. Brown
Lt. René Karrière (*René Maître*)
Sgt. G. N. "Smithy" Smith, W/T

ALEC
Deployed from Harrington, England, to the Loire-et-Cher department
of Central France on the night of 9–10 August 1944.
1st Lt. George C. Thomson
Lt. Alain Bordes (*Bernard Allet*)
S/Sgt. John Augustine White, W/T

ALEXANDER
Deployed from Tempsford, England, to the Creuse department of
Central France on the night of 12–13 August 1944.
Lt. René de la Tousche (*Richard Thouville*)
1st Lt. Stewart J. O. Alsop
1st Sgt. Norman R. "Dick" Franklin, W/T

ALFRED
Deployed from England to the Oise department of Northern France
on the night of 24–25 August 1944.
Capt. Lewis D. MacDonald (*Leslie MacDougall*)
Lt. Jean-Pierre Herenguel (*G. de Wavrant*)
Sgt. Albert W. Key, W/T

---

* All ranks are as of the date of deployment and do not reflect later promotions.
Most of the American radio operators were promoted to the rank of first sergeant
by the time their missions were completed. Many officers also were promoted
while in the field.

American ranks in the table above include: **Lt. Col.** (lieutenant colonel), **Maj.**
(major), **Capt.** (captain), **1st Lt.** (first lieutenant), **2d Lt.** (second lieutenant), **1st Sgt.**
(first sergeant), **M/Sgt.** (master sergeant), **T/Sgt.** (technical sergeant), **S/Sgt.** (staff
sergeant), **T/3** (technician, 3d grade), **Sgt.** (sergeant), **S3Cl.** (seaman third class [U.S.
Navy]).

Code Name	Nationality	Remarks
Ariège	French	
Pembroke	British	Wounded in action
Kroner	French	
Kent	British	
Donegall	French	
Lincoln	British	
Cromarty	American	
Oxford	French	Died of wounds
Colorado	American	
Leix	French	
Rona	American	
Cork	American	
Argyll	British	
Aude	French	
Wampum	British	

British ranks include: **Lt. Col.** (lieutenant colonel), **Maj.** (major), **Capt.** (captain), **1st Lt.** (first lieutenant), **2d Lt.** (second lieutenant), **CQMS** (quartermaster sergeant), **Sgt.** (sergeant), **LAC** (leading aircraftman [Royal Air Force]).

French ranks include: **Col.** (colonel), **Cmdt.** (commandant [major]), **Capt.** (capitaine [captain]), **Lt.** (lieutenant [first lieutenant]), **S/Lt.** (sous-lieutenant [second lieutenant]), **Asp.** (aspirant [officer cadet]).

Mission
Rank, Name & (*Nom-de-guerre*)

AMMONIA
Deployed from Blida, Algeria, to the Lot department of Southwest
France on the night of 9–10 June 1944.
Capt. Benton McDonald "Mac" Austin
Capt. Raymond Lecompte (*R. Conte*)
Sgt. Jacob B. "Jack" Berlin, W/T

ANDREW
Deployed from England to the Ardennes department of Northeast
France on the night of 15–16 August 1944.
Maj. A. H. S. "Henry" Coombe-Tennant
Lt. Édouard C. Antoine, Comte d'Oultrement
Sgt. Frank Harrison, W/T

ANDY
Deployed from Harrington, England, to the Haute-Vienne department
of South Central France on the night of 11–12 July 1944.
Maj. Ronald A. Parkinson
Cmdt. J. Verneuil (*J. Vermeulen*)
Sgt. Glyn R. Loosmore, W/T

ANTHONY
Deployed from Keevil, England, to the Saône-et-Loire department
of Central France on the night of 14–15 August 1944.
Capt. Maurice Stasse (*Claude Deprez*)
1st Lt. Mason B. "Buz" Starring
T/Sgt. John L. Bradner, W/T

ARCHIBALD
Deployed from Harrington, England, to the Meurthe-et-Moselle
department of Northeast France on the night of 25—26 August 1944.
Maj. Arthur du P. Denning
Lt. François Costes (*A. Montlac*)
M/Sgt. Roger L. Pierre, W/T

ARNOLD
Deployed from Tarrant Rushton, England, to the Marne department
of Northeast France on the night of 24–25 August 1944.
Capt. Michel de Carville (*Michel Coudray*)
Capt. James H. F. Monahan
Sgt. Alan de Ville, W/T

Code Name	Nationality	Remarks
Gaspard	American	
Ludovic	French	
Marcial	American	
Rupel	British	
Demer	Belgian	Wounded in action
Nethe	British	
Fife	British	Fractured leg on jump
Carlow	French	Fractured ankle on jump
Lundy	British	Joined Jed Hamish in the field
Perth	French	
Nebraska	American	
Pfennig	American	
Cumberland	British	Wounded in action
Montgomery	French	Wounded in action
Sen	American	
Sussex	French	
Londonderry	British	
Escudo	British	

Mission
Rank, Name & (*Nom-de-guerre*)

ARTHUR
Deployed from Tempsford, England, to the Côte-d'Or department
of Eastern France on the night of 18–19 August 1944.
Capt. Cecil F. "Skip" Mynatt, Jr.
S/Lt. Xavier Humblet (*Louis Hache*)
T/Sgt. Albert Victor Bacik, W/T

AUBREY
Deployed from Harrington, England, to the Seine-et-Marne
department of Northern France on the night of 11–12 August 1944.
Capt. Godfrey Marchant
Lt. Adrien Chaigneau (*J. Telmon*)
Sgt. Ivar Hooker, W/T

AUGUSTUS
Deployed from England to the Aisne department of Northern France
on the night of 15–16 August 1944.
Maj. John Halsey Bonsall
Capt. Jean Delviche (*Jean Dechville*)*
T/Sgt. Roger E. Côté, W/T

BASIL
Deployed from Harrington, England, to the Doubs department of
Eastern France on the night of 25–26 August 1944.
Capt. Robert Rivière (*R. Raincourt*)
Capt. Thomas A. "Tom" Carew
T/Sgt. John L. Stoyka, W/T

BENJAMIN
Deployed from Fairford, England, to the Meuse department of
Northeast France on the night of 20–21 August 1944.
Maj. Hubert "Terry" O'Bryan-Tear (*A. J. Forrest*)
Lt. Paul Moniez (*P. Marchand*)
S/Lt. Henri Kaminski, W/T (*J. Camouin*)

BERNARD
Deployed from Fairford, England, to the Meuse department of
Northeast France on the night of 20-21 August 1944.
Capt. Jocelyn de W. "Jock" Waller
Capt. Étienne Nasica (*E. Prato*)
Sgt. Cyril M. Bassett, W/T

* Although the Augustus mission report found in the Office of Strategic Services
War Diary shows this name spelled "Delwich," I have followed the spelling used
in French documents provided to me by General (Ret.) Paul Aussaresses.

Code Name	Nationality	Remarks
Connecticut	American	Fractured spine on jump
Smabrère	French	
Millième	American	
Rutland	British	
Kildare	French	Killed in action
Thaler	British	
Arizona	American	Captured and executed
Hérault	French	Captured and executed
Indiana	American	Captured and executed
Amblève	French	
Sutherland	British	
Ore	American	
Stirling	British	Wounded in action
Ulster	French	
Serre	French	Wounded in action
Tipperary	British	
Argens	French	Wounded in action
Lancashire	British	Wounded in action

Mission
Rank, Name & (*Nom-de-guerre*)

BRIAN
Deployed from Harrington, England, to the Doubs department of
Eastern France on the night of 27–28 August 1944.
Maj. Francis P. C. Johnstone
Capt. Roger Crétin (*R. Francomte*)
Sgt. Norman A. Smith, W/T

BRUCE
Deployed from Harrington, England, to the Yonne department of
Central France on the night of 14–15 August 1944.
Maj. William Egan "Bill" Colby
Lt. Camille M. Lelong (*Jacques P. Favel*)
S/Lt. Roger Villebois, W/T (*Louis Giry*)

BUGATTI
Deployed from Blida, Algeria, to the Hautes-Pyrénées department of
Southwest France on the night of 28–29 June 1944.
Maj. (USMCR) Horace W. "Hod" Fuller
Capt. Guy de la Roche du Rousset (*G. Rocher*)
S/Lt. Martial Sigaud, W/T (*J. Guillemot*)

BUNNY
Deployed from England to the Haute-Marne department of
Northeast France on the night of 17–18 August 1944.
Capt. J. F. D. Radice
Lt. Maurice Geminel (*M. Gerville*)
Sgt. James T. Chambers, W/T

CECIL
Deployed from Harrington, England, to the Aube department of
Central France on the night of 25–26 August 1944.
Maj. David J. Nielson
Capt. Alfred Keser (*A. Frayant*)
Sgt. Ronald "Boxer" Wilde, W/T

CEDRIC
Deployed from England to the Doubs department of Eastern
France on the night of 27–28 August 1944.
Capt. Douglas DeWitt "Doug" Bazata
Capt. Louis Lesne (*F. Chapel*)
T/Sgt. Richard C. "Dick" Floyd, W/T

Code Name	Nationality	Remarks
Illinois	British	
Orkney	French	Wounded in action
Lira	British	
Berkshire	American	
Galway	French	
Piastre	French	
Kansul	American	
Hopei	French	
Chekiang	French	Killed in action
Peso	British	Died of wounds
Yen	French	Wounded in action
Drachma	British	
Delaware	British	
Lys	French	
Centavo	British	
Vesdre	American	Wounded in action
Dendre	French	
Guilder	American	

Mission
Rank, Name & (*Nom-de-guerre*)

CHLOROFORM
Deployed from Algeria to the Drôme and Hautes-Alpes
departments of Southeast France on the night of 29–30 June 1944.
Capt. Jacques Martin (*Jacques Martino*)
1st Lt. Henry Deane McIntosh
S/Lt. Jean Sassi, W/T (*Jean H. Nicole*)

CHRYSLER
Deployed from Blida, Algeria, to the Ariège department of
Southwest France on the night of 16–17 August 1944.
Capt. Cyril H. Sell
Lt. Paul Louis Aussaresses (*Jean Soual*)
Sgt. Ronald E. "Ron" Chatten, W/T

CINNAMON
Deployed from Blida, Algeria, to the Var department of Southeast
France on the night of 13–14 August 1944.
Capt. Robert Harcourt
Capt. Henri Lespinasse-Fonsegrive (*F. L. Ferandon*)
S/Lt. Jacques Morineau, W/T (*J. G. Maurin*)

CITROËN
Deployed from Algeria to the Vaucluse department of Southeast
France on the night of 13–14 August 1944.
Capt. John E. Saint C. Smallwood
Capt. Pierre Bloch (*René-Clément Alcée*)
Sgt. Frederick A. "Fred" Bailey, W/T

COLLODION*
Deployed from Algeria to the Aveyron department of Southwest
France on the night of 6–7 August 1944.
Capt. Harold Hall
Lt. Henri Marsaudon (*P. Morgan*)
Sgt. Theodore "Theo" Baumgold, W/T

DANIEL
Deployed from Fairford, England, to the Côtes-du-Nord department
of Brittany in Western France on the night of 4–5 August 1944.
Capt. Kemys D. "Ed" Bennett
Lt. Albert P. de Schonen (*Pierre de Schonen*)
Sgt. Ron Brierley, W/T

* Team also known as **Loch**.

Code Name	Nationality	Remarks
Joshua	French	
Lionel	American	
Latimer	French	
Elie	British	
Bazin	French	
Artus	British	
Louis	British	Fractured both legs on jump
Orthon	French	
Luc	French	
Anne	British	
Laurent	French	
Rétif	British	
Augustine	British	
Benoît	French	Wounded in action
Jules	American	
Apôtre	British	
Argentier	French	
Florin	British	

Mission
Rank, Name & (*Nom-de-guerre*)

DESMOND
Deployed from Harrington, England, to the Côte-d'Or department
of Eastern France on the night of 3–4 September 1944.
Capt. William H. "Bill" Pietsch, Jr.
Capt. Gilles Maunoury (*Henri Bourriot*)
M/Sgt. Robert R. "Bob" Baird, W/T

DODGE
Deployed from Algeria to the Drôme department of Southeast
France on the night of 24–25 June 1944 (reinforced Jed Veganin).
Maj. Cyrus E. "Cy" Manierre, Jr.
Sgt. L. T. Durocher, W/T

DOUGLAS
Deployed from Keevil, England, to the Morbihan department of
Brittany in Western France on the night of 6–7 August 1944.
Capt. Richard A. "Dick" Rubinstein
Lt. Jean Roblot (*Jean Ronglou*)
Sgt. John D. Raven, W/T

DOUGLAS II
Deployed from Harrington, England, to the Doubs department of
Eastern France on the night of 15–16 September 1944.
Capt. Richard A. "Dick" Rubinstein
Capt. Jean Roblot (*Jean Ronglou*)
T/Sgt. John T. Van Hart, W/T

EPHEDRINE
Deployed from Blida, Algeria, to the Savoie department of Southeast
France on the night of 12–13 August 1944.
1st Lt. Lawrence E. "Larry" Swank
Lt. Louis Donnard (*Louis Rabeau*)
S/Lt. Robert Desplechin, W/T (*J. Bourgoin*)

FELIX
Deployed from Fairford, England, to the Côtes-du-Nord department
of Brittany in Western France on the night of 8–9 July 1944.
Capt. Jean-Paul Souquet (*J. Kernevel*)
Capt. John J. Marchant
Sgt. Peter M. Colvin, W/T

Code Name	Nationality	Remarks
Skerry	American	
Shetland	French	
Hampshire	American	
Rupert	American	Captured-POW, liberated 1945
Oswald	Canadian	
Augure	British	
Anachorere	French	
Half Crown	British	
Augure	British	
Anachorere	French	Killed in action
Half Crown	American	
Gantor	American	Killed in accidental shooting
Julien	French	
Léon	French	
Carnavon	French	
Somerset	British	
Middlesex	British	

Mission
Rank, Name & (*Nom-de-guerre*)

FRANCIS
Deployed from Harrington, England, to the Finistère department of
Brittany in Western France on the night of 9–10 July 1944.
Maj. Colin M. Ogden-Smith
Lt. Guy Le Borgne (*Guy Le Zachmeur*)
Sgt. Arthur J. Dallow, W/T

FRANK
Deployed by sea from Plymouth, England, to the Vendée department
of Western France on 27–28 September 1944.
Capt. Idris Isaac
Lt. Alexandre Martelli (*A. Massoni*)
Sgt. Thomas Henney, W/T

FREDERICK
Deployed from Fairford, England, to the Côtes-du-Nord department
of Brittany in Western France on the night of 9–10 June 1944.
Maj. Adrian W. Wise
S/Lt. Paul Bloch-Auroch (*Paul Aguirec*)
T/Sgt. Robert R. "Bob" Kehoe, W/T

GAVIN
Deployed from Harrington, England, to the Ille-et-Vilaine department
of Brittany in Western France on the night of 11–12 July 1944.
Cmdt. Joseph Jean Carbuccia (*Daniel Jean-Claude*)
Capt. William B. "Bill" Dreux
S/Lt. Paul Valentini, W/T (*G. Masson*)

GEORGE
Deployed from Fairford, England, to the Morbihan department of
Brittany in Western France on the night of 9–10 June 1944.
Capt. Philippe Ragueneau (*P. Erard*)
Capt. Paul Cyr
S/Lt. Pierre Gay, W/T (*Christien Lejeune*)

GEORGE II
Deployed from Harrington, England, to the Loire-Inférieure
department of Western France on the night of 7–8 Sept. 1944.
Capt. Philippe Ragueneau (*P. Erard*)
Capt. Paul Cyr
S/Lt. Pierre Gay, W/T (*Christien Lejeune*)

Code Name	Nationality	Remarks
Dorset	British	Killed in action
Durance	French	
Groat	British	
Westmoreland	British	
Dumbarton	French	
Cheshire	British	
Kinros	British	
Vire	French	
Peseta	American	
Shilling	French	
Sixpence	American	
Halfpenny	French	
Save	French	
Wigton	American	
Rupee	French	
Save	French	Fractured leg on jump
Wigton	American	
Rupee	French	

Mission
Rank, Name & (*Nom-de-guerre*)

GERALD
Deployed from Harwell, England, to the Morbihan department of
Brittany in Western France on the night of 18–19 July 1944.
Capt. Stephen J. "Steve" Knerly
Lt. Claude l'Herbette (*Jean-Luc Beaumont*)
1st Sgt. Berent E. Friele, Jr., W/T

GILBERT
Deployed from Harrington, England, to the Finistère department of
Brittany in Western France on the night of 9–10 July 1944.
Capt. Christopher Gillian W. Blathwayt
Lt. Paul Carron de la Carrière (*P. Charron*)
Sgt. Neville Wood, W/T

GILES
Deployed from Harrington, England, to the Finistère department of
Brittany in Western France on the night of 8–9 July 1944.
Capt. Bernard M. W. "Bernie" Knox
Capt. Paul Grall (*Paul Lebel*)
Sgt. Gordon H. Tack, W/T

GODFREY
Deployed from Harrington, England, to the Haut-Rhin department
of Northeast France on the night of 11–12 September 1944.
1st Lt. Ian Forbes
Lt. Pierre Laval (*Jacques Morhange*)
Sgt. Frank A. Hanson, W/T

GRAHAM
Deployed from Algeria, via Corsica and Italy, to the Basses-Alpes
department of Southeast France on the night of 8–9 August 1944.
Maj. Michael C. M. "Bing" Crosby
Capt. Pierre "Papa" Gavet (*P. Gouvet*)
1st Sgt. William H. "Bill" Adams, W/T

GREGORY
Deployed from Harrington, England, to the Doubs department of
Eastern France on the night of 4–5 September 1944.
Capt. Kemys D. "Ed" Bennett
Capt. Albert P. de Schonen (*Pierre de Schonen*)
Sgt. Ron Brierley, W/T

Code Name	Nationality	Remarks
Norfolk	American	
Suffolk	French	
Selkirk	American	
Surrey	British	
Ardèche	French	
Doubloon	British	
Kentucky	American	
Loire	French	
Tickie	British	
Rhode Island	American	
Roscommon	French	
Roxburgh	American	
Huge	British	
Crispin	French	
Desire	American	Did not deploy to the field with team
Apôtre	British	Wounded in action
Argentier	French	Wounded in action
Florin	British	

Mission
Rank, Name & (*Nom-de-guerre*)

GUY
Deployed from Harrington, England, to the Ille-et-Vilaine department
of Brittany in Western France on the night of 11–12 July 1944.
Capt. André Duron (*A. Dhomas*)
Capt. Aubrey A. E. "Troff" Trofimov
S/Lt. Roger Groult, W/T (*J. Deschamps*)

HAMISH
Deployed from Harrington, England, to the Indre department
of Central France on the night of 12–13 June 1944.
1st Lt. Robert M. "Bobby" Anstett
Lt. René Schmitt (*Lucien Blachère*)
Sgt. Lee J. Watters, W/T

HAROLD
Deployed from Fairford, England, to the Vendée department of
Western France on the night of 15–16 July 1944.
Maj. Valentine E. Whitty
Lt. Pierre Jolliet (*Pierre Rimbaut*)
Sgt. Harry Verlander, W/T

HARRY
Deployed from Tempsford, England, to the Nièvre department of
Central France on the night of 6–7 June 1944.
Capt. Duncan Dunbar Guthrie
Lt. Pierre E. Rousset (*Pierre Etienne Dupont*)
S/Lt. René Couture, W/T (*Roger Legrand*)

HENRY
Deployed from Harrington, England, to the Belfort department of
Eastern France on the night of 9–10 September 1944.
Capt. Stephane Jean-Moncler (*S. Montcler*)
1st Lt. Raymond E. "Ray" Moore
T/Sgt. Vincent M. Rocca, W/T

HILARY
Deployed from Tempsford, England, to the Finistère department of
Brittany in Western France on the night of 17–18 July 1944.
Lt. Edgar Mautaint (*E. Marchant*)
1st Lt. Philip H. "Phil" Chadbourne, Jr.
S/Lt. Roger Hervouet, W/T (*R. Pariselle*)

Code Name	Nationality	Remarks
Dronne	French	
Gironde	British	
Dordogne	French	
Alabama	American	
Louisiana	French	
Kansas	American	
Ross	British	
Tyrone	French	
Sligo	British	
Denby	British	
Gapeau	French	
Centime	French	
Anglesey	French	
New Mexico	American	
West Virginia	American	
Charente	French	
Nevada	American	
Kopek	French	

Mission
Rank, Name & (*Nom-de-guerre*)

HORACE
Deployed from Tempsford, England, to the Finistère department of
Brittany in Western France on the night of 17–18 July 1944.
Maj. John W. Summers
Lt. Georges Leclercq (*C. Levalois*)
T/3 William F. Zielski, Jr., W/T

HUGH
Deployed from Tempsford, England, to the Indre department of
Central France on the night of 5–6 June 1944.
Capt. William R. "Bill" Crawshay
Capt. Louis l'Helgouach (*Louis Legrand*)
S/Lt. René Meyer, W/T (*Robert Mersiol*)

IAN
Deployed from Harrington, England, to the Vienne department of
Central France on the night of 20–21 June 1944.
Maj. John J. Gildee, Jr.
Capt. Alexandre Desfarges (*Yves Delorme*)
Sgt. Lucien J. Bourgoin, W/T

ISAAC*
Deployed from Fairford, England, to the Nièvre department of
Central France on the night of 10–11 June 1944.
Col. F. G. Viat (*Dubac*)
Lt. Col. James R. H. Hutchison (*John L. Hastings*)
Sgt. John Sharpe, W/T

IVOR
Deployed from Harrington, England, to the Cher department of
Central France on the night of 6–7 August 1944.
Capt. John H. Cox
Lt. Robert Colin (*Yves M. Dantec*)
1st Sgt. Lewis F. "Lew" Goddard, W/T

JACOB
Deployed from England to the Vosges department of Eastern France
on the night of 12–13 August 1944.
Capt. Albert Victor Gough

Lt. Maurice Boissarie (*Guy Baraud*)
Sgt. Kenneth Roy "Ken" Seymour, W/T

* Team name changed to **Verveine** after deployment; team deployed as the core
of a larger special inter-Allied mission. Col. Viat, not a Jedburgh, was the mission
leader.

Code Name	Nationality	Remarks
Wyoming	American	
Somme	French	
Dime	American	
Crown	British	
Franc	French	
Yonne	French	
Oklahoma	American	
Maine	French	
Mayo	American	Killed in action
Diagramme	French	Joined team in the field on 22 July
Télémètre	British	
	Canadian	
Monmouth	British	Injured on jump
Selune	French	Injured, accidental gunshot wound
Oregon	American	Killed on jump (parachute failed)
Arran	British	Captured-POW, executed November 1944
Connaught	French	Killed in action
Skye	British	Captured-POW, liberated 1945

Mission
Rank, Name & (*Nom-de-guerre*)

JAMES
Deployed from Fairford, England, to the Corrèze department of
Southwest France on the night of 10–11 August 1944.
1st Lt. John K. "Jack" Singlaub
Lt. Jacques Le Bel de Penguilly (*Dominique Leb*)
T/Sgt. Anthony J. "Tony" Denneau, W/T

JEREMY
Deployed from Blida, Algeria, to the Haute-Loire department of
Southern France on the night of 24–25 August 1944.
Capt. George M. Hallowes
Capt. Henri-Charles Giese (*H. Fontcroise*)
Sgt. Roger A. Leney, W/T

JIM
Deployed from Harrington, England, to the Ain department of
Eastern France on the night of 15–16 September 1944.
Capt. Philip W. "Phil" Donovan
Lt. Joseph A. "Joe" de Francesco (*Jean Lavige*)
T/Sgt. Michael F. "Mike" Henely, W/T

JOHN
Deployed from Blida, Algeria, to the Ariège department of
Southwest France on the night of 16–17 August 1944.
Capt. David L. Stern
Lt. Maurice de Galbert (*J. Lerocher*)
Sgt. Donald Gibbs, W/T
S/Lt. Jean Verneuil

JUDE
Deployed from Fairford, England, to the Loire department of
Southeast France on the night of 14–15 August 1944.
Capt. William L. O. Evans
Capt. Jean Larrieu (*J. Lavisme*)
Sgt. Alfred E. Holdham, W/T

JULIAN
Deployed from Harrington, England, to the Indre-et-Loire
department of Central France on the night of 10–11 August 1944.
Maj. A. H. Clutton
Lt. Marcel Joseph Vermot (*Joseph Brouillard*)
CQMS James S. Menzies, W/T

Code Name	Nationality	Remarks
Mississippi	American	Wounded in action
Michigan	French	
Massachusetts	American	
Aimable	British	
Dur	French	
Ferne	British	
Pennsylvania	American	
Leitrim	French	
Wexford	American	
Beau	British	
Lucide	French	
Silencieux	British	
Marcellin	French	W/T replacement for Jed Ammonia
Glamorgan	British	
Rence	French	
Guinea	British	
Stafford	British	
Vermont	French	
Essex	British	

Mission
Rank, Name & (*Nom-de-guerre*)

JULIAN II
Deployed from Tarrant Rushton, England, to the Haut-Rhin department of Northeast France on the night of 18–19 November 1944.
Capt. Jean-Paul Souquet (*J. Kernevel*)
S/Lt. Paul Scherrer (*Sauvage*)
S/Lt. René Meyer, W/T (*Robert Mersiol*)

LEE
Deployed from Keevil, England, to the Haute-Vienne department of Southwest France on the night of 9–10 August 1944.
Capt. Charles E. Brown III
Lt. Pierre Angoulvent (*N. Viguier*)
S/Lt. Maurice Pirat, W/T (*André Chevalier*)

MARK
Deployed from Blida, Algeria, to the Tarn-et-Garonne department of Southwest France on the night of 16–17 August 1944.
1st Lt. Lucien E. "Lou" Conein
Lt. Joannés Thévenet (*F. G. de Thévenet*)
Sgt. James J. Carpenter, W/T

MARTIN
Deployed from Blida, Algeria, to the Gers department of Southwest France on the night of 16–17 August 1944.
Capt. Thomas Anthony "Tony" Mellows
Lt. Georges Redonnet (*G. Rémond*)
Sgt. Neville E. S. Carey, W/T

MASQUE
Deployed from Maison Blanche, Algeria, to the Isère department of Southeast France on the night of 27–28 August 1944.
Capt. Nelson E. Guillot
Lt. Jacques Bouvery (*J. René Gramont*)
Sgt. Francis M. "Jack" Poché, Jr., W/T

MAURICE
Deployed from Tempsford, England, to the Jura department of Eastern France on the night of 31 August–1 September 1944.
Capt. Charles MacArthur Carman, Jr.
Lt. Hubert Reveilhac (*Hubert Dumesnil*)
T/Sgt. Francis J. Cole, W/T

Code Name	Nationality	Remarks
Carnavon	French	
[none]	French	
Yonne	French	
Pice	American	
Sous	French	Killed in action
Reis	French	
Intrepide	American	
Sympathique	French	
Leste	American	
Blasé	British	Captured, died of wounds
Substantif	French	
Placide	British	
Harmonieux	American	
Succulent	French	
Idéal	American	
Utah	American	
Virginia	French	
Georgia	American	

Mission
Rank, Name & (*Nom-de-guerre*)

MILES
Deployed from Blida, Algeria, to the Gers department of Southwest
France on the night of 16–17 August 1944.
Capt. Everett T. "Ev" Allen
Lt. René Estève (*Pierre Fourcade*)
T/Sgt. Arthur "Art" Gruen, W/T

MINARET
Deployed from Blida, Algeria, to the Lozère department of Southern
France on the night of 13–14 August 1944.
Maj. Lancelot C. M. Hartley-Sharpe
Capt. Pierre Cros (*Pierre Mutin*)
Sgt. John W. Ellis, W/T

MONOCLE
Deployed from Blida, Algeria, to the Vaucluse department of Southeast
France on the night of 13–14 August 1944.
Capt. Jacques Fiardo (*J. Tozel*)
1st Lt. Ray H. Foster
T/Sgt. Robert J. Anderson, W/T

NICHOLAS
Deployed from England to the Vosges department of Northeast
France on the night of 10–11 September 1944.
Capt. John C. C. Maude
Lt. Henri Penin (*H. Puget*)
Sgt. Maurice A. Whittle, W/T

NORMAN
Deployed from Harrington, England, to the Jura department of
Eastern France on the night of 27–28 August 1944.
Lt. Konrad C. Dillow
Lt. Marc Lautier (*Frederic Bataille*)
1st Sgt. Lucien E. "Lou" Lajeunesse, W/T

NOVOCAINE
Deployed from Blida, Algeria, to the Hautes-Alpes department of
Southeast France on the night of 6–7 August 1944.
1st Lt. Charles J. Gennerich
Lt. Jean-Yves Pronost (*Jean-Yves Lelann*)
Sgt. William T. "Bill" Thompson, W/T

Code Name	Nationality	Remarks
Libre	American	
Lumineux	French	
Fidèle	American	
Edmond	British	
Hector	French	Did not deploy due to illness
Arsène	British	
Immense	French	
Solide	American	
Raieux	American	
Leiccster	British	
Breaknock	French	
Northumberland	British	
Minnesota	American	
Washington	French	
Tennessee	American	
Mathieu	American	
Herve	French	
Gilles	American	

Mission
Rank, Name & (*Nom-de-guerre*)

PACKARD
Deployed from Blida, Algeria, to the Lozère department of
Southern France on the night of 31 July–1 August 1944.
Capt. Aaron Bank
Capt. Henri Denis (*C. Boineau*)
Lt. Marcel F. Montfort, W/T

PAUL
Deployed from Tempsford, England, to the Côte-d'Or department
of Eastern France on the night of 18–19 August 1944.
Maj. Ernest Hugo Migesson Hood
Lt. Michel Vallée (*François Cormier*)
Sgt. Kenneth John Wilde Brown, W/T

QUENTIN
Deployed by sea from Plymouth, England, to the Vendée
department of Western France on 27–28 September 1944.
Capt. Ronald S. "Ronnie" Fenton
Lt. Jean Raux (*J. Lasserre*)
Sgt. David Rawson, W/T

QUININE
Deployed from Blida, Algeria, to the Cantal department of
Southwest France on the night of 8–9 June 1944.
Maj. R. Thomas "Tommy" MacPherson
Asp. Michel de Bourbon-Parme (*Maurice Bourdon*)
Sgt. O. Arthur Brown, W/T

RAYMOND
Deployed by sea from Plymouth, England, to the Vendée
department of Western France on 27–28 September 1944.
Capt. R. Dehosses (*R. Waguet*)
Lt. Henri H. L. Cadilhac (*H. Chaulais*)
Sgt. Walter Adams, W/T

RODERICK
Deployed from England to the Doubs department of Eastern
France on the night of 31 August–1 September 1944.
Capt. Jean Preziosi (*Albert Paoli*)
Lt. William C. "Bill" Boggs
T/Sgt. Charles P. Mersereau, W/T

Code Name	Nationality	Remarks
Chechwan	American	
Fukien	French	
Formosa	British	
Shropshire	British	
Durthe	French	
Limerick	British	
Cornwall	British	
Wicklow	French	
Mcrioneth	British	
Anselme	British	
Aristide	French	
Felicien	British	
Waterford	French	
Gloucester	French	
Kincardine	British	
Nairn	French	
New Hampshire	American	
Stronsay	American	

Mission
Rank, Name & (*Nom-de-guerre*)

RONALD
Deployed from England to the Finistère department of Brittany in Western France on the night of 4–5 August 1944.
1st Lt. Shirly Ray Trumps
Lt. Georges Desseilligny (*J. Dartigues*)
T/Sgt. Elmer B. "El" Esch, W/T

RUPERT*
Deployed from Harrington, England, to the Vosges department of Northeast France on the night of 31 August–1 September 1944.
Capt. C. Jean Liberos (*J. G. de Rouen*)
1st Lt. Robert A. "Bob" Lucas
S3Cl. (USN) Joseph M. Gergat,†W/T

SCEPTRE
Deployed from Blida, Algeria, to the Var department of Southeast France on the night of 13–14 August 1944.
1st Lt. Walter C. "Walt" Hanna, Jr.
Lt. François G. Franceschi (*François Tévenac*)
T/Sgt. Thomas J. Tracy
M/Sgt. Howard V. Palmer, W/T

SCION
Deployed from Maison Blanche, Algeria, to the Isère department of Southeast France on the night of 29–30 August 1944.
Maj. Osborne P. Grenfell
Lt. Roger Gruppo (*G. Revard*)
Sgt. Thomas F. "Cobber" Cain, W/T

SIMON
Deployed by sea from Plymouth, England, to the Vendée department of Western France on 27–28 September 1944.
Capt. Anthony W. C. Coomber
Capt. Maurice Fouéré (*M. Fontaine*)
LAC (RAF) Claud Somers, W/T

---

* Name changed to **Philip** after deployment.

† U.S. Navy Seaman Third Class Joseph Gergat's name is spelled "Grgat" in official records. The family of Mr. Gergat, who is now deceased, provided this version to the author as the correct spelling.

Code Name	Nationality	Remarks
Boursier	American	Wounded in action
Boutton	French	
Pound	American	
Kintyre	French	
Caithness	American	
Leincester	American	Became separated from team
Vaillant	American	
Intense	French	
[none]	American	Did not deploy due to illness
Dévoux	American	Replacement for Sgt. Tracy
Scintillating	British	
Vif	French	
Vibrant	British	
Coustard	British	
Fernard	French	
Stephane	British	

Mission
Rank, Name & (*Nom-de-guerre*)

STANLEY
Deployed from Tempsford, England, to the Haute-Marne department
of Northeast France on the night of 31 August–1 September 1944.
Capt. Oswin E. Craster
Lt. Robert Cantais (*Robert Carlière*)
Sgt. Eric J. "Jack" Grinham, W/T

TIMOTHY
Deployed from Harrington, England, to the Doubs department of
Eastern France on the night of 10–11 September 1944.
Capt. Louis Moutte (*L. Ambel*)
1st Lt. Robert E. "Bob" Heyns
1st Lt. Robert G. Mundinger

1st Sgt. Donald A. Spears, W/T

TONY
Deployed from Harrington, England, to the Vendée department of
Western France on the night of 17–18 August 1944.
Maj. Robert K. "Bob" Montgomery
Lt. Lucien Paris (*Mark Devailly*)
T/Sgt. John E. McGowan, W/T

VEGANIN
Deployed from Algeria to the Drôme department of Southeast
France on the night of 8–9 June 1944.
Maj. H. Neil Marten
Capt. Gaston Vuchot (*Claude L. Noir*)
Sgt. Dennis "Jesse" Gardner, W/T

WILLYS
Deployed from Blida, Algeria, to the Ardèche department of
Southeast France on the night of 28–29 June 1944.
Capt. Georges Marchal (*P. J. Granier*)
Capt. John C. C. Montague
Sgt. F. A. "Ted" Cornick, W/T

Code Name	Nationality	Remarks
Yorkshire	British	
Meath	French	
Worcestershire	British	
Nesque	French	
Dyle	American	Fractured both ankles on jump
Marcelin	American	Joined team on 13 September 1944
Escaut	American	
Dollar	American	
Écu	French	
Quarter	Amcrican	
Cuthbert	British	
Derek	French	
Ernest	British	Killed on jump (parachute failed)
Simon	French	
Honan	British	
Chansi	British	

NOTES

PROLOGUE

1. Gen. Dwight D. Eisenhower, letter to Maj. Gen. Colin Gubbins, executive director of SOE, 31 May 1945, in *SOE in France: An Account of the Work of the British Special Operations Executive in France, 1940–1944*, by M. R. D. Foot (London: Her Majesty's Stationery Office, 1966), pp. 441–42; and Eisenhower, letter to Col. David K. E. Bruce, chief of OSS, European Theater of Operations, 31 May 1945, in *The Overseas Targets: War Report of the OSS (Office of Strategic Services), Volume 2*, intro. by Kermit Roosevelt (Washington, DC: Carrollton Press; New York: Walker & Company, 1976), p. 222.
2. Harry C. Butcher, *My Three Years with Eisenhower: The Personal Diary of Captain Harry C. Butcher, USNR, Naval Aide to General Eisenhower, 1942 to 1945* (New York: Simon & Schuster, 1946), p. 654.
3. Office of Strategic Services (OSS), London Office, *OSS/London: Special Operations Branch and Secret Intelligence Branch War Diaries* (1945), ed. Paul Kesaris, (Frederick, MD: University Publications of America, 1985), vol. 13, pp. 1–6, gives the total number of Jedburgh operators deployed as 281 (103 French, 90 British, 83 Americans, 4 Dutch, and 1 Belgian).
4. OSS/London, *OSS/London: Special Operations Branch War Diary*, vol. 13, pp. 1–6; and Associated Press, "D-Day Chutists Rate as Heroes: South Bend Officer One of International Secret Unit," unidentified Indiana newspaper, September 27, [1945?].
5. Ernie Pyle, *Brave Men* (New York: Henry Holt, 1944), p. 416.

CHAPTER 1

1. OSS/London, *OSS/London: Special Operations Branch War Diary*, vol. 4, bk. 1, p. 13.
2. Robert Kehoe, telephone conversation with the author, January 19, 2004.
3. Robert R. Kehoe, "Jed Team Frederick, 1944: An Allied Team With the French Resistance" (1997), article on the Central Intelligence Agency's Center for the Study of Intelligence webpage, http://www.cia.gov/csi/ studies/winter98_99/art03.html (accessed January 13, 2005).
4. Walter Bedell Smith, *Eisenhower's Six Great Decisions* (New York: Longmans, Green, 1956), pp. 41–51.
5. Roy Berkeley, *A Spy's London* (London: Leo Cooper, 1994), pp. 164–76.
6. Paul McCue, *SAS Operation Bulbasket: Behind the Lines in Occupied France, 1944* (London: Leo Cooper, 1996), pp. 1–2; and M. R. D. Foot, *Resistance: European Resistance to Nazism, 1940–1945* (New York: McGraw-Hill, 1977), pp. 53–55.
7. Robert Kehoe, telephone conversation with the author, January 19, 2004.
8. OSS/London, *OSS/London: Special Operations Branch War Diary*, vol. 4, bk. 1, report on Team Frederick, pp. 33–35, 143; SO Branch War Diary, vol. 4, bk. 1, report on Team George, pp. 39–42, 157; and Kehoe, "Jed Team Frederick, 1944."
9. Smith, *Eisenhower's Six Great Decisions*, pp. 28–29; and Stephen E. Ambrose, *D-Day, June 6, 1944: The Climactic Battle of World War II* (New York: Simon & Schuster, 1994), p. 189.
10. Robert Kehoe, telephone conversation with the author, January 19, 2004.
11. Kehoe, "Jed Team Frederick, 1944."
12. OSS/London, *OSS/London: Special Operations Branch War Diary*, vol. 4, bk. 1, report on Team George, pp. 157–58; and Kehoe, "Jed Team Frederick, 1944."

CHAPTER 2

1. Squadron and flight details are taken from the Royal Air Force WWII 38 Group website, http://www.raf38group.org (accessed September 21, 2004).
2. Kehoe, "Jed Team Frederick, 1944."
3. OSS/London, *OSS/London: Special Operations Branch War Diary*, vol. 4, bk. 1, report on Team Frederick, p. 143; and Kehoe, "Jed Team Frederick, 1944."
4. Robert Kehoe, telephone conversation with the author, January 19, 2004.

5. Kehoe, "Jed Team Frederick, 1944."
6. Roger Ford, *Fire from the Forest: The SAS Brigade in France, 1944* (London: Cassell, 2003), p. 255.
7. OSS/London, *OSS/London: Special Operations Branch War Diary*, vol. 4, bk. 1, report on Team Frederick, p. 144.
8. Special Operations Executive, *Secret Agent's Handbook: The WWII Spy Manual of Devices, Disguises, Gadgets, and Concealed Weapons*, reproduction of two wartime volumes with intro. by Mark Seaman (Guilford, CT: The Lyons Press, 2001), pp. 163–65.
9. OSS/London, *OSS/London: Special Operations Branch War Diary*, vol. 4, bk. 1, report on Team Frederick, p. 36; and Kehoe, "Jed Team Frederick, 1944."
10. Kehoe, "Jed Team Frederick, 1944."
11. Ibid.
12. This account of the incident at the farm on the evening of June 11 is based on Major Wise's after-action report and Bob Kehoe's account. In his book *Fire from the Forest* (p. 256), author Roger Ford gives a slightly different account based on Captain Leblond's report. All three of these reports, of course, are second-hand as neither Wise, Kehoe, nor Leblond was present at the farmhouse during the attack.
13. OSS/London, *OSS/London: Special Operations Branch War Diary*, vol. 4, bk. 1, report on Team Frederick, p. 144.
14. Julian Thompson, *The Imperial War Museum Book of War Behind Enemy Lines* (Washington, DC: Brassey's, 2001), p. 307.
15. Robert Kehoe, telephone conversation with the author, January 19, 2004.
16. William Colby and Peter Forbath, *Honorable Men: My Life in the CIA* (New York: Simon & Schuster, 1978), p. 26.
17. OSS/London, *OSS/London: Special Operations Branch War Diary*, vol. 4, bk. 1, report on Team Frederick, pp. 145–46; and Kehoe, "Jed Team Frederick, 1944."

CHAPTER 3

1. William Manchester, *The Last Lion: Winston Spencer Churchill; Alone, 1932–1940* (Boston: Little, Brown, 1988), p. 13; and Winston S. Churchill, *The Second World War*, vol. 2, *Their Finest Hour* (Boston: Houghton Mifflin Company, 1949), p. 128.
2. Winston Churchill, quoted in *The Last Lion: Winston Spencer Churchill; Visions of Glory, 1874–1932*, by William Manchester (Boston: Little, Brown, 1983), p. 650.
3. Nigel West [Rupert Allason], *MI6: British Secret Intelligence Service Operations, 1909–45* (New York: Random House, 1983), p. 60.

4. Foot, *SOE in France*, p. 11.

5. The fact that Donovan was a prominent Republican was of little concern to Roosevelt. The previous summer he had appointed two Republicans to fill the key defense positions in his bipartisan cabinet—Frank Knox as secretary of the Navy and Henry L. Stimson as secretary of war, as the Army's civilian leadership was then called. Donovan had actually been considered for the War Department post.

6. The complete text of Churchill's December 1941 strategy documents are in *Churchill and Roosevelt, The Complete Correspondence*, ed. Warren F. Kimball (Princeton: Princeton University Press, 1984), vol. 1, pp. 294–309; also see Winston S. Churchill, *The Second World War*, vol. 3, *The Grand Alliance* (Boston: Houghton Mifflin, 1950), pp. 582, 588.

7. Peter Wilkinson, *Foreign Fields: The Story of an SOE Operative* (London: I. B. Tauris, 1997), p. 128.

8. OSS/London, *OSS/London: Special Operations Branch War Diary*, vol. 4, bk. 1, p. i.

9. Churchill, *The Second World War*, vol. 5, *Closing the Ring* (Boston: Houghton Mifflin, 1951), pp. 580, 583.

10. See M. R. D. Foot, *SOE: An outline history of the Special Operations Executive, 1940–46* (London: British Broadcasting Corp., 1984), p. 127, for more on how code names were assigned. Foot also explains how entire blocks of approved code names were allocated to Special Force Headquarters (SFHQ) for use with Jedburgh and other special forces teams. This accounts for the many Jed teams that were assigned men's first names as code names, while other teams were assigned code names from other blocks—names of automobiles or drugs, for example. OSS Operational Groups were mostly assigned code names from a block of women's first names.

11. Arthur Brown, "The Jedburghs: A Short History," April 1991, photocopy of unpublished manuscript provided to the author by Mr. Brown, p. 5.

12. Bruce Marshall, *The White Rabbit* (Boston: Houghton Mifflin, 1952), pp. 84–85.

13. Stanley Cannicott, *Journey of a Jed* (Cheddar, UK: Cheddar Valley Press, 1986), pp. 12–13.

14. Gen. Paul Aussaresses, letter to the author, September 19, 1989.

15. Bernard Knox, *Essays Ancient and Modern* (Baltimore: Johns Hopkins University Press, 1989), p. xxiii.

16. Ibid.

17. Roger Hall, *You're Stepping on My Cloak and Dagger* (New York: W. W. Norton, 1957), p. 32.

18. Ibid.

19. Edmund F. Wehrle, *Catoctin Mountain Park: A Historic Resource Study* (2000), on National Park Service website, http://www.nps.gov/cato/hrs/hrs.htm, chap. 6, "War and Politics Shape the Park" (accessed January 24, 2005).
20. William L. Cassidy, ed., *History of the Schools and Training Branch, Office of Strategic Services* (San Francisco: Kingfisher Press, 1983), p. 72.
21. Albert Hemingway, "The Great Parachute Drop," *Military History*, April 1990, p. 48.
22. John K. Singlaub and Malcolm McConnell, *Hazardous Duty: An American Soldier in the Twentieth Century* (New York: Summit Books, 1991), p. 32.
23. Kehoe, "Jed Team Frederick, 1944."
24. Ibid.
25. Steve Harding, *Gray Ghost: The R.M.S. Queen Mary at War* (Missoula, MT: Pictorial Histories, 1982), p. 78.
26. Gen. Paul Aussaresses, letters to the author, September 17, 18, and 19, 1989, and January 24, 1990; and Michel de Bourbon, letter to the author, January 3, 1990.
27. OSS/London, *OSS/London: Special Operations Branch War Diary*, vol. 4, bk. 1, p. xxii; vol. 9, p. 8; Office of Strategic Services Assessment Staff, *Assessment of Men: Selection of Personnel for the Office of Strategic Services* (New York: Rinehart & Company, Inc., 1948); and M. G. M. Crosby, *Irregular Soldier* (United Kingdom: XB Publications, 1993), pp. 88–91. Col. Crosby served as a member of the assessments board and later deployed as part of a Jedburgh team.
28. OSS/London, *OSS/London: Special Operations Branch War Diary*, vol. 4, bk. 1, p. xxii.
29. Brown, "The Jedburghs: A Short History," p. 6.
30. Norman Longmate, *The G.I.'s: The Americans in Britain, 1942–1945* (New York: Charles Scribner's Sons, 1975), pp. 36, 38.
31. OSS/London, *OSS/London: Special Operations Branch War Diary*, vol. 4, bk. 1, p. xxii; and Thompson, *The Imperial War Museum Book of War Behind Enemy Lines*, p. 301.
32. Knox, *Essays Ancient and Modern*, p. xxiii.
33. James Hutchison, *That Drug Danger* (Montrose, Scotland: Standard Press, 1977), p. 86.
34. Cannicott, *Journey of a Jed*, p. 22.
35. Gen. Paul Aussaresses, letter to the author, September 1989.
36. OSS/London, *OSS/London: Special Operations Branch War Diary*, vol. 4, bk. 1, pp. 1–3.
37. Cannicott, *Journey of a Jed*, p. 23.
38. Ibid., p. 25.
39. Butcher, *My Three Years with Eisenhower*, pp. 510, 538, 544.

40. Ibid., p. 538.

41. Frederick Morgan, *Overture to Overlord* (Garden City, NY: Doubleday, 1950), pp. 155–56; Churchill, *The Second World War*, vol. 5, pp. 69–70, 327; and Hastings Lionel Ismay, *The Memoirs of General Lord Ismay* (New York: Viking, 1960), p. 311.

42. Stephen E. Ambrose, *Ike's Spies: Eisenhower and the Espionage Establishment* (Jackson: University Press of Mississippi, 1999), pp. 88, 97.

43. Col. C. S. Vanderblue, commander, Office of Strategic Services Detachment Third Army, memorandum to Gen. William J. Donovan, subject: Report of C. S. Vanderblue on OSS Operations with the Third Army, November 15, 1944, p. 5 (National Archives, Washington History Office, Record Group (RG) 226, OP–23, entry 99, folder 50, box 12), photocopy in author's files.

44. Maj. Gen. Harold R. Bull, operations officer (G–3), Supreme Headquarters Allied Expeditionary Force (SHAEF), memorandum to Chief, Plans and Operations Section, subject: "SOE/SO Assistance to Overlord," April 6, 1944 (National Archives, Washington History Office, RG 331, entry 23, box 47), photocopy in author's files.

45. Chief of Staff to the Supreme Allied Commander, Designate (COSSAC), "Operation 'Overlord'," app. P, "Support of Military Operations by Resistance Groups in Europe," July 15, 1943 (National Archives, Washington History Office, RG 331, entry 23, box 47), photocopy in author's files; and Butcher, *My Three Years with Eisenhower*, p. 510.

46. Butcher, *My Three Years with Eisenhower*, pp. 515, 540.

47. Joint Psychological Warfare Committee, minutes of 24th meeting (August 24, 1942) with attached Jedburgh concept paper, minutes of 33rd meeting (September 2, 1942), and minutes of 35th meeting (September 16, 1942); Gen. Walter B. Smith, memorandum to Operations Div., War Dept., subject: "Jedburghs," September 3, 1942; Gen. Eisenhower, message to War Dept., subject: "Jedburghs," September 16, 1942 (National Archives, Washington History Office, RG 218, box 8), photocopies in author's files; Dwight D. Eisenhower, *The Papers of Dwight David Eisenhower: The War Years*, ed. Alfred D. Chandler, Jr. (Baltimore: The Johns Hopkins Press, 1970), vol. 5, p. 76.

48. SHAEF, Office of the G–3, directive, subject: "Open Title for Headquarters, SOE/SO," May 1, 1944, copy in OSS/London: Special Operations Branch War Diary, vol. 12, p. 85; vol. 1, pp. 1–2, 4, 11–12; vol. 4, bk. 1, p. 14; vol. 12, p. 33.

CHAPTER 4

1. OSS/London, *OSS/London: Special Operations Branch War Diary*, vol. 4, bk. 1, report on Team George, p. 43.

2. Ibid., pp. 158–60; Ford, *Fire from the Forest*, p. 252; André Hue and Ewen Southby-Tailyour, *The Next Moon: The remarkable true story of a British agent behind the lines in wartime France* (London: Viking, 2004), p. 19.

3. OSS/London, *OSS/London: Special Operations Branch War Diary*, vol. 11, p. 589; and "Keeping Posted," *Saturday Evening Post*, 23 March 1946, p. 4.

4. Hue, *The Next Moon*, pp. 47, 64.

5. Special Force Headquarters (SFHQ) G–3 Periodic Report no. 9 (June 13, 1944), p. 2 (National Archives, Washington History Office, RG 226, OP–23, entry 99, box 93), provides numbers which conflict with those taken from Jedburgh team George's report, citing 85 SAS troops and 250 containers.

6. SFHQ G–3 Periodic Report no. 12 (June 16, 1944), p. 1.

7. OSS/London, *OSS/London: Special Operations Branch War Diary*, vol. 4, bk. 1, report on Team George, pp. 160–63.

8. OSS/London, *OSS/London: Special Operations Branch War Diary*, vol. 3, bk. 3, p. 14.

9. Ibid., vol. 3, bk. 1, pp. 6–7.

10. Foot, *SOE in France*, p. 388; Foot, "Special Operations," in *The D-Day Encyclopedia*, ed. David G. Chandler and James Lawton Collins, Jr. (New York: Simon & Schuster, 1994), p. 524; Maurice J. Buckmaster, *They Fought Alone: The Story of British Agents in France* (New York: W. W. Norton, 1958), pp. 219–20; Max Hastings, *Das Reich: The March of the 2nd SS Panzer Division Through France* (New York: Holt, Rinehart and Winston, 1982), p. 5.

11. The Reader's Digest Association, *Secrets and Spies: Behind-the-Scenes Stories of World War II* (Pleasantville, NY: Reader's Digest Assn., 1964), p. 387.

12. David Eisenhower, *Eisenhower at War, 1943–1945* (New York: Vintage Books, 1987), p. 255; and Alfred Goldberg, "Air Campaign Overlord: To D-Day," in *D-Day: The Normandy Invasion in Retrospect* (Lawrence: The University Press of Kansas, 1971), pp. 66–68.

CHAPTER 5

1. Kehoe, "Jed Team Frederick, 1944."

2. OSS/London, *OSS/London: Special Operations Branch War Diary*, vol. 4, bk. 1, report on Team Frederick, p. 36; and Kehoe, "Jed Team Frederick, 1944."

3. Richard Floyd, telephone conversation with the author, September 13, 2004.

4. Kehoe, "Jed Team Frederick, 1944."

5. Kehoe, "Jed Team Frederick, 1944"; and SFHQ G–3 Periodic Report no. 20 (June 24, 1944), p. 4.
6. OSS/London, *OSS/London: Special Operations Branch War Diary*, vol. 4, bk. 1, report on Team Frederick, p. 152.
7. Ibid., p. 37.
8. Ibid., p. 139.
9. OSS/London, *OSS/London: Special Operations Branch War Diary*, vol. 4, bk. 1, report on Team Frederick, pp. 140, 147–48; vol. 4, bk. 2, report on Team Giles, p. 328; vol. 4, bk. 2, report on Team Felix, p. 365; and Kehoe, "Jed Team Frederick, 1944."
10. Kehoe, "Jed Team Frederick, 1944."

CHAPTER 6

1. André Hue, who was with Bourgoin throughout this period, refers to him by that rank in his book *The Next Moon*.
2. SFHQ G–3 Periodic Report no. 12 (June 16, 1944), p. 1.
3. OSS/London, *OSS/London: Special Operations Branch War Diary*, vol. 4, bk. 1, report on Team George, pp. 163, 169.
4. Ibid., p. 44; and Hue, *The Next Moon*, p. 82.
5. OSS/London, *OSS/London: Special Operations Branch War Diary*, vol. 4, bk. 1, report on Team George, pp. 167–68; Hue, *The Next Moon*, pp. 134–35; and Ford, *Fire from the Forest*, pp. 253–54. While team George's report states that this attack was made by 150 German feldgendarmes screened by civilians, Hue's account calls it 50 Germans and makes no mention of the civilians. Ford cites French sources which described the German force as 125 infantrymen and also mentions the civilian screen.
6. Roger Ford, *Steel from the Sky: The Jedburgh Raiders, France, 1944* (London: Weidenfeld & Nicolson, 2004), pp. 67–68.
7. SFHQ G–3 Periodic Report no. 20 (June 24, 1944), p. 4; and Hue, *The Next Moon*, p. 151.
8. OSS/London, *OSS/London: Special Operations Branch War Diary*, vol. 4, bk. 1, report on Team George, p. 45.
9. SFHQ G–3 Periodic Report no. 26 (June 30, 1944), p. 3.
10. OSS/London, *OSS/London: Special Operations Branch War Diary*, vol. 4, bk. 1, report on Team George, p. 45.
11. OSS/London, *OSS/London: Special Operations Branch War Diary*, vol. 3, bk. 2, p. 160; and vol. 3, bk. 3, pp. 268–79.
12. Dwight D. Eisenhower, *D Day to VE Day, 1944–45: General Eisenhower's Report on the Invasion of Europe* (London: The Stationery Office, 2000), p. 97.
13. Ambrose, *Ike's Spies*, p. 106.

14. Samuel W. Mitcham, Jr., *Retreat to the Reich: The German Defeat in France, 1944* (Westport, CT: Praeger, 2000), pp. 13–14.
15. Foot, *SOE in France*, p. 411.
16. Sidney C. Moody and the Associated Press, *War in Europe* (Novato, CA: Presidio Press, 1993), p. 135.
17. Wilhelm Tieke, *In the Firestorm of the Last Years of the War: II SS-Panzerkorps with the 9 and 10 SS-Divisions "Hohenstaufen" and "Frundsberg,"* trans. Frederick Steinhardt (Winnipeg: Fedorowicz, 1999), pp. 80–81.
18. Arthur L. Funk, "French Resistance," in *The D-Day Encyclopedia*, ed. Chandler and Collins, p. 264.
19. Eisenhower, *The Papers of Dwight David Eisenhower*, vol. 3, pp. 1926–27.
20. Ambrose, *Ike's Spies*, p. 107.

CHAPTER 7

1. Etat-major des Forces Francaises de l'Interieur (EMFFI) [General Headquarters of the French Forces of the Interior], "A Short History of the Organization of the Command of Operations Undertaken by the French Forces of the Interior," (1945), p. 12 (National Archives, Washington History Office, RG 226), photocopy in author's files; and OSS/London, *OSS/London: Special Operations Branch War Diary*, vol. 3, bk. 2, p. 364.
2. Eisenhower, *D Day to VE Day, 1944–45*, p. 117.
3. Robert S. Allen, *Lucky Forward: The History of Patton's Third U.S. Army* (New York: Vanguard Press, 1947), p. 89; and OSS/London: Special Operations Branch War Diary, vol. 2, p. 64.
4. OSS/London, *OSS/London: Special Operations Branch War Diary*, vol. 3, bk. 2, p. 374.
5. OSS/London, *OSS/London: Special Operations Branch War Diary*, vol. 4, bk. 1, report on Team Frederick, p. 140; and Kehoe, "Jed Team Frederick, 1944."
6. Vanderblue, OSS Detachment Third Army, memorandum to Gen. Donovan, subject: "Report of C. S. Vanderblue on OSS operations with Third Army," November 15, 1944, p. 9.
7. Jonathan Gawne, *The Americans in Brittany, 1944: The Battle for Brest* (Paris: Histoire & Collections, 2002), p. 19.
8. Ralph Ingersoll, *Top Secret* (New York: Harcourt, Brace, 1946), pp. 184–85.
9. Edward Bautz, interview posted on the Rutgers Oral History Archives of World War II website, http://fas-history.rutgers.edu/oralhistory/Interviews/bautz_edward.html (accessed October 18, 2004).
10. Brenton G. Wallace, *Patton and his Third Army* (Mechanicsburg, PA:

Stackpole Books, 2000), pp. 16–20; Allen, *Lucky Forward*, p. 96; and Vanderblue, "memorandum to Gen. Donovan," November 15, 1944, p. 9.

11. Special Force Detachment 11, Headquarters, Third United States Army, G–3 Section, "Operations Report," p. 3 (National Archives, Washington History Office, RG 226, entry 115, box 50), photocopy in author's files; and Gawne, *The Americans in Brittany*, p. 26.

12. Robert B. Asprey, *War in the Shadows: The Guerrilla in History* (Garden City, NY: Doubleday, 1975), p. 319.

13. OSS/London, *OSS/London: Special Operations Branch War Diary*, vol. 4, bk. 1, report on Team Frederick, p. 154.

14. OSS/London, *OSS/London: Special Operations Branch War Diary*, vol. 4, bk. 1, report on Team George, p. 204.

15. Ibid., p. 216; Charles M. Province, *Patton's Third Army: A Daily Combat Diary* (New York: Hippocrene Books, 1992), p. 20; and 12th Army Group, *Report of Operations, G–3 Section, 12th Army Group (Final After Action Report)*, (1945), photocopy in author's files, p. 75.

16. Allen, *Lucky Forward*, p. 50.

17. Foot, "Special Operations," in *The D-Day Encyclopedia*, ed. Chandler and Collins, p. 525.

18. Robert LeBlanc papers, U.S. Army Military History Institute Archives, Carlisle Barracks, PA, WWII–7396, box OSS/LONDON, WWII survey; and Vanderblue, "memorandum to Gen. William J. Donovan," November 15, 1944, p. 28.

19. SFHQ G–3 Periodic Report no. 69 (August 12, 1944), app. A, p. 1.

20. OSS/London, *OSS/London: Special Operations Branch War Diary*, vol. 4, bk. 1, report on Team George, p. 233.

21. SFHQ G–3 Periodic Report no. 66 (August 9, 1944), app. B, p. 1.

22. Omar N. Bradley, *A Soldier's Story* (New York: Henry Holt, 1951), p. 365.

23. Eisenhower, *D Day to VE Day*, p. 138.

24. Ibid., p. 154.

25. Ingersoll, *Top Secret*, pp. 186–87.

CHAPTER 8

1. William E. Colby, letter to the author, March 27, 1989; Colby and Forbath, *Honorable Men*, pp. 26–35; and OSS/London, *OSS/London: Special Operations Branch War Diary*, vol. 11, p. 564.

2. Camille Lelong, telephone conversation with the author, August 13, 2004.

3. Foot, *SOE in France*, p. 292.

4. E. H. Cookridge, *Set Europe Ablaze* (New York: Crowell, 1967), pp. 181–5.

5. Ibid., p. 185.
6. Jean Overton Fuller, *The German Penetration of SOE: France, 1941–1944*, rev. ed. (Maidstone, UK: George Mann Books, 1996), pp. 33–35.
7. Hugo Bleicher, *Colonel Henri's Story: The War Memoirs of Hugo Bleicher: Former German Secret Agent*, ed. Ian Colvin (London: William Kimber, 1954), pp. 139–41; and Cookridge, *Set Europe Ablaze*, pp. 190–5.
8. William E. Colby, interview with the author, July 28, 1989, in Washington, DC.
9. Camille Lelong, telephone conversation with the author, August 13, 2004.
10. Colby and Forbath, *Honorable Men*, pp. 23–24.
11. Ibid., pp. 39–40.
12. Ibid., p. 41.
13. Ibid., p. 42.
14. Richard Harris Smith, *OSS: The Secret History of America's First Central Intelligence Agency* (Berkeley: University of California Press, 1972), p. 196.
15. Special Force Detachment 11, "Operations Report," p. 16.
16. Ibid.
17. Province, *Patton's Third Army*, p. 29.
18. George S. Patton, Jr., *War as I Knew It* (Boston: Houghton Mifflin, 1947), p. 361.
19. George S. Patton, Jr., quoted in Allen, *Lucky Forward*, p. 85.
20. Smith, *Eisenhower's Six Great Decisions*, pp. 81–82.
21. Ingersoll, *Top Secret*, p. 196.
22. OSS/London, *OSS/London: Special Operations Branch War Diary*, vol. 4, bk. 4, report on Team Bruce, app. 1, p. 860.
23. 5th Infantry Division, United States Army, *The 5th Division in France* (Metz: La Lorraine Press, 1944), pp. 9, 13–14; and James A. Huston, *Biography of a Battalion: The Life and Times of an Infantry Battalion in Europe in World War II* (Mechanicsburg, PA: Stackpole Books, 2003), p. 76.
24. OSS/London, *OSS/London: Special Operations Branch War Diary*, vol. 4, bk. 4, report on Team Bruce, pp. 853–54.
25. Eisenhower, *The Papers of Dwight David Eisenhower*, vol. 4, pp. 2100–01.
26. Ibid., vol. 4, pp. 2100–03.
27. Butcher, *My Three Years with Eisenhower*, p. 654.
28. Robert Hayden Alcorn, *No Bugles for Spies: Tales of the OSS* (New York: Popular Library, 1964), p. 95.

Chapter 9

1. Ford, *Steel from the Sky*, p. 257.
2. Gen. Paul Aussaresses, letter to the author, September 21, 1989.
3. Background material on John Bonsall was provided by Sarah Drake (John Bonsall's niece), during a telephone interview with the author on November 8, 2004, and by Katherine Strong (John Bonsall's sister) and Sarah Drake during a telephone interview with the author on November 14, 2004.
4. OSS/London, *OSS/London: Special Operations Branch War Diary*, vol. 4, bk. 6, report on Team Augustus, p. 2; and SFHQ G–3 Periodic Report no. 76 (August 19, 1944), p. 5.
5. Violette Desmarais (Roger Côté's sister), telephone interview with the author, November 13, 2004, and letter to the author, November 22, 2004.
6. Unless otherwise indicated in footnotes, the account of Jedburgh team Augustus in this chapter was constructed using the following sources: Gaston Costeaux and Émile Fortier, "Rapport sur l'activité de la mission Auguste," first-person account dated October 5, 1944 (a photocopy of the report, which is also on file at the National Archives, was provided to the author by Jedburgh veteran Charles Carman, then serving as Jedburgh archivist at the Hoover Institution, Stanford University); Gen. Paul Aussaresses, letter to the author, September 25, 1989, with an enclosed map annotated with a chronology of the movements and activities of team Augustus; Gen. Paul Aussaresses, letter to the author, October 25, 1989, relating details provided to him by resistance veterans and others who had first-hand knowledge of the team's final days, including Armand Rot; and Armand Rot, "Compte-Rendu," statement written in 1944.
7. OSS/London, *OSS/London: Special Operations Branch War Diary*, vol. 4, bk. 6, report on Team Augustus, pp. 2–3. While Jedburgh after-action reports found in the *OSS/London: Special Operations Branch War Diary* were normally written by the team members, principally the team leader, the Augustus report was written by someone on the SFHQ staff. The report includes the text of radio messages received from the team and a report by Maj. William T. Hornaday, dated October 23, 1944, on the results of an investigation into the team's fate.
8. Costeaux and Fortier, "Rapport sur l'activité de la mission Auguste," p. 3.
9. Ibid.
10. Hans von Luck, *Panzer Commander: The Memoirs of Colonel Hans von Luck* (New York: Praeger, 1989), p. 184.
11. H. R. Knickerbocker, et. al., *Danger Forward: The Story of the First Division in World War II* (Atlanta: Albert Love, 1947), p. 270.

12. Gordon A. Harrison, *Cross-Channel Attack*, United States Army in World War II series (Washington, DC: Center of Military History, 1993), p. 412.

13. Helmut Ritgen, *The Western Front 1944: Memoirs of a Panzer Lehr Officer*, trans. Joseph Welsh (Winnipeg: Fedorowicz, 1995), pp. 121, 198–99.

14. OSS/London, *OSS/London: Special Operations Branch War Diary*, vol. 4, bk. 6, report on Team Augustus, p. 4; and SFHQ G–3 Periodic Report no. 84 (August 27, 1944), p. 5. The SFHQ G–3 Periodic Report indicates that 15 containers were dropped to the Aisne department on the night of August 24–25, another 24 containers the following night, 48 more the night after that, and another 60 on the night of August 27–28. It is unclear whether any of these were intended for Jedburgh team Augustus.

15. Martin Blumenson, *Breakout and Pursuit*, United States Army in World War II (Washington, DC: Center of Military History, 1961, 1984), p. 668.

16. Vincent J. Esposito, ed., *The West Point Atlas of American Wars*, vol. 2, *1900–1953* (New York: Praeger, 1959), pp. 55–56.

17. Blumenson, *Breakout and Pursuit*, p. 661.

18. Ritgen, *The Western Front 1944*, p. 201.

19. Costeaux and Fortier, "Rapport sur l'activité de la mission Auguste," p. 6.

20. Ritgen, *The Western Front 1944*, p. 201; and Robert A. Miller, *August 1944: The Campaign for France* (Novato, CA: Presidio Press, 1988), p. 249.

21. 3rd Armored Division, United States Army, "Spearhead History G–3 Supplement," in *Spearhead in the West: The Third Armored Division, 1941–45* (Nashville: Battery Press, 1980), p. 205.

22. Tieke, *In the Firestorm*, pp. 209–10; Heinz Günther Guderian, *From Normandy to the Ruhr: With the 116th Panzer Division in World War II*, trans. Ulrich Abele, Esther Abele, and Keith E. Bonn; ed. Keith E. Bonn (Bedford, PA: Aberjona Press, 2001), pp. 97–103, 592; and Robert J. Kershaw, *"It Never Snows in September": The German View of Market-Garden and the Battle of Arnhem, September 1944* (New York: Sarpedon, 1999), p. 14.

23. Guderian, *From Normandy to the Ruhr*, pp. 97–103, 592.

24. 3rd Armored Division, *Spearhead in the West*, p. 86.

CHAPTER 10

1. Arthur Layton Funk, *Hidden Ally: The French Resistance, Special Operaions, and the Landings in Southern France, 1944* (Westport, CT: Greenwood Press, 1992), pp. 46–55.

2. OSS/London, *OSS/London: Special Operations Branch War Diary*, vol. 1, pp. 28–29; vol. 3, bk. 2, pp. 162–63; and Martin Thomas, "The Massingham Mission: SOE in French North Africa, 1941–1944," *Intelligence and National Security* 11, no. 4 (October 1996): 696–721.

3. OSS/London, *OSS/London: Special Operations Branch War Diary*, vol. 1, p. 31; vol. 2, pp. 31, 47–51; vol. 3, bk. 2, p. 164; vol. 4, bk. 1, pp. 3, 14.

4. Henry McIntosh, interview with the author, November 10, 2003, in Lakeland, FL.

5. Foot, *SOE in France*, pp. 253–56; and Patrick Howarth, *Undercover: The Men and Women of the SOE* (London: Phoenix Press, 2000), pp. 79–80.

6. Fuller, *The German Penetration of SOE*, p. 33.

7. Arthur Funk, telephone conversation and e-mail with the author, February 22, 2005.

8. Funk, *Hidden Ally*, p. 19.

9. Office of Strategic Services, "OSS Aid to the French Resistance in World War II," report no. 980, Jedburgh Team Chloroform (1945), p. 2, photocopy on file at the Marquat Memorial Library, U.S. Army John F. Kennedy Special Warfare Center and School, Fort Bragg, NC, and in the author's files.

10. Jacques Martin, letter to the author, March 1, 1989.

11. OSS/London, "OSS Aid to the French Resistance in World War II," report 980, Jedburgh Team Chloroform, pp. 3–4; and Jacques Martin, letter to the author, March 1, 1989.

12. OSS/London, "OSS Aid to the French Resistance in World War II," report 980, Jedburgh Team Chloroform, p. 4; and Funk, *Hidden Ally*, pp. 123–25.

13. Gen. Sir Henry Maitland Wilson, *Report by the Supreme Allied Commander Mediterranean to the Combined Chiefs of Staff on the Operations in Southern France, August 1944* (London: His Majesty's Stationery Office, 1946), pp. 14, 26.

14. OSS/London, *OSS/London: Special Operations Branch War Diary*, vol. 3, bk. 2, p. 365.

15. Wilson, *Report by SACMED to the CCS*, p. 26.

16. OSS/London, *OSS/London: Special Operations Branch War Diary*, vol. 3, bk. 13, p. 378.

17. F. W. Winterbotham, *The Ultra Secret* (New York: Dell Publishing, 1975), p. 227.

18. John A. Hyman, ed., *From the Riviera to the Rhine: 36th Division in World War II* (1945), unit history, Texas Military Museum website, http://www.kwanah.com/txmilmus/36division/hyman.htm (accessed April 12, 2000).

19. L. K. Truscott, Jr., *Command Missions: A Personal Story* (New York: Dutton, 1954), p. 426.
20. Leo V. Bishop, Frank J. Glasgow, and George A. Fisher, eds., *The Fighting Forty-Fifth: The Combat Report of an Infantry Division* (Baton Rouge: Army and Navy Publishing Company, 1946), p. 97.
21. Clifford H. Peek, Jr., ed., *Five Years, Five Countries, Five Campaigns . . . with the 141st Infantry Regiment* (Munich: 1945), unit history, Texas Military Museum website, http://www.kwanah.com/txmilmus/36division/141con.htm, chap. 7 (accessed 4 December 2000).
22. Audie Murphy, *To Hell and Back* (New York: Henry Holt, 2002), p. 183.
23. Stan Swinton, "Thunderbirds Soar Over South France," *The Stars and Stripes* (Mediterranean Edition), September 4, 1944, quoted in George A. Fisher, *The Story of the 180th Infantry Regiment* (San Angelo, TX: Newsfoto, 1947), chap. 8.

CHAPTER 11

1. Knox, *Essays Ancient and Modern*, p. xxiii.
2. Richard Floyd, telephone conversation with the author, September 13, 2004.
3. Foot, *SOE in France*, pp. 286–87; and E. H. Cookridge, *They Came from the Sky* (New York: Crowell, 1967), pp. 40–41.
4. Howarth, *Undercover*, p. 79; and Cookridge, *They Came from the Sky*, pp. 2–3, 11–69.
5. George Millar, *Maquis* (London: Heinemann, 1945), pp. 30–51.
6. Ibid, p. 264.
7. Ibid., pp. 301–02.
8. George Millar, *Road to Resistance: An Autobiography* (Boston: Little, Brown, 1979), p. 378; and *Maquis*, p. 312.
9. Millar, *Maquis*, pp. 314–15, 319–20.
10. Office of Strategic Services, "Report of Jedburgh Cedric," (1944), p. 3 (National Archives, Washington History Office, RG 226), photocopy in author's files.
11. Millar, *Road to Resistance*, pp. 383–84.
12. Ronald B. Sorobey, "Ukrainians' Fight for France," *World War II*, September 2004, pp. 44–46.

CHAPTER 12

1. Millar, *Road to Resistance*, p. 385; *Maquis*, pp. 322–23.
2. Millar, *Road to Resistance*, pp. 386–87.
3. Millar, *Maquis*, pp. 347, 349.
4. Millar, *Road to Resistance*, p. 391.

5. Ibid., p. 392.
6. Richard Floyd, telephone conversation with the author, September 13, 2004, and letter to the author, October 28, 2004.
7. "20,000 Nazis Surrender," *83rd Spearhead*, vol. 1, no. 7 (September 25, 1944), p. 1.
8. Richard Floyd, telephone conversation with the author, September 13, 2004.
9. Foot, *SOE in France*, p. 133.
10. Millar, *Maquis*, p. 362.
11. Staff of Trailblazers Weekly, *Trailblazer: The 70th Division in Action* (Nancy, France: Trailblazers Weekly, [1945?]), p. 8.

Epilogue

1. OSS/London, *OSS/London: Special Operations Branch War Diary*, vol. 1, p. 111; vol. 4, bk. 1, p. 63; vol. 9.
2. Captain Paul Grall, "Report of Mission Landa-Sar-Sin," July 4, 1946, copy provided to the author by OSS veteran Caesar Civitella.
3. Ibid.
4. Document on post-war careers of French Jedburghs, copy provided to the author by OSS veteran Caesar Civitella.
5. Col. Jean Sassi, "Report on Experiences in the Far East, 1945–46," April 6, 1996; and document on post-war careers of French Jedburghs, both provided to the author by OSS veteran Caesar Civitella.
6. Associated Press, "Soldiers Remember Life Behind Enemy Lines," *Times Herald-Record*, (Middletown, NY), May 12, 1988, p. 25.
7. Buckmaster, *They Fought Alone*, p. 52.
8. Foot, *SOE in France*, p. xxii.
9. Ingersoll, *Top Secret*, pp. 181–82.
10. Allen, *Lucky Forward*, p. 96.
11. Ibid., p. 134.
12. Maj. Melvin A. Hoherz, Headquarters, XX Corps, letter to commanding general, Third U.S. Army, subject: "Report of assistance of SF personnel," August 31, 1944 (enclosure to Special Force Detachment 11 "Operations Report").
13. Special Force Detachment 11, "Operations Report," p. 18.
14. Brig. Gen. Frederick B. Butler, quoted in Funk, *Hidden Ally*, p. 121, from Frederick Butler, "Task Force Butler," *Armored Cavalry Journal*, January-February 1948, p. 15.
15. OSS/London, *OSS/London: Special Operations Branch War Diary*, vol. 3, bk. 2, p. 380.
16. Donald G. Taggart, ed., *History of the Third Infantry Division in World War II* (Nashville: Battery Press, 1987), p. 217.

17. Fisher, *The Story of the 180th Infantry Regiment*, ch. 8.
18. Warren P. Munsell, Jr., *The Story of a Regiment: A History of the 179th Regimental Combat Team* (Germany, 1946), p. 73.
19. Seventh United States Army, *Report of Operations, The Seventh United States Army in France and Germany, 1944–1945* (Heidelberg: Aloys Gräf, 1946), vol. 1, p. 168.
20. Truscott, *Command Missions*, p. 420.
21. Gen. Sir Henry Maitland Wilson, quoted in Foot, *SOE in France*, p. 442.
22. Ingersoll, *Top Secret*, p. 182–83.
23. Ibid.
24. Ritgen, *The Western Front 1944*, p. 201.
25. Field Marshal Gerd von Rundstedt, quoted in Foot, *SOE in France*, p. 233.
26. Ibid, p. 356.
27. Field Marshal Walther Model to Gen. Warlimont, June 11, 1944, from a captured journal of enemy telephone conversations, quoted in Butcher, *My Three Years with Eisenhower*, p. 667.
28. Dwight D. Eisenhower, *Crusade in Europe* (Garden City, NY: Doubleday, 1948), p. 296.
29. Eisenhower, letters to the executive director of SOE and to the director of OSS London, May 31, 1945 (see Prologue Note 1).
30. Lt. Gen. Walter Bedell Smith and Lt. Gen. Sir Frederick E. Morgan to the Combined Chiefs of Staff, July 1945, quoted in Foot, *SOE in France*, p. 442.
31. Gen. George C. Marshall, 1946, quoted in Blake Ehrlich, *Resistance: France, 1940–1945* (Boston: Little, Brown, 1965), p. 194.
32. Lt. Col. James R. H. Hutchison, "Report on operations of Mission Verveine," October 6, 1944, p. 13 (National Archives, Washington History Office, RG 226), photocopy in author's files.
33. Robert J. Jakeman, "Air Special Operations," in *The D-Day Encyclopedia*, eds. Chandler and Collins, p. 29; and Paul Gaujac, *Special Forces in the Invasion of France*, trans. Janice Lert (Paris: Histoire & Collections, 1999), p. 93.
34. Kermit Roosevelt, ed., *The Overseas Targets*, pp. xii, 199.

SOURCES

I. Documents and Unpublished Sources

Bautz, Edward. Interview posted on the Rutgers Oral History Archives of World War II Website, http://fas-history.rutgers.edu/oralhistory/Interviews/bautz_edward.html (accessed October 18, 2004).

Brown, Arthur. "The Jedburghs: A Short History." April 1991, photocopy. Unpublished manuscript.

Bull, Harold R. Memorandum to Chief, Plans and Operations Section, subject: "SOE/SO Assistance to Overlord." April 6, 1944 National Archives, Washington History Office, record group 331, entry 23, box 47).

Chief of Staff to the Supreme Allied Commander, Designate (COSSAC). "Operation 'Overlord.'" Appendix P, "Support of Military Operations by Resistance Groups in Europe." July 15, 1943. National Archives, Washington History Office, record group 331, entry 23, box 47.

Colby, William E. Letter to Chief, Special Operations Branch, Office of Strategic Services. May 23, 1945. Photocopy provided to the author by Mr. Colby.

Costeaux, Gaston and Emile Fortier. "*Rapport sur l'activite de la mission 'Auguste.'*" October 5, 1944. Photocopy in author's files.

Etat-major des Forces Francaises de l'Interieur (EMFFI). "A Short History of the Organization of the Command of Operations Undertaken by the French Forces of the Interior." 1945. National Archives, Washington History Office, record group 226 (Office of Strategic Services records).

Hoherz, Melvin A. "Report of assistance of SF personnel." August 31,

1944 (enclosure to Special Forces Detachment 11, "Third Army G–3 Section, 11ᵗʰ Special Force Detachment Operations Report," December 18, 1944).

Hutchison, James R. H. "Report on operations of Mission Verveine." October 6, 1944. National Archives, Washington History Office, record group 226.

Joint Psychological Warfare Committee. Meeting minutes and associated documents. National Archives, Washington History Office, record group 218 (Joint Chiefs of Staff records), Central Decimal File 1942–45, box 8.

Kehoe, Robert R. "Jed Team Frederick, 1944: An Allied Team With the French Resistance." Article on the Central Intelligence Agency's Center for the Study of Intelligence website, 1997. http://www.cia.gov/csi/studies/winter98_99/art03.html (accessed January 13, 2005).

LeBlanc, Robert. World War II veteran survey and other papers. United States Army Military History Institute Archives, Carlisle Barracks, PA, WWII–7396, box OSS, WWII survey.

Office of Strategic Services. "OSS Aid to the French Resistance in World War II." Report 980, "Jedburgh Team Chloroform," 1945. Photocopy on file at Marquat Memorial Library, U.S. Army John F. Kennedy Special Warfare Center and School, Fort Bragg, NC.

———. OSS/London: Special Operations Branch and Secret Intelligence Branch War Diaries, 1945. 13 vols. on 8 reels of microfilm. Edited by Paul Kesaris. Frederick, MD: University Publications of America, 1985. Also found in National Archives Microfilm Publication M1623.

———. "Report of Jedburgh Cedric." 1944. National Archives, Washington History Office, record group 226.

Rot, Armand. "Compte-Rendu." Statement about Jedburgh team Augustus written in 1944, photocopy in author's files.

Special Force Detachment 11. "Plan for Resistance Movements in Brittany." With attached operations summary. August 10, 1944. National Archives, Washington History Office, record group 226, London SO, entry 115, box 50.

———. "Third Army G–3 Section, 11th Special Force Detachment Operations Report." December 18, 1944. National Archives, Washington History Office, record group 226, entry 115, box 50.

Special Force Headquarters. SFHQ G–3 Periodic Reports, published and submitted daily to Supreme Headquarters Allied Expeditionary Force G–3 from June 5, 1944, to May 7, 1945. National Archives, Washington History Office, record group 226, OP–23, entry 99, folders 116–118, box 93.

Twelfth Army Group. Report of Operations, G–3 Section, 12th Army Group (Final After Action Report). 1945. Photocopy in author's files.

Vanderblue, C. C. Memorandum to General William J. Donovan, subject:

Report of C. S. Vanderblue on OSS Operations with the Third Army. November 15, 1944. National Archives, Washington History Office, record group 226, OP–23, entry 99, folder 50, box 12.

II. UNIT HISTORIES

3rd Armored Division. *Spearhead in the West: The Third Armored Division, 1941–45*. Nashville: Battery Press, 1980.

5th Infantry Division. *The 5th Division in France*. Metz: La Lorraine Press, 1944.

Seventh United States Army. *Report of Operations: The Seventh United States Army in France and Germany, 1944–1945*. 2 vols. Heidelberg: Aloys Gräf, 1946.

Bishop, Leo V., Frank J. Glasgow, and George A. Fisher, eds. *The Fighting Forty-Fifth: The Combat Report of an Infantry Division*. Baton Rouge: Army and Navy Publishing, 1946.

Colby, Elbridge. *The First Army in Europe, 1943–1945*. Nashville: Battery Press, 1993.

Fisher, George A. *The Story of the 180th Infantry Regiment*. San Angelo, TX: Newsfoto, 1947.

Hyman, John A., ed. *From the Riviera to the Rhine: 36th Division in World War II*. 1945. Unit history online at the Texas Military Museum website, http://www.kwanah.com/txmilmus/36division/hyman.htm (accessed April 12, 2000).

Knickerbocker, H. R., et. al. *Danger Forward: The Story of the First Division in World War II*. Atlanta: Albert Love, 1947.

Munsell, Warren P., Jr. *The Story of a Regiment: A History of the 179th Regimental Combat Team*. Germany: 1946.

Peek, Clifford H., Jr., ed. *Five Years, Five Countries, Five Campaigns . . . with the 141st Infantry Regiment*. Munich: 141st Infantry Regiment Association, 1945. Online at Texas Military Museum website, http://www.kwanah.com/txmilmus/36division/141con.htm (accessed December 4, 2000).

Taggart, Donald G., ed. *History of the Third Infantry Division in World War II*. Nashville: Battery Press, 1987.

Trailblazers Weekly (Staff). *Trailblazers: The 70th Division in Action*. Trailblazers Weekly, [n.d.].

III. BOOKS

Alcorn, Robert Hayden. *No Bugles for Spies: Tales of the OSS*. New York: Popular Library, 1964.

Allen, Robert S. *Lucky Forward: The History of Patton's Third U.S. Army*. New York: Vanguard Press, 1947.

Alsop, Stewart, and Thomas Braden. *Sub Rosa: The OSS and American Espionage*. New York: Harcourt, Brace & World, 1964.

Ambrose, Stephen E. *D-Day, June 6, 1944: The Climactic Battle of World War II*. New York: Simon & Schuster, 1994.

Ambrose, Stephen E., with Richard H. Immerman. *Ike's Spies: Eisenhower and the Espionage Establishment*. Jackson: University Press of Mississippi, 1999.

Asprey, Robert B. *War in the Shadows: The Guerrilla in History*. Garden City, NY: Doubleday, 1975.

Bank, Aaron. *From OSS to Green Berets*. Novato, CA: Presidio Press, 1986.

Berkeley, Roy. *A Spy's London*. London: Leo Cooper, 1994.

Bleicher, Hugo. *Colonel Henri's Story: The War Memoirs of Hugo Bleicher: Former German Secret Agent*. Edited by Ian Colvin. London: William Kimber, 1954.

Blumenson, Martin. *Breakout and Pursuit*. United States Army in World War II. Washington, DC: Center of Military History, 1984.

Bradley, Omar N. *A Soldier's Story*. New York: Henry Holt, 1951.

Bruce, David K. E. *OSS against the Reich: The World War II Diaries of Colonel David K. E. Bruce*. Edited by Nelson D. Lankford. Kent, Ohio: Kent State University Press, 1991.

Buckmaster, Maurice J. *They Fought Alone: The Story of British Agents in France*. New York: Norton, 1958.

Butcher, Harry C. *My Three Years with Eisenhower: The Personal Diary of Captain Harry C. Butcher, USNR, Naval Aide to General Eisenhower, 1942 to 1945*. New York: Simon & Schuster, 1946.

Butler, Daniel Allen. *Warrior Queens: The Queen Mary and Queen Elizabeth in World War II*. London: Leo Cooper, 2002.

Calvocoressi, Peter. *Top Secret Ultra*. New York: Pantheon Books, 1980.

Cannicott, Stanley M. *Journey of a Jed*. Cheddar, Somerset, UK: Cheddar Valley Press, 1986.

Cassidy, William L., ed. *History of the Schools and Training Branch, Office of Strategic Services*. San Francisco: Kingfisher Press, 1983.

Chandler, David G., and James Lawton Collins, Jr., eds. *The D-Day Encyclopedia*. New York: Simon & Schuster, 1994.

Churchill, Winston S. *The Second World War*. 6 vols. Boston: Houghton Mifflin, 1949–53.

Churchill, Winston S., and Franklin D. Roosevelt. *Churchill and Roosevelt, The Complete Correspondence*. Edited by Warren F. Kimball. Princeton: Princeton University Press, 1984.

Clarke, Jeffrey J., and Robert Ross Smith. *Riviera to the Rhine*. United States Army in World War II. Washington, DC: Center of Military History, 1993.

Colby, William, and Peter Forbath. *Honorable Men: My Life in the CIA*. New York: Simon & Schuster, 1978.

Cookridge, E. H. *Set Europe Ablaze*. New York: Crowell, 1967.

———. *They Came from the Sky*. New York: Crowell, 1967.

Crosby, M. G. M. *Irregular Soldier*. United Kingdom: XB Publications, 1993.

Dolan, Anne Reilly. *Congressional Country Club, 1924–1984*. Baltimore: MacLellan and Associates, [n.d.].

Dreux, William B. *No Bridges Blown*. Notre Dame: University of Notre Dame Press, 1971.

Ehrlich, Blake. *Resistance: France, 1940–1945*. Boston: Little, Brown, 1965.

Eisenhower, David. *Eisenhower at War 1943–1945*. New York: Vintage Books, 1987.

Eisenhower, Dwight D. *Crusade in Europe*. Garden City, NY: Doubleday, 1948.

———. *D Day to VE Day, 1944–45: General Eisenhower's Report on the Invasion of Europe*. London: The Stationery Office, 2000.

———. *The Papers of Dwight David Eisenhower, The War Years*. 5 vols. Edited by Alfred D. Chandler, Jr. Baltimore: Johns Hopkins Press, 1970.

Esposito, Vincent J., ed. *The West Point Atlas of American Wars*, vol. 2, *1900–1953*. New York: Praeger, 1959.

Foot, M. R. D. *Resistance: European Resistance to Nazism, 1940–1945*. New York: McGraw-Hill, 1977.

———. *SOE: An Outline History of the Special Operations Executive, 1940–46*. London: British Broadcasting Corp., 1984.

———. *SOE in France: An Account of the Work of the British Special Operations Executive in France, 1940–1944*. London: Her Majesty's Stationery Office, 1966.

Ford, Roger. *Fire From the Forest: The SAS Brigade in France, 1944*. London: Cassell, 2003.

———. *Steel From the Sky: The Jedburgh Raiders, France 1944*. London: Weidenfeld & Nicolson, 2004.

Fuller, Jean Overton. *The German Penetration of SOE: France, 1941–1944*. Revised edition. Maidstone, UK: George Mann Books, 1996.

Funk, Arthur Layton. *Hidden Ally: The French Resistance, Special Operaions, and the Landing in Southern France, 1944*. Westport, CT: Greenwood Press, 1992.

Gaujac, Paul. *Special Forces in the Invasion of France*. Trans. by Janice Lert. Paris: Histoire & Collections, 1999.

Gawne, Jonathan. *The Americans in Brittany, 1944: The Battle for Brest*. Paris: Histoire & Collections, 2002.

Guderian, Heinz Günther. *From Normandy to the Ruhr: With the 116th Panzer Division in World War II*. Translated by Ulrich Abele, Esther Abele, and Keith E. Bonn. Edited by Keith E. Bonn. Bedford, PA: Aberjona Press, 2001.

Hall, Roger. *You're Stepping on My Cloak and Dagger*. New York: Norton, 1957.

Harding, Steve. *Gray Ghost: The R.M.S. Queen Mary at War*. Missoula, MT: Pictorial Histories, 1982.

Harrison, Gordon A. *Cross-Channel Attack*. United States Army in World War II. Washington, DC: Center of Military History, 1993.

Hastings, Max. *Das Reich: The March of the 2nd SS Panzer Division Through France*. New York: Holt, Rinehart and Winston, 1982.

Howarth, Patrick. *Undercover: The Men and Women of the SOE*. London: Phoenix Press, 2000.

Hue, André, and Ewen Southby-Tailyour. *The Next Moon: The Remarkable True Story of a British Agent Behind the Lines in Wartime France*. London: Viking, 2004.

Huston, James A. *Biography of a Battalion: The Life and Times of an Infantry Battalion in Europe in World War II*. Mechanicsburg, PA: Stackpole Books, 2003.

Hutchison, James. *That Drug Danger*. Montrose, Scotland: Standard Press, 1977.

Ingersoll, Ralph. *Top Secret*. New York: Harcourt, Brace, 1946.

Ismay, Hastings Lionel. *The Memoirs of General Lord Ismay*. New York: The Viking Press, 1960.

Kershaw, Robert J. *"It Never Snows in September": The German View of Market-Garden and the Battle of Arnhem, September 1944*. New York: Sarpedon, 1999.

Knox, Bernard. *Essays Ancient and Modern*. Baltimore: The Johns Hopkins University Press, 1989.

Ladd, James, and Keith Melton. *Clandestine Warfare: Weapons and Equipment of the SOE and OSS*. London: Blandford Press, 1988.

Longmate, Norman. *The G.I.'s: The Americans in Britain, 1942–1945*. New York: Scribner, 1975.

Lorain, Pierre. *Clandestine Operations: The Arms and Techniques of the Resistance, 1941–1944*. New York: Macmillan, 1983.

Mackenzie, W. J. M. *The Secret History of SOE: The Special Operations Executive 1940–1945*. London: St. Ermin's Press, 2002.

Manchester, William. *The Last Lion: Winston Spencer Churchill; Alone, 1932–1940*. Boston: Little, Brown, 1988.

———. *The Last Lion: Winston Spencer Churchill; Visions of Glory, 1874–1932*. Boston: Little, Brown, 1983.

Marshall, Bruce. *The White Rabbit*. Boston: Houghton Mifflin, 1952.

McCue, Paul. *SAS Operation Bulbasket: Behind the Lines in Occupied France, 1944*. London: Leo Cooper, 1996.

Millar, George. *Maquis*. London: Heinemann. 1945.

———. *Road to Resistance: An Autobiography*. Boston: Little, Brown, 1979.

Miller, Robert A. *August 1944: The Campaign for France*. Novato, CA: Presidio Press, 1988).

Miller, William H., and David F. Hutchings. *Transatlantic Liners at War: The Story of the Queens*. New York: Arco, 1985.

Mitcham, Samuel W., Jr. *Retreat to the Reich: The German Defeat in France, 1944*. Westport, CT: Praeger, 2000.

Moody, Sidney C., and the Associated Press. *War in Europe*. Novato, CA: Presidio Press, 1993.

Morgan, Frederick. *Overture to Overlord*. Garden City, NY: Doubleday, 1950.

Murphy, Audie. *To Hell and Back*. New York: Henry Holt, 2002.

Obolensky, Serge. *One Man in His Time: The Memoirs of Serge Obolensky*. New York: McDowell, Obolensky, 1958.

Office of Strategic Services Assessment Staff. *Assessment of Men: Selection of Personnel for the Office of Strategic Services*. New York: Rinehart, 1948.

———. *The Overseas Targets: War Report of the OSS (Office of Strategic Services), Volume 2*. Introduction by Kermit Roosevelt. Washington, DC: Carrollton Press; New York: Walker, 1976.

Parnell, Ben. *Carpetbaggers: America's Secret War in Europe*. Austin: Eakin Press, 1987.

Patton, George S. *War as I Knew It*. Boston: Houghton Mifflin, 1947.

Province, Charles M. *Patton's Third Army: A Daily Combat Diary*. New York: Hippocrene Books, 1992.

Pyle, Ernie. *Brave Men*. New York: Henry Holt, 1944.

Reader's Digest Association, The. *Secrets and Spies: Behind-the-Scenes Stories of World War II*. Pleasantville, NY: Reader's Digest Assn., 1964.

Ritgen, Helmut. *The Western Front 1944: Memoirs of a Panzer Lehr Officer*. Translated by Joseph Welsh. Winnipeg: Fedorowicz, 1995.

Roosevelt, Kermit, ed. *War Report of the OSS*. New York: Walker, 1976.

Singlaub, John K., and Malcolm McConnell. *Hazardous Duty: An American Soldier in the Twentieth Century*. New York: Summit Books, 1991.

Smith, Richard Harris. *OSS: The Secret History of America's First Central Intelligence Agency*. Berkeley: University of California Press, 1972.

Smith, Walter Bedell. *Eisenhower's Six Great Decisions*. New York: Longmans, Green, 1956.

Special Operations Executive. *Secret Agent's Handbook: The WWII Spy Manual of Devices, Disguises, Gadgets, and Concealed Weapons*. Reproduction of SOE's 1944 *Descriptive Catalogue of Special Devices and Supplies*, with an introduction by Mark Seaman. Guilford, CT: The Lyons Press, 2001.

Thompson, Julian. *The Imperial War Museum Book of War Behind Enemy Lines*. Washington, DC: Brassey's, 2001.

Tickell, Jerrard. *Moon Squadron*. Garden City, N Y: Doubleday, 1958.

Tieke, Wilhelm. *In the Firestorm of the Last Years of the War: II SS-Panzerkorps with the 9 and 10 SS-Divisions "Hohenstaufen" and "Frundsberg"*. Translated by Frederick Steinhardt. Winnipeg: Fedorowicz, 1999.

Truscott, L. K., Jr. *Command Missions: A Personal Story*. New York: Dutton, 1954.

von Luck, Hans. *Panzer Commander: The Memoirs of Colonel Hans von Luck*. New York: Praeger, 1989.

Wallace, Brenton G. *Patton and his Third Army*. Mechanicsburg, PA: Stackpole Books, 2000.

Wehrle, Edmund F. *Catoctin Mountain Park: A Historic Resource Study*. March 2000. On National Park Service website, http://www.nps.gov/cato/hrs/hrs.htm (accessed January 24, 2005).

West, Nigel [Rupert Allason]. *MI6: British Secret Intelligence Service Operations, 1909–45*. New York: Random House, 1983.

———. *Secret War: The Story of SOE, Britain's Wartime Sabotage Organisation*. London: Hodder & Stoughton, 1992.

Wilkinson, Peter. *Foreign Fields: The Story of an SOE Operative*. London: I. B. Tauris, 1997.

Wilson, Henry Maitland. *Report by the Supreme Allied Commander Mediterranean to the Combined Chiefs of Staff on the Operations in Southern France, August 1944*. London: His Majesty's Stationery Office, 1946.

Winterbotham, F. W. *The Ultra Secret*. New York: Dell Publishing, 1975.

IV. ARTICLES

"20,000 Nazis Surrender." *83rd Spearhead* 1, no.7 (September 25, 1944).

Associated Press. "D-Day Chutists Rate as Heroes: South Bend Officer One of International Secret Unit." Unidentified Indiana newspaper, September 27, 1945.

Goldberg, Alfred. "Air Campaign Overlord: To D-Day." In *D-Day: The Normandy Invasion in Retrospect* (Lawrence: University Press of Kansas, 1971).

Hemingway, Albert. "The Great Parachute Drop." *Military History* 6, no. 5 (April 1990): 46–52.

"Keeping Posted." The *Saturday Evening Post*, March 23, 1946, p. 4.

Sorobey, Ronald B. "Ukrainians' Fight for France." *World War II*, September 2004, pp. 42–48.

Thomas, Martin. "The Massingham Mission: SOE in French North Africa, 1941–1944." *Intelligence and National Security* 11, no. 4 (October 1996): 696–721.

V. Correspondence and Interviews

Americans
Everett T. Allen
Col. (USA, Ret.) Aaron Bank
Rev. Jacob B. Berlin
John L. & Anne Bradner
Franklin O. Canfield
Charles M. Carman, Jr.
Philip H. Chadbourn, Jr.
William E. Colby
Lucien E. Conein
Paul & Donna J. Cyr
Violette A. (Côté) Desmarais
Sarah Drake
René A. Dussaq
Richard C. Floyd
Ray H. Foster
Dick Franklin
Brig. Gen. (USMCR, Ret.) Horace W. Fuller
Jean Gildee
Mary D. Hanson
Dr. Robert R. Kehoe
Dr. Bernard M. W. Knox
Lucien E. Lajeunesse
Robert A. Lucas
Dr. Henry D. & Harriet McIntosh
Robert K. Montgomery
Cecil F. Mynatt, Jr.
Gordon Nelson
John M. & Elisabeth Olmsted
William H. Pietsch, Jr.
Jack Shannon
Maj. Gen. (USA, Ret.) John K. Singlaub
Donald A. Spears
Katherine B. (Bonsall) Strong
William T. Thompson
Allan & Amanda Todd
Thomas & Norma Tracy
Col. (USA, Ret.) S. Ray Trumps
George M. Verhaeghe

British
Arthur Brown
Stanley Cannicott
John C. C. Montague
Richard A. Rubinstein
Cyril H. Sell

French
Gen. (Ret.) Paul Aussaresses
Col. (Ret.) Robert Cantais
Gen. (Ret.) Jean Joseph Carbuccia
Robert Clause
Prince Michel de Bourbon de Parme
Lt. Col. (Ret.) René de la Tousche
Gen. (Ret.) Roland de Mecquenem
Baron Albert de Schonen
Mme. Hubert Dumesnil
René Estève
François G. Franceschi
Joe de Francesco
Col. (Ret.) Maurice Geminel
Adrien Grafeville
Col. (Ret.) Paul Grall
Xavier Humblet
Lt. Col. (Ret.) Pierre Jolliet
Col. (Ret.) Marc Lautier
Gen. (Ret.) Guy Le Borgne
Camille Lelong
Col. (Ret.) Claude l'Herbette
Georges Marchal
Jacques Martin
Edgar Mautaint
René Meyer
Jacques Morineau
Étienne Nasica
Mme. Paule Perraud
Maurice Pirat
Philippe Ragueneau
Jacques Robert
Gen. (Ret.) Robert Toussaint
François C. Verger
Marcel Vermot

ACKNOWLEDGMENTS

I was a captain on the staff of the John F. Kennedy Special Warfare Center at Fort Bragg when I was asked to help host a reunion of Jedburgh veterans in 1985. I had known what the Jedburgh project was from classes I'd sat through during Special Forces training. But when I met the veterans and heard their stories, my interest in their experience grew, and I began what would turn out to be two decades of research.

In 1988, former CIA director and Jedburgh veteran William E. Colby wrote me suggesting that I come to Washington for a reunion of Jedburghs scheduled to take place there that summer. He thought it would be a good opportunity for me to get to know more of them. So when he called me a few days later to see if I was coming, I said yes and packed my bags. And I was thus able to enjoy a few more days with the Jeds and get to know some of their families as well. I hoped someday to be able to write about them, but I knew that it would have to wait until my retirement from the service, when I could devote all of my time and energy to the project. In the meantime, I began writing to many of the Jeds or interviewing them whenever an opportunity presented itself. Eventually, I spoke or corresponded with more than sixty Jedburgh veterans—American, British, and French.

I wish to thank the many people who have helped in some way to make this book possible. Dr. Samuel J. Lewis of the Combat Studies Institute at the U.S. Army Command and General Staff College was generous with his time and Jedburgh expertise when I was a student of his in 1990–91. His assistance was not limited to academic guidance; he also provided me with copies of many archival documents and photographs.

John Taylor and Will Mahoney at the Military History Branch of the U.S. National Archives (in downtown Washington, D.C., when I began this, and later at College Park, Maryland) helped immeasurably in locating documents and photographs. Fred Fuller, at the Marquat Memorial Library of the U.S. Army John F. Kennedy Special Warfare Center and School, was very helpful in sharing with me Jedburgh after-action reports and other documents during my time there in the 1980s.

Dr. John Sweets, my faculty advisor during my brief time at the University of Kansas, gave me guidance on research approaches and shared his expertise on the French resistance. Dr. Arthur Layton Funk, retired professor of history at the University of Florida, took time to answer my questions and share his knowledge of resistance and Allied special forces activities in France. And Colonel Brian McMillan, friend and former boss, generously provided me copies of OSS training manuals.

I also want to thank those who read portions of early versions of the manuscript and provided many valuable comments and suggestions: Colonel Gordon Atcheson, John Hunt, Rick Brown, Robert E. Kehoe, and Dr. Henry D. McIntosh.

Thanks also go to the staffs at the Combined Arms Research Library of the United States Army Command and General Staff College at Fort Leavenworth, Kansas; the Watson Library at the University of Kansas; the Hoover Institution at Stanford University; the United States Army Europe Library and Research Center in Heidelberg, Germany; the United States Army Military History Institute Archives at Carlisle Barracks, Pennsylvania; the RAND Library in Santa Monica, California; the United States Special Operations Command Library at MacDill Air Force Base, Florida; and the public libraries in Redondo Beach, California, and Tampa, Florida. The staff members of these institutions showed both commendable perseverance in helping me locate source materials and remarkable patience with my delinquent returns.

I am grateful for the photographs provided by Donna J. Cyr, Violette A. Desmarais, Richard C. Floyd, Robert E. Kehoe, Michael G. Leemhuis and the Congressional Country Club, Dr. Henry D. McIntosh, Katherine B. Strong and Sarah Drake, and the Time Warner Book Group.

Thanks to Jedburgh wife Joann Henely for putting me in touch with the families of John Bonsall and Roger Côté, to OSS veteran Caesar Civitella for information on the activities of the French Jedburghs following their missions in France, and to Kathleen Price for providing translations of many of the French documents I used.

My most profound debt of gratitude, of course, is owed to the many former Jeds and their families who have given so freely of their time for interviews and correspondence and who have provided so much in the way of source documents and photographs. Their names are included in the list of sources provided in this book.

Special thanks go to my agent, John A. Ware, and to my editor at Public-Affairs, Clive Priddle. Needless to say, this book never would have seen the light of day without them. They were constant sources of encouragement, and they taught me much about turning a truly rough draft into something readable.

Finally, thanks go to my wife, Angie, and my sons, Donovan, Thomas, and William, for their many sacrifices and unwavering support.

INDEX

PUBLICAFFAIRS is a publishing house founded in 1997. It is a tribute to the standards, values, and flair of three persons who have served as mentors to countless reporters, writers, editors, and book people of all kinds, including me.

I. F. STONE, proprietor of *I. F. Stone's Weekly*, combined a commitment to the First Amendment with entrepreneurial zeal and reporting skill and became one of the great independent journalists in American history. At the age of eighty, Izzy published *The Trial of Socrates*, which was a national bestseller. He wrote the book after he taught himself ancient Greek.

BENJAMIN C. BRADLEE was for nearly thirty years the charismatic editorial leader of *The Washington Post*. It was Ben who gave the *Post* the range and courage to pursue such historic issues as Watergate. He supported his reporters with a tenacity that made them fearless, and it is no accident that so many became authors of influential, best-selling books.

ROBERT L. BERNSTEIN, the chief executive of Random House for more than a quarter century, guided one of the nation's premier publishing houses. Bob was personally responsible for many books of political dissent and argument that challenged tyranny around the globe. He is also the founder and was the longtime chair of Human Rights Watch, one of the most respected human rights organizations in the world.

· · ·

For fifty years, the banner of Public Affairs Press was carried by its owner Morris B. Schnapper, who published Gandhi, Nasser, Toynbee, Truman, and about 1,500 other authors. In 1983 Schnapper was described by *The Washington Post* as "a redoubtable gadfly." His legacy will endure in the books to come.

Peter Osnos, Publisher